THE AGE OF THE MASSES

Ideas and Society in Europe since 1870

THE AGE
OF THE MASSES

Ideas and Society in
Europe since 1870

MICHAEL D. BIDDISS

HUMANITIES PRESS, NEW JERSEY

HUMANITIES PRESS INC.,
ATLANTIC HIGHLANDS
NEW JERSEY 07716, U.S.A.

First published in this edition
in 1977 by Humanities Press Inc., in the U.S.A.
and by The Harvester Press Ltd., in England
by agreement with Penguin Books Ltd.,
Harmondsworth, Middlesex, England.

Library of Congress Cataloguing in Publication Data
Biddiss, Michael Denis.
The age of the masses.

(The Pelican history of European thought; 6)
Includes bibliographical references and indexes.
1. Europe—Intellectual life.   2. Philosophy, Modern—
19th century.   3. Philosophy, Modern—20th century.
I. Title.
CB417.B47   199'.4   77-7542
ISBN 0-391-00736-X

Printed in Great Britain by
REDWOOD BURN LIMITED
Trowbridge & Esher

For Sarah,
Kate, and Clare

CONTENTS

PREFACE

ANY general history of European thought over the last hundred years or so cannot fail to betray its author's audacity. As my Introduction suggests, the writer confronts substantial problems of method and a potentially unlimited range of source materials. His boldness is all the more marked when the account must be compressed into a single volume such as this. Throughout its preparation I have been very conscious of matter regretfully omitted, and of a certain rawness of argument conditioned by the need for conciseness. However, within these dimensions, I have sought to respond positively to the challenge of providing a broad survey. It is as such that I hope the book will be judged, and perhaps enjoyed.

Readers may find it helpful to keep in mind a few points about presentation. I have added the original title of a foreign book only when this differs significantly in sense from the heading of a published English version. Works still untranslated have usually been presented in my own English titling. Unless otherwise indicated, any cited date of publication refers to a work's appearance in its original language. I have recorded few dates of birth and death in the main text. Instead I have compiled, with the kind assistance of Miss Susan Woods, a full list of these for incorporation within the Index of Names.

Many of the arguments presented here were elaborated first in the ordinary course of my university teaching duties. I doubt whether my recent pupils in Cambridge and Leicester realize just how far their reactions, favourable or otherwise, have helped me to settle what to say and how to say it. I must acknowledge also the help which many friends have given over particular sections and chapters. Now that there is a rounded text for them to see they may at last understand why they were pestered so often for such seemingly disparate kinds of information or comment. Among those who have read the work as a whole I must certainly make a special mention of Professor Jack Plumb: the book was begun at his invitation, and its completion is in no small way due to his sustained advice and generous encouragement. I am grateful too for the offer made by my colleague Dr Aubrey Newman to scrutinize the full final draft. Such of his marginalia as he and I were later able to decipher went far in improving my text. This has benefited also from the editorial acumen of Mr Peter Carson and Mrs Lucy Pinney. My wife has been responsible, above all, for creating an environment in which both the activity of writing and the necessary relaxation from writing are possible and pleasurable. She has acted, additionally, as the doughtiest champion that the so-called general reader could wish for. Without her critical good sense far fewer rough places would have been made plain.

Responsibility for the book's shortcomings is mine alone. But to those persons I have just mentioned must go a large measure of the credit for such virtue it may possess as a guide to the rich complexities of the modern European mind. I myself would be satisfied were readers to find here some real stimulus towards exploring at first hand the work of those discussed.

July 1976   M. D. B.

THE STUDY
OF IDEAS AND SOCIETY
IN THE MODERN AGE

IN the range and power of its intellectual achievements
Europe has been for many centuries unsurpassed. Yet in no
previous age has it produced ideas of such richness and complexity as those which mark the last hundred years. In this
period European thought has developed alongside changes in
society that are themselves of unprecedented magnitude.
Obviously there must be connections between those ideas and
that society, but the nature of these links remains highly
disputable. No formulation of predominantly unidirectional
influences is altogether convincing. To see society as moulded
overwhelmingly by mind is no more helpful than to regard
intellect as some mere side-effect of dominant material conditions. There is a vastly more complex and fluctuating
dialectic between given social circumstances and man himself,
who perceives them so variously and strives to transform them
according to a wealth of competing aspirations. Few efforts
recorded in this book are more valuable than Max Weber's
subtle and essentially tentative explorations through the intricate nexus between thought as a social symptom and ideas as
creative influences upon society. Any truly systematic treatment of such interplay would require a much larger volume
than the present one. Even so, I accept the challenge of attempting to make here a good number of convincing suggestions about the relationship between ideas and society
during this incomparably exciting historical epoch.

The title page carries perhaps the most important of these

suggestions. Recurrent throughout the book is the theme of mass socialization, as the most fundamental fact confronting those in dialogue with the historical situation of the last hundred years. The relative unity of a period of intellectual history is best evoked on a plane deeper than that concerned with what thinkers may positively affirm. It emerges rather through indicating, amidst the sheer variety of their perceptions and responses, what problems they have been forced to face in common. Within the intellectual matrix of any era this seems the best approach to understanding the elements both of coherence and, no less significant, of disjunction. From the shared dilemmas, if from anywhere, may be derived the *Zeitgeist* or 'spirit of the age', that elusive but not altogether illusory mingling of perceived relevances, habits of mind, modes of expression, and so forth, which helps us to characterize an epoch. In the context of European history it is the emergence of mass society, and the associated development of mass politics and culture, which most essentially and dramatically distinguishes this period from what has gone before. Moreover, this same emergence has presented intellectuals with their most persistent challenge. Nothing marks the age more clearly than their heightening sense of constriction and asphyxia amidst a herd whom they sought to abuse, exploit, or redeem. In the words of Søren Kierkegaard, that once-neglected prophet resurrected for the twentieth century: 'The crowd is the lie.'

The mass mediocrity which so many intellectuals perceived and feared as a peril to any improvement of the European mind has stimulated some of them to great things. But the battle has been fierce, the loss heavy. Much of the strife involved an extension and sharpening of important eighteenth-century debates, especially concerning the nature and status of reason. At their best the *philosophes* were acutely aware of many of its limitations, but about its powers they maintained generally a degree of optimism that has been repeatedly questioned in this later period not merely by devotees of irrationalism but also by increasingly sceptical rationalists themselves. Nineteenth-century European society certainly pursued many of the intimations of Enlightenment, including that 'rationalization' of processes which was central to Weber's characterization of Western development. Yet, simultaneously, it was becoming ever more evident that herd values emphasized both the frailties of reason and the scope of dynamic passion. The theme of mass socialization is therefore inseparable from that of the challenge which it has issued, above all, to conventions about rationality itself. This liaison – no merely retrospective and structural device of the historian – has been a conscious concern of the greatest minds of this era.

In the classic model mass society is differentiated from what precedes it by an enlargement in the scale of activities, institutions, and loyalties. For an understanding of it there is still much to commend in Ferdinand Tönnies' *Community and Association* (1887). This was a timely pioneering analysis of the shifting emphasis from small and close-knit groupings (*Gemeinschaften*, or 'communities') to large, bureaucratized, impersonal, and anonymous aggregations (*Gesellschaften*, or 'associations'). Within the latter, Tönnies claimed, the significance of similarities between attitudes, thoughts, and behaviour is enhanced at the expense of everything distinctively individualistic. As these structures are transformed so too is the framework of authority. The individual finds his social and moral bearings alike thrown into confusion. His plight, a recurrent concern of social theorists in Tönnies' time and beyond, was best crystallized in Émile Durkheim's concept of 'anomie', the state of normlessness. Henceforth intellectuals would address themselves not merely to these problems of disorientation but also to those produced by the equalizing tendencies of mass society in every field. To the liberal-minded a reduction of political and even economic inequalities had some attractions that compensated for its readily perceptible drawbacks. The success of government or marketing might be assessed roughly by counting votes or sales. Yet in how many other areas should the growing worship of numerical supremacy be countenanced? Was high culture, for instance, to be a mere commodity whose quality must be related closely to size of audience?

Pleas for the preservation of judicious discrimination amid the universal levelling threatened by mass society have echoed down from the age of Alexis de Tocqueville and Jakob Burckhardt to our own. But in such an environment the survival of cultural and intellectual élitism has become more than ever before a matter of conscious and strenuous contrivance. It is a sign of the times that intellectuals should have become so conscious about being such. This self-consciousness is corollary to a crisis in self-confidence. It may seem, at first, curious that the caste of intellectuals should have grown so defensive during an age in which their own accomplishments have been immense and in which there has been overall such an improvement in the literacy and basic education of Europeans, such an acceleration in the rate at which knowledge can be accumulated, and such an enlargement in the scale of its diffusion. None would deny these as benefits, but the most self-critical intellectuals have appreciated at what high price they have been purchased.

Such thinkers have shown awareness that over the last century some of the finest achievements of the European mind point towards the limitations of reason itself or towards the illusory nature of 'progress' in spheres outside that of basic material subsistence. Viewing the democratization of intellect they have often recognized, alongside some undoubted gains, real elements of debit going even beyond the tyranny of number and of equalization. For instance, extensive parts of the traditional corpus of European high culture, such as its classical legacy, have been allowed to atrophy, and many other aspects have been imperilled by excessive vulgarization. Media of communication unique to this period – a press at last truly popular, films, radio, and television – have evolved as immense, though ultimately incalculable, influences upon the ideas current in mass society. As vehicles for successful propaganda in the hands of the unscrupulous they have proved their power. The development of half-knowledge has turned out often more dangerous than the preceding ignorance, and there is force in the argument that a century of educational revolution has scarcely begun to solve the problems of mass gullibility. Consciously cultivated for millennia, this is perhaps at its most insidious when we are tempted wrongly to believe that it has been banished by the forces of progress. Sceptical good sense, the best of the Enlightenment tradition, has not won a mass audience.

The remarks made so far have important bearings on the intellectual historian's methodological problems. For any period these are complicated enough, and this is not the place to compose a general essay about them. But it is appropriate to mention here the difficulties that are, relatively speaking, peculiar to our hundred years – the matter of proximity, and the sheer bulk of source materials. Of course historians of every genre working on this period are faced with them, but it may be helpful to suggest a few of the implications they have for the study of intellectual development in particular.

In the first place, a sense of comparative familiarity with the ideas of recent times is not tantamount to a philosophical or historical understanding of them. Our more immediate empathy with the world-picture of Henrik Ibsen or Bertrand Russell than with that of Molière or Spinoza may lead us simply into mental laxity. On the other hand relative proximity, combined with the welter of accessible sources, is less likely to encourage such laxity when we come to decide which figures and themes to highlight. One of the commonest failings in many intellectual histories dealing with earlier times derives from the greater temptations there to prejudge just what and who is 'significant'. It relates also to the development of a traditionalized corpus of relevances, often in the form of 'classic' thinkers who then become too easily the symbols of whole epochs – Aquinas of the Middle Ages, Machiavelli of the Renaissance, and so forth. The tradition can become so rigid as severely to restrict open-mindedness about creative revisions of the structure. In relation to the last hundred years the tyranny of tradition, though not entirely absent, is as yet less marked. But here the greater fluidity of debate about significances imposes strains of a different sort – not least, the feeling that the historian's preferences for inclusion or emphasis may seem personal to the point of short-lived idiosyncrasy. Of some continuing high stature for Sigmund Freud or Marcel Proust he need have little doubt, but about Miguel de Unamuno or Boris Pasternak he may be less sure. To the extent that legislation for future intellectual judgements is certainly not his purpose this does not matter. Yet it can be appreciated how heavy will weigh the onus of discrimination in situations where, amidst a horde of potentially relevant materials, the processes of winnowing have only just begun.

All forms of written matter, from abstruse philosophical treatises to the products of the daily or even hourly press, fall ideally within the ambit of the intellectual historian. And throughout this period their bulk has grown exponentially. So has every kind of source, written or unwritten, about the social fabric to which ideas must be related. Understandably the sociology of knowledge has still to attain maturity. Especially in a general survey such as this careful selection is both a necessity and a nightmare. We need also to remember that – again, ideally – the historian of thought must accept as potentially relevant all forms of human expression, including those not conveyed directly by written or oral utterance. In short, his subject matter is part of that totality of relationships out of which human behaviour is compounded. Indeed, elucidation of the ultimate inseparability of thought, emotion, and action has been one of the most impressive intellectual endeavours of this epoch, carried on even in fields beyond that of its most explicit and dramatic study by Freud and the post-Freudians. The existence of this nexus reinforces the argument that in the last resort the web of history is seamless in terms both of chronology and of genres. So long as this is kept in mind, there is much convenience and no necessary harm in the historians' divisions of labour under labels such as 'political', 'diplomatic', 'economic', and 'social'. With them the 'intellectual' genre can satisfactorily co-exist. But, especially regarding the era of mass society, there is value in enlarging upon its relationship to one other kind – the notoriously imprecise realm of 'cultural' history.

Sorting out the many possible nuances of the term 'culture' would be here beside the point. It is enough to suggest the broad distinction between an anthropological and a more popular use. In the former case, culture denotes the whole nexus just mentioned, being the sum total of the ways of life which characterize a particular society. In popular usage the word has a scope that is less extensive though not necessarily more exact. It directs prime attention to matters of aesthetics and intellect, to the verbal constellation of taste, elegance, urbanity, and refinement. This latter sense is the one ordinarily employed in the present book. Under this meaning the phrase 'mass culture' – evoking the meretricious world of *kitsch* – may be rendered ironical, and even self-contradictory. The contrasting product has then to be described through such a term as 'high culture', which has appeared here already. Thus history that is 'cultural', either in the anthropological or the popular sense, can quite explicitly incorporate the study of ideas but need not keep them in centre-focus. The intellectual historian's main field of view is, then, somewhat narrower. But there are two caveats. Firstly, as stressed before, the significance of ideas cannot be assessed in substantial isolation from the greater nexus embraced by the anthropologist's conception of culture, and least of all under modern conditions of communication. Secondly, it must be recognized that, parallel to the disparities between high and mass culture, there exists a range of distinctions for the various levels of sophistication at which ideas themselves are couched; and, further, that in mass society we find the interaction between these levels at its most complex.

This interaction is especially important in so far as the history of ideas tolerates no general law suggesting that either influence or conscious sophistication stands directly proportionate to worth. Intellectual blind-alleys can be of the highest significance. The fact that prevalent error may be not infrequently more accurately representative of the spirit of an age than ultimately more profitable ideas presents the historian with a problem of balance that is particularly pressing in the context of general survey. The difficulty is clearest in the history of the natural sciences where metaphors of advance are less vulnerable than in, say, the study of philosophy or literature. For example, in any account touching upon scientific thought shortly before the First World War the aberrations of Ernst Haeckel, so popularly and influentially solving 'the riddle of the universe', can well claim as much attention as the more esoteric but truly valuable achievements of Max Planck. Under such circumstances the historian of ideas, concerned also adequately to expound the developments that provided foundations for real progress, may reasonably make some mild concessions to 'Whiggishness'. That is, he may give some artificial weighting to the genesis and development of those features of his contemporary intellectual scene that he himself cherishes as valid or inspiring. But this procedure is defensible only if used very selectively and if adopted with sufficient judiciousness to preserve a live impression of the countervailing forces of misguided pretentiousness, of half-truth, and of downright error.

Within the space available I have chosen to stress ideas emanating from those with pretensions, normally but not invariably justified, to a certain sophistication. This emphasis does not necessarily involve neglecting the wider scene. As Jacques Barzun comments:

It is beside the point to argue that millions of our fellow men live and die without bothering their heads about the work of Einstein or Freud or Bernard Shaw. Either the indifferent masses will ultimately feel the impact – the bomb will explode over their heads – or their existence is demonstrably related to mankind's articulate thought through their acting as background, subject matter, or chief obstacle.

In considering primarily scientists, philosophers, theologians, theorists of society and politics, creative authors and artists, I have tried to treat their work in a way that might capture something of the interaction between refined thought and popular conceptions, and still more generally between ideas and the broader social fabric. Sometimes, indeed, it is vulgarity rather than any real sophistication that stands well to the fore. The implications of Nazism, for example, are among the central concerns of this study – and for the very reason that the doctrines of Hitler's movement quite calculatedly debased the best parts of the European intellectual tradition and made a far from unsuccessful appeal to vulgarity in thought and action alike.

Among the repercussions of the temporary triumph of Nazi political and intellectual tyranny was a notable exodus of intellectuals from the Germanic world. To this we shall return in due course, but it is worth mentioning here as symptomatic of a more general problem with methodological implications for the historian of ideas over the last hundred years. This concerns what we might call roughly the geography of thought, the spatial elaboration of the dual tendencies towards diversity and uniformity in intellectual development. In some cases, we need to recognize nuances of differentiation on a relatively local scale. The history of ideas in Germany under the Second Reich cannot disregard real tensions between north and south, between the Prussian intellectual arrogance epitomized by Heinrich von Treitschke in Berlin and the freer atmosphere quite self-consciously engineered by the intelligentsia of Munich or Freiburg. As an instance of diversity on a much broader scale, we need to recognize in the context of twentieth-century philosophical developments the remarkable division between countries where versions of logical empiricism have become fashionable and those where more metaphysical forms have continued to hold sway. Or, again, there are distinctions, not all of them simply attributable to the triumph of communist ideology, which have to be made concerning intellectual evolution as between Eastern and Western Europe. There is much in the well-tried notion that through a thousand years the area of Western and Central Europe originally circumscribed by the boundaries of Charlemagne's empire has been a heartland for intellectual achievement. Indeed the present account, while seeking to avoid any severe neglect of other parts, must have that region as the clearest object of focus.

At the intermediate level of nuances between individual nations there appears at once a paradox indicating the delicacy of balance between intellectual diversities and uniformities. On one hand, nationalism has been amongst the strongest forces in this period and intellectuals have been often in the vanguard of its advance. On the other hand, there has been across the continent such a notable internationalization of ideas as to suggest that we must treat with caution many claims about distinctively national schools of philosophy, social science, and so forth. We are still confronted with numerous difficulties in the communication of ideas but, as I shall try to explain towards the end of the book, the major ones are not now primarily the result of national barriers. The accentuation of the international element must be related closely to the relative homogeneity of social developments throughout the continent during the last century or so. No country has escaped the forces of mass socialization, which has had as one of its features the encouragement of mobility on an unprecedented scale. This has been plainly reflected in the physical restlessness of intellectuals, who in every age have been more inclined to travel than most of their neighbours. To such mobility must everywhere be added the revolutionary technical improvements that have so speeded and enlarged the international communication of ideas themselves. Where the transmission has been delayed in significant cases, such as those of Kierkegaard or Gregor Mendel, our surprise at the exceptions may be itself testimony to the generality of the rule.

In dealing with 'European' thought, we must not only keep in mind its diversities within the continent but also appreciate the extent to which, ideally, attention might be given to its impact beyond. As global traders and colonists Europeans have affected deeply the thought and culture of the wider world. It will be obviously beyond the scope of this book to detail such interaction. But some of its features will be touched on, especially in relation to the United States whose culture has maintained for 200 years some very significant ties with that of Europe. As a haven for numerous gifted refugees and migrants from the old continent, the United States has provided the geographical setting for many intellectual developments which cannot be regarded either as solely American or as exclusively European. Again, it would be wrong to overlook America's contributions to a general enlargement of scale in scientific activities everywhere, with all that this implies for the furtherance of fundamental theorizing in these fields. Not least, the experience of the United States impinges insistently on our imagination once we derive a certain thematic unity from the concept of mass socialization. For it is there that many of its processes have developed furthest; and there too that we see, alongside self-consciously lavish endowments of intellectual and artistic activity, some of the most painful examples of the better aspects of Western thought and culture undergoing extensive and even irrevocable vulgarization. Moreover, these are the examples which Western Europeans have in the forefront of their minds when they speak of 'Americanization' as a peril on their own doorstep.

To these remarks about geographical lines and limits must be added, in conclusion, brief comment on the analogous problems of chronological demarcation. Periodization is essential to the historian's activity, but it must never be the foundation merely for specious tidiness. It is helpful in elucidating the intelligible disorder of history only so long as we recognize its status as a structure whose imposition is predominantly retrospective and artificial. This structure, already demonstrably vulnerable when employed for the history of 'events', is even less solid when applied to the study of ideas. Indeed, as a rough starting point for this book '1870' is very advantageous – precisely because, for the intellectual rather than the political historian, it lacks the dramatic significance that might dull sensitivity to the continuities with the preceding period. Within the relevant span of a hundred years or so the chronological structuring has been influenced chiefly by the two World Wars. Although neither in intellectual nor in any other terms can they be regarded as causative of all that followed, these wars seem structurally crucial – as crises, relatively precise in date, which were so vast as to prove immediately inescapable to the consciousness of Europeans at every level of sophistication.

In consequence the bulk of the volume is organized in two broad chronological swathes, the earlier running to the eve of the First World War and the later reaching from there to the conclusion of the Second. By beginning the former period around 1870 it is possible properly to elaborate the significance of those elements of intellectual contrast – even, in some forms, of intellectual revolution – that became increasingly evident from the pivotal decade of the 1890s onward. Politically, on both the domestic and the international planes, the forty years or so before 1914 would come in due course to be characterized with some justification as an epoch of relative peace. Certainly, ever since, there have been many willing to view it as the last phase of a golden age. In contrast, the second chronological span – from 1914 to 1945 – was marked by more open strife, being dominated not merely by war and tenuous peace but also by the growth of massive ideological confrontation. For the purposes of intellectual history there is within this period too, roughly around 1930, a point of notable modulation.

After the earlier comments on ideas and mass society it should be clear why, in treating each main time-span, I have started with a brief contextual chapter. The argument then proceeds topically – though the order of treatment differs somewhat as between the two periods – through the fields of natural science, philosophical and religious thought, social and political ideas, literature and the arts, thereby encompassing the major areas of intellectual and imaginative endeavour. This procedure is not adopted however in the briefer coverage of a third and final chronological segment, concerning the years since 1945. Both the sheer quantity and the close proximity of the relevant source materials have prompted me to treat this last period within the much looser structure of a single general essay.

In all these essentially preliminary remarks about the chief problems to be faced and the sort of strategy here adopted to cope with them, my natural emphasis has been upon the difficulties associated with the study of recent European thought. But something of its potential for excitement may also have begun to emerge. By the end of the book I hope to have made quite abundantly clear what makes the whole subject so attractive, compelling, and rewarding.

PART ONE

1870 – 1914

Chapter 1

THE
SOCIAL AND POLITICAL
ENVIRONMENT

AN unprecedented rate of growth in population was the most significant precondition for the enlargement of scale centrally characteristic of mass society. In 1800 Europe, including Russia, was inhabited by some 190 million people. Over the next seventy years the figure rose to nearly 300 million, and the 400-million mark was reached around the beginning of the twentieth century. By 1914, quite exclusive of some 200 million persons of European birth or descent living outside a continent that throughout the preceding century had been a massive exporter of migrants and colonists, the inhabitants probably exceeded 460 million. As nearly always with demographic change, the causes were complex. But the increase was manifested chiefly in a falling rate of mortality. From 1870 at least, the most important factor seems to have been a series of rapid advances in preventive medicine. These demonstrated clearly a connection between modifications in ideas and changes in social conditions. The germ theory of disease involved considerable revisions in biological thinking, which will be examined later. Yet these could not have been turned to much practical benefit without new conceptions of social planning as well. Diseases such as cholera, typhoid, and small-pox – hitherto seemingly unavoidable facts of ordinary existence – were understood and in great measure controlled. After 1900 even the rate for mortality at the especially vulnerable stage of infancy began to fall sharply. It is hard to exaggerate the impact that such advances towards a longer and healthier life had upon a whole range of human expectations and aspirations, not least regarding an improved standard of everyday existence. They were a dramatic instance of man's ability now to tame forces which for long had mastered him in seemingly inevitable fashion. Age-old enemies were retreating before the march of science and progress.

The medical advances were particularly relevant to the health of town-dwellers. This was all the more important because, even despite exceptions in Eastern Europe, it was within urban centres that most of the population increase was being assimilated. In 1870 there had been some seventy European towns of at least 100,000 inhabitants, but by the turn of the century there were nearly 200. Within the same period Berlin, Vienna, Moscow, and St Petersburg joined London and Paris as conurbations of a million or more. For vastly increasing numbers the 'swarming city', which already Charles Baudelaire had explored so sensitively in literature, was becoming the environment for everyday life. It was the focus for the markedly anonymous and standardized existence characteristic of mass society. Drastically to reduce the incidence of epidemic disease was one thing; it was quite another to cope with the individual and collective psychological strains and pressures imposed by the clamour or the physical density of urban life on this unprecedented scale. Not surprisingly, it was within the context of the towns and cities that European intellectuals perceived most clearly those elements of rootlessness, alienation, and disorientation which were so recurrent both in their introspective meditation and in their assessment of the wider contemporary human condition. Often their critique of urban life spilt over into an indictment of modern civilization at large.

Patterns of life and labour were necessarily intertwined. From the last third of the nineteenth century the processes and products of mass manufacture were progressively more essential elements in the trend towards an existence that was standardized and, even beyond the factory, moulded by the master images of the machine and the conveyor belt. Between 1870 and 1914 the industrialization already dominant in Britain and Belgium took a decisive grip upon the economic life of most of the continent, doing so in a form now substantially characterized by mechanization. It was this feature which in part encouraged the integration of manufacturing processes, the enlargement in the average size of factory units, and the amalgamation of firms into great new complexes and virtual monopolies. But there were other pressures in this direction, not least those of ruthless competition. For employers and financiers, quite apart from the mass proletariat itself, the growth process was accompanied by strains. The expansion of industrial capacity, allied to the fuller exploitation of world agricultural potential, soon led to a severe bout of overproduction. For two decades from 1873 there was a depression in prices and a crisis in profits and investment, which marked a retardation but certainly not a reversal of overall economic growth. Though the cake was expanding there were for a time simply too many firms slicing at it. Under these conditions a high incidence of commercial failure, with consequential unemployment and labour unrest, was inevitable even in the midst of plenty.

Not only the ways but also the material products of industrial capitalism appeared to many as wondrous strange. To the last decades of the nineteenth century must be traced the invention or first significant diffusion of such now unexceptional phenomena as electrical lighting and transportation, the bicycle and the internal combustion engine, the telephone and the wireless, synthetic fibres and artificial dyes. The range of industrial products for mass consumption was moving rapidly towards its present complexity. As Geoffrey Barraclough suggested during the 1960s, 'On the purely practical level of daily life, a person living today who was suddenly put back into the world of 1900 would find himself on familiar ground, whereas if he returned to 1870, even in industrialized Britain, the differences would be more striking than the similarities.' Qualitative change was characteristic of this phase of industrialization also at a deeper level, in so far as the period's major advances tended to rest less on piecemeal technological improvements than on new ideas of a fundamentally scientific nature. In this context the chemical and electrical sciences were outstanding, and their achievements were put to use most speedily in Germany. As with the victories over disease so too in these further cases a greater sophistication in science was the bedrock for improvements in the material and physical conditions of living. But in all such matters as health or industrial production scientific advance would have been inoperative for most practical purposes if left unaccompanied by major changes of attitude towards social and economic organization.

Central here were conflicting ideas about the proper extent of state involvement. With population booming, cities mushrooming, industrialization advancing, all in such a vast degree, any rigid subscription to laissez-faire conceptions would have been a recipe for social anarchy. Governments, together with municipal organs, amplified the scale of their activities to deal with the challenge of ordering and serving societies formed of larger, denser, and more mobile agglomerations of people than previously experienced. Everywhere there was an enlargement of state bureaucracy, a multiplication of records and statistics, to an extent which seemed to threaten the privacy and freedoms of the individual. Governmental responses to the new circumstances involved enormous budgetary expansion, and by 1914 income tax was at last the rule rather than the exception in Europe as a whole. The firmer hold that the state took on economic strategy was also demonstrated clearly in a general shift of stress back to tariff protectionism between countries from the 1870s onward. Domestically, tighter controls were required for the maintenance of public order, and for the maximization of the benefits associated with improved methods of transport and communication. Stricter regulations about such matters as sanitation and urban planning had to be made and enforced before epidemiological advances could be fully exploited. In the context of labour there was much legislative progress regarding both factory conditions and workers' insurance. While British precedent inspired much of the action on the former front, it was Bismarck's Reich which proffered a model on the latter. By 1914 the German enactments of the 1880s in regard to sickness, accident, and old age provision had been reflected, to varying degree, in Austria, Denmark, Italy, Switzerland, France, and Britain. In all countries each instance of enlarged state responsibility met with accusations of unnecessary encroachment and interference, but the volume of opposition tended to diminish over the period as a whole.

The practical and ideological problems associated with greater state intervention are nowhere better seen than in relation to education – an area obviously of the utmost importance in studying the interaction of ideas and society. It was a field in which liberal qualms about interference were often muted by the thought that state control was preferable to the preceding tendencies towards ecclesiastical domination. Throughout the period, during which it was still easy to postulate a general parallelism between progress in the diffusion of knowledge and improvement in social behaviour, there were advances at every educational level. These were in large part a state-guided response to the requirements of a more complex industrial society. Moreover they were speeded by the economies of scale made possible by patterns of denser urban living. In secondary and higher education – still sectors available only to relatively few – curricula were adapted increasingly to practical social demands. Scientific and modern-language studies thrived at the expense of the ancient classics. From the enlarging number of high schools and universities would emerge the engineers and technicians, the scientists and doctors, the lawyers and administrators to service the intricate mechanisms of modern life. At this level the rapid development of higher technical schooling in Germany was the clearest and most efficient reply to this demand. In a political context too it appeared desirable that élites, old or new, should be better equipped to discharge responsibilities growing ever more complex, not least under the impact of popular aspirations towards more democratic forms of government.

It also seemed plain that there were economic and political advantages attached to a wider diffusion of at least rudimentary knowledge amongst the masses. Indeed, the great progress in elementary schooling was the period's most remarkable achievement on the educational scene. It involved tackling a truly revolutionary task – that of removing the mass illiteracy which had been hitherto a constant of European social history. Like the Scandinavian countries, Prussia had been well on the road to universal elementary education even before 1870. Under the new Reich her provisions were extended to Germany at large, and free schooling was introduced in 1888. In France too the already relatively advanced arrangements were consolidated through the 1880s into a system of universal, free, and secular primary instruction. Between 1874 and 1880 Switzerland, Italy, the Netherlands, Belgium, and Britain had legislated for compulsory elementary school attendance, though there was variation between the countries in their provisions regarding age span and financing. By the turn of the century there was no European government that failed to acknowledge in theory its responsibility for some form of elementary school system, and in the western and central parts of the continent such provision was also well established in practice.

Similar regional variations are important in assessing the illiteracy figures themselves. Throughout the period these were lowest in Scandinavia and North-Western Europe generally, and highest in Italy, Spain, Portugal, Hungary, the Balkans, and Russia. But everywhere there was some improvement and, even if we exclude the particularly perilous statistics of similar progress in Russia, its overall scale was such that between 1850 and 1930 the proportion of European adults unable to read fell roughly from fifty to ten per cent. It was a quantitative reduction massive enough to have great qualitative implications for society as a whole. In many ways such changes had left the masses more vulnerable than responsible. Certainly contemporary ideologists were not blind to the new opportunities for manipulation unleashed by mass suscepti-bility to the printed word. Political parties and other interest groups were quick to exploit the fact that in most countries by the 1880s the battle for press freedom was substantially won. Technical factors such as improved communications, better typesetting, and cheaper newsprint were further aids to the emergence at last of a popular press, financially bolstered by advertising as much as by subscription. But the success and influence of this first truly mass medium would have been unthinkable without the revolution in schooling.

Under all these conditions the significance of educational control was accentuated. It was here that the Churches, already faced both with much intellectual hostility and with the tre-mendous problem of adapting their ministration to a markedly urban environment, came into the severest conflict with secularizing tendencies. Educational issues were prominent in, for example, the German *Kulturkampf* of the 1870s and the sustained French tussle between Church and State which led to their formal separation in 1905. Everywhere the broad out-come was, on the one hand, some sort of grudging toleration of church schools and, on the other, a distinctively anti-clerical or even anti-religious flavour in the education provided within the greatly expanding sector of state instruction. Amidst the unprecedented flux of contemporary life both sides recognized the need for social discipline. Its inculcation had been traditionally a major objective of ecclesiastical bodies. But there was in principle no reason why it should not be nurtured just as well in a secular context. Durkheim, for instance, viewed the establishment of a comprehensive secular morality as the crucial palliative, or even the cure, for anomic disorientation. It was realized that such features of modern society as the standardized conditions of factory labour and the regimentation involved in the trend towards mass military service might contribute to a process of secular discipline. But still more crucial seemed school training, experienced as this was at an even earlier stage of life. If defenders of Christian education fell the more readily into the traditional error of mere indoctrination, there were certainly also many secularists who had their own brands of intolerance scarcely concealed behind the banners of rational free inquiry. Excess on both sides was understandable. The battle was for nothing less than a sphere of fundamental influence over the moral values of mass society.

In this same context of a focus for authority the position of the family, like that of the Churches, was becoming less secure. The change bulked large in Tönnies's analysis of the problems of transition from *Gemeinschaft* to *Gesellschaft*. Although modern psychology would certainly underline the parental part in the processes of early socialization and personality formation, there was over this period a reduction in the familial contribution to general education and material welfare. The formal school system became the main repository for that rapidly growing corpus of basic technical and scientific knowledge which parental instruction could no longer encompass; and the progress of state and factory welfare schemes was at once effect and accelerating cause of the diminished likelihood of the smaller, less stable urban family making the relevant provisions on the extensive scale customary in earlier times. The age-old currents of revolt against

parental authority and the deeply felt stresses between generations were accentuated by these developments and by the
related and crucial fact that the family was becoming less
important as a determinant of social status. Society was more
than ever before geared to being on the move and on the make.
It was thus natural that smaller store should be put on family
background than on education or, still more especially,
occupation, earnings, and similar criteria susceptible to predominantly meritocratic and materialistic evaluation.

The mobility of social status was unprecedented in scope
and speed of action. With aristocratic values receding before
the advance of bourgeois ones, the broad principles of
stratification became those appropriate to a market hierarchy
that had progressively smaller reference to 'orders' or 'estates'.
This trend, though understandably productive of much
tension in the socially and politically backward areas dominated by Ottoman, Romanov, and Habsburg rule, was
clearest in Western and parts of Central Europe. It was there
that social divisions were becoming structured most rapidly in
terms of essentially economic 'class', not least as between the
owners of industrial and commercial capital and the labouring
mass of wage-earners. While the expropriation of the former
by the latter was the aim of many resentful of bourgeois
society, there were no fewer workers who accepted as an
economic and ethical postulate that by striving, saving, and
self-help they might more readily than ever before aspire
rather to be assimilated within the ranks of the middle classes.
What was most significantly common to both cases was a
sense of acceleration in the beat of time, a feeling of greater
proximity to the moment at which hope might be fulfilled.
This is one of the keys to appreciating the urgency that
radiates from the social thinking of the age.

These aspirations and confrontations were associated too
with the processes of political democratization. By the 1870s
parliamentary institutions in some form or other had been

adopted by most European countries, but they had substantial checking effects on executive power only in Britain, France, and Belgium. Moreover, although there was general accept-ance of the principle of equality before the law, there was still much opposition to political egalitarianism. Every franchise arrangement embodied discrimination on grounds of sex and normally also of property. However, on balance and in despite of a number of ingenious and quite successful stalling actions by conservative rearguards fearful of an incompatibility be-tween democracy and order, there was during the period firm general advance towards mass politics through extensions both of parliamentary functions and of popular voting rights. For present purposes it will suffice to suggest the stages in the triumph of universal manhood suffrage – though we have to remember that it varied in actual significance as between countries according to its place within a total context of constitutional provisions referring, for example, to age quali-fications, plural voting, or the composition and powers of a second less democratic chamber.

All male Germans were enfranchised in 1871, for national Reichstag elections at least. Universal manhood suffrage was reintroduced in France in the same year, and implemented by Switzerland in 1874, by Spain, Belgium, and Norway in the 1890s, and by Sweden, Austria, and Portugal too before 1914. Over the same period, the British, Dutch, and Italian elector-ates were also enlarged; Russia and Turkey, albeit only in the aftermath of revolutions, introduced for the first time some form of parliament and franchise in 1905 and 1908 respec-tively; and between 1907 and 1913 the first European vic-tories for female suffrage were registered in Finland, Norway, and Denmark. The political thinkers of the time interpreted these developments variously, but none could deny their immense significance either for better or worse. The progress of democracy, and of parliamentarianism, was certainly not tantamount to an unequivocal triumph for liberalism. As we shall see, the ability of this political creed to respond adequately to needs that were changing so rapidly was severely questioned through much of the speculation of the epoch. Some of the acutest criticism came from liberals themselves, but there were also explicit assaults from those standing either to right or left of a moderate tradition increasingly endangered by the passions of mass politics. In principle franchise extension, like .enlargement of educational opportunities, had potential for intensifying popular involvement and responsibility in society. But in certain contexts it was also available to élites as an instrument for manipulating the populace on a scale hitherto unknown. Certainly it hastened the evolution of a more demagogic political style, adapted not merely to wider electorates but also to conditions of denser urbanization and of improved literacy and communications.

The development of this style was accompanied by the emergence, on a mass basis, of firmly institutionalized and relatively disciplined political parties whose organization and functions provided contemporary theorists with much food for thought. For instance, in the Marxist setting the heightening of such concerns was one of the chief features of contrast between Lenin's generation and the preceding one. The most outstanding example of a mass party was that of the German Social Democrats which was more than a million strong by 1914. As foci for a sense of loyalty and belonging amidst the flux of mass society, the party organizations have to be viewed within the broader context of a general boom in the popularity of a whole range of voluntary associations organized for economic, social, or cultural purposes. Such bodies as credit associations, women's leagues, sporting organizations, and youth movements – with or without explicit political affiliations – burgeoned profusely in the period. Perhaps most notable was growth amongst trade unions, which by 1890 had gained in Britain, France, Austria, Germany, and Spain some form of legal recognition and were progressing towards federation at the national and international levels.

Amidst all these generalizations about aspects of European society and politics in the half-century before the First World War it has been impossible to linger on the relevance of geographical nuancing. But the suggestion of some marked homogeneity of development across the continent can be beneficial only so long as it is recognized for what it is – a judgement essentially relative, used principally to convey a certain contrast with the rather more heterogeneous situation of earlier times. In any case, even in the treatment thus far of the years from 1870 to 1914 there have emerged very clearly some broad patterns of differentiation concerning the incidence of social, economic, and political advance. Most particularly there is a continuation, though not necessarily an intensification, of age-old distinctions between the western and eastern parts of the continent. For contemporaries the persistence of variations of this kind seemed no less significant than the elements of similarity found in pan-continental developments. Moreover their awareness of distinctions must be associated also with their obsessive attachment to nationalism – a political doctrine which, though ironically being yet another force influential across Europe as a whole, was overall divisive in its implications.

Aspirations towards national independence in the German and Italian states and in the Habsburg Empire at large had been among the main features of the revolutionary pandemic of 1848–9. Over the following twenty years nationalism gained ground rapidly, playing a central role in the brief wars forced upon Austria by France in 1859 and by Prussia in 1866. Although a Polish revolt was put down by the Russians, the 1860s saw the political unification of the Italian peninsula, the concession of a large degree of domestic autonomy to at least the Magyar minority within the Habsburg Empire, and great strides towards the fulfilment of Bismarck's version of a united Germany. His successful war against France in 1870–71 allowed him to annex Alsace-Lorraine and to bind together most non-Austrian Germans in a Prussianized Reich. The victory also gave the new Kingdom of Italy an opportunity of tidying up its territory through the expropriation of nearly all the remaining papal domain. In the following two decades Bismarck sought with qualified success to stabilize the international order which his own diplomacy had done so much to fashion.

Although general war was avoided for nearly fifty years after 1870, this balance of power was constantly imperilled. The French, even if demoralized by both acute defeat and chronic failure to share significantly in the general population boom, were willing to seize any likely opportunity of taking revenge on the enemy across the Rhine. Especially after Bismarck's removal in 1890 there were within the new Reich and also in Austria many ready to purvey visions wider than his as to what was properly German in territory and culture. For them the so-called national unification of 1871 was partial and far from clearly definitive. Many of their pan-German aspirations and of the competing ones emanating from Russian-led Slavs focused on the Balkans. The area smouldered with nationalist resentments against what was left of Ottoman domination. It was also a sphere where the Habsburg and Romanov Empires stood in active rivalry both with each other and with the smaller ethnic groups. From the Russo–Turkish War begun in 1877 and the Berlin Congress of 1878 through to the Balkan Wars of 1912 and 1913 the region was an arena of nationalist conflict. And eventually it was the confrontation between Germany and Slav concerns over the fate of Serbia that provided the occasion for the outbreak of general European war in 1914.

The events of that summer revealed the depths of nationalistic hysteria all over the continent. They came as the culmination of more than a decade of frantic competition in armament production. In 1914 most of the highly vocal socialist opposition to internationally divisive war was silenced, and the people of Europe went to battle nation by nation rather than class by class. As symbols of loyalty for the members of mass secular society both class and nation had grown in stature throughout the previous century, but at this time of general crisis it was the latter that won out decisively. The already deeply emotive appeal of nationalism to societies in need of new sources of authority had been fortified, and in many ways transcended, by the rapid permeation of modes of thought and action connected with belief in racial superiorities. With support from many contemporary scientists of repute, politicians and publicists readily invoked racist arguments both in national rivalries and in spheres that were more than anything supra-national, like that associated with the broad collision between pan-Slav and pan-German aspirations. The intensified political anti-semitism of the time, exemplified by the Russian pogroms or by aspects of the Dreyfus Affair in France, also drew increasingly on a biologized racism. At many levels of confrontation the visceral myth of blood was revealing clearly its profound attractions for the masses.

National rivalries and racial confrontations also had relevance in an extra-European setting. In the long history of European colonial imperialism there is for sheer explosive expansion no period comparable to the thirty years from 1870. The main force was in the direction of Eastern Asia and still more especially of the African continent which by 1895 had been within a generation carved up into European colonies. There the British and French made vast extensions from their previous holdings, while on a lesser scale Germany, Belgium, and Italy sought for the first time to establish African empires of their own. In the same setting the Portuguese consolidated their existing influence, and this was also the case with the Dutch in Asia. However, in the latter continent it was the growth of Russian claims and the competing challenge from Japan which stood out. There were some conscious efforts to ensure that these expansionist developments did not unduly aggravate antagonism between the powers. Most notably, the Berlin Conference of 1884–5 attempted to establish working rules for the peaceful dissection of Africa. But it became increasingly unrealistic to separate colonial confrontations from national rivalries and other tensions within the politics of the European continent itself. The Anglo–French Fashoda episode of 1898, the British fears of German influence in South Africa and of Russian influence in Persia, and the successive crises arising from Franco–German antagonism over the future of Morocco were all clear examples of this inter-relationship. It also had much to do with that naval race, principally as between Germany and Britain, which so stirred the popular imagination. More generally still, colonial issues were part of the fabric of that system of alliances and confrontations between the powers which was developed in the ten years or so before 1914. When major war came between Germany and Austria on one side and Britain, France, and Russia upon the other it could scarcely fail to have certain truly global dimensions.

The motivations behind imperialism were immensely complex and cannot be pursued here. Yet it must be said that the commonest error has been to depict them too predominantly in economic terms. Factors such as the search for new markets, the investigation of openings where surplus capital might be invested, or the demand for raw materials are all noteworthy. But explanation primarily on these lines, though it has a certain plausibility overall, normally becomes severely inadequate when a particular area of expansion is examined in detail. Competition for naked political power was no less significant, nor can the wellsprings of imperialism be traced adequately without substantial reference to the realms of cultural and even spiritual mission. In short, any sweeping·

generalization about the overall relationship between, for example, trade, flag, and Bible is perilous. It is however quite indisputable that, in political, economic, and cultural contexts alike, imperialism emerged from and then itself intensified a long-established sense of European superiority. In ages past this feeling had contributed to the fundamental painlessness of such modes of self-criticism as those reliant upon contrast with noble savagery and primitive virtue. Here too – on a scale of continental self-flattery – by the end of the nineteenth century supremacy was being expressed, to a degree hitherto unknown, in terms of innate racial hierarchization. This was now one of the chief symptoms of belief in the essential timelessness and immutability of European hegemony. In the years around 1900 the healthy continuance of such supremacy seemed to most people unquestionable. With hindsight we can clearly see their error. In political terms at the very least, Europe had reached a point of apogee beyond which extended a curve of decline. The victory of Abyssinians over an Italian expeditionary army at Adowa in 1896, the Boxer Rebellion of 1900 in China, the defeat of Russia by Japanese land and sea forces in the war of 1904–5, and the growing involvement of the United States in Central and South America, the Pacific, and the Far East were all straws in a wind of change.

Those who perceived the real significance of these varied external challenges to hegemony were a minority. So too were those who fully appreciated the self-destructive potentia growing within European civilization itself. Yet the importance of this minority is out of all proportion to its number once we seek to trace the history of intellectual developments. For there it must be emphasized that disaffection, doubt, and despair, manifested in modes ranging from passive gloom to active denunciation, characterized many of Europe's acutest minds in the generation before the First World War. But certainly until Armageddon itself their prophecies went generally unhonoured amongst those masses which were now more self-conscious and socially self-assertive than ever before. Even the outbreaks of anarchist violence, or the nationalistic fevers running high nearly everywhere from the Balkans to Ireland, or the multiplication of armaments had not dissolved the popular adherence to certain vague ideas of progress. The masses had the clearest vested interests in the continued plausibility of beliefs about the inexorable forward march of civilization. This creed had given consolation, had enlarged aspirations, and indeed – in the mode of self-fulfilling prophecy – had inspired real gains. Eventually the manifestations of progress even came to be regarded as matters less of faith than of the most ordinary everyday experience.

It was only when there were massive reverses at this very level of the mundane, amidst the carnage and waste of the Great War, that more general disillusionment set in. Not until then did the symbiosis between material growth and the advance of civilization become, for a time at least, the object of widespread scepticism. Its previous dominance over the popular mind had been related in no small way to the contemporary worship of natural science, both as a model of cumulative knowledge and as a dramatic contributor to general welfare. But this was an image with important areas of superficiality, not least because, in the very generation before 1914, science was a sphere essentially of dissolving certainties. Ironically, it was becoming – at least for experts and perceptive laymen – in many respects a paradigm of doubt. For understanding the relationship between ideas and society in and beyond this period there is no more significant point of departure than an examination of the course of this truly revolutionary transformation.

Chapter 2

THE
NATURAL SCIENCES

ALREADY by 1870 the natural sciences seemed well on the way to consolidating a dominant and unifying intellectual status of the kind enjoyed by theology in the high Middle Ages and to a lesser extent by other forms of philosophy through to the early eighteenth century. Secular science's tangible contribution to social and material advances was reinforcing both its intellectual respectability and its institutional foundations. Though the scientist had emerged already as fairly distinct from the philosopher, it was not until the final decades of the nineteenth century that the European universities came to view the natural sciences as major academic pursuits in their own right. The chief exceptional case of earlier recognition, in Prussia, enabled the Germans to provide a model for scientific teaching and research elsewhere and to maintain down to 1914 a pre-eminence in many fields. Science was now asserting itself as a major intellectual and social force, and over the period as a whole an ever-increasing number of the sharpest intellects were being attracted by its problems. Money too came its way, most notably to support such centres of excellence as the Cavendish Laboratory at Cambridge and the Kaiser Wilhelm Institute for the Advancement of Science at Berlin. Industry and government were beginning to take a more active interest in physical science especially, and the laboratory, though typically still organized on a small scale, was well on the way to rivalling the humanistic library as a focus for higher educational activity.

The rising stock of science cannot be discussed apart from

the contemporary cult of positivism – a term so protean as to have been associated with much confusion then and since. The matter is complex but, for present purposes, it should suffice to make a single broad distinction between its critical and uncritical forms. The word had been coined earlier in the century by the social philosopher Auguste Comte. As the founder also of a self-consciously positivist movement he propounded a theory of progress which broadly conveyed the processes whereby science had triumphed over theology and metaphysics. Every branch of human knowledge came under his 'law of three stages'. In the theological state it is postulated that phenomena are produced by the immediate action of supernatural beings. At the transitional metaphysical stage the latter are replaced by abstract forces. Finally, in the positive state the vanity of all absolute notions and underlying causes is recognized and the mind applies itself through rational observation to studying more modestly the invariable relations of succession and resemblance among phenomena. Unfortunately, especially in the years towards his death in 1857, Comte's writings and behaviour suggested to the critical that his law was cyclical, that his positivist 'religion of humanity' (including even a secularized Blessed Virgin) was itself boundless in pretensions, and that within it the scientist had taken over the arrogance as well as the explanatory functions of an earlier priesthood. Positivists were characterized by their wariness of metaphysics, but its age-old spell could not be dissolved at a stroke.

Most brands of positivism, however close or remote their particular relationship to Comte, embodied some such contest between critical modesty and sublime assertiveness – a tension which had once strained the foundations of the Enlightenment itself. In its subtle empiricist forms positivism aimed merely to establish rules about the conditions and methods proper to the pursuit of knowledge. In the late nineteenth century this essentially normative attitude was

fundamental to such positivistic philosopher-scientists as the
Austrian Ernst Mach and the Frenchman Pierre Duhem. But
those who regarded a consistency in the sources and methods
of cognition as the major sign of scientific maturity were confronted by others who sought that maturity above all in the
unitary pattern which would inevitably emerge from the
actual findings of science. In the 1870s the latter version of
positivism was dominant, its overweening ambitions nurtured by the temptation to counter on the same plane the no
less foolhardy blanket denunciations of science emanating
especially from certain religious circles. More profoundly, its
cult of synthesis responded to two needs actively felt. The
first was that of keeping some conception of unity within the
sciences themselves, which amidst their rapid progress might
tend otherwise to set unbridgeable gulfs between, say, the
physical and the biological or the observational and the
experimental. The second need, demonstrable from the angles
of scientific and social thought alike, was to provide intellectual orientation and stability within the wider setting of an
unprecedentedly volatile society. Comte's positivist aim of
'generalizing our scientific conceptions and systematizing the
art of social life' was later reflected by others aspiring to bring
the superficially non-scientific within the world view of the
natural sciences themselves.

Central to the most ambitious expectations of synthesis was
the image presented by contemporary physical science. As we
shall see shortly in more detail, it depicted the universe as a
giant machine made up of material bodies in dynamic inter-
relationship. Formulated earlier in the century, the First and
Second Laws of thermodynamics – of the energy in the
cosmos being constant in quantity and yet diminishing in
availability for use – provided one of the master images of
unity. In principle even the new advances in evolutionary
biology might come to be subsumed within a physics that
could tie the activities of living organisms to the framework of

atomic motion as cases of mechanical and chemical energy. There was belief in the external reality of nature as a harmonious whole. This embodied – within itself, and quite independently of projections or impositions from the mind of the scientist – an order that was rational and logically necessary. It seemed that in time this order would be susceptible to total explanation, and with such explanation would come an intellectual and practical mastery of man's environment. In these words of 1878 from Emil Du Bois-Reymond, Berlin professor and important scientific popularizer, the note of confidence rings clear: 'If there is one criterion which for us indicates the progress of humanity, it is the level attained of power over nature ... Only in scientific research and power over nature is there no stagnation; knowledge grows steadily, the shaping strength develops unceasingly.' Such encomia to science as the self-evident centre of intellectual security and material advancement were highly influential. The need for this unifying image was such that, until the 1890s at least, the anomalies it contained were largely overlooked or regarded as testimony to transient failures in perception. But in time, and at the very heart of physics itself, they would grow in significance and become crucial to a shattering of the comfortable consensus of uncritical positivism.

Although physical law reigned supreme, it was generally the biological fields which attracted greater intellectual debate over the last three or four decades of the century. In quite large degree this excitement was due to the stimulus of Charles Darwin. His *Origin of Species* attracted immediate fame and infamy upon its appearance in 1859. As a feat of synthesis offering a key to variety and development throughout the natural order it was the culmination of a long tradition of speculation in evolutionary biology. Darwin was claiming that his detailed observational evidence squared best not only with an assertion of mutability in species but also with a particular theory about its mode of operation. Of the mutability he was convinced even before a chance reading in 1838 of Malthus on population provoked realization of the mechanism whereby new species might originate and existing ones develop or die. Henceforth he believed that there was a bitter struggle for existence, operating within and between species against the broader setting of a potentially hostile environment, and that those variations in inheritance which happened to be most favourably adapted to its circumstances would tend to be preserved at the expense of others less profitable to the organism.

This was the core of the theory of 'natural selection' as the principal, though not quite exclusive, mechanism for the transformation of species. It could strike final and fatal blows against conceptions of ideal forms in the animate world. Moreover – though here the causal process was still mysterious – the manifest randomness of the variations inherited by offspring from their parents seemed to refute ideas of purposeful direction within nature. Even programmes of controlled breeding could not create variations but only fortify those that happened to occur. So keen was Darwin to stress the general impersonality of evolutionary development that he eventually preferred the phrase 'survival of the fittest' over the somewhat ambiguous 'natural selection'. His conception of evolution had an almost godly omnicompetence. It operated right across the biological realm and was also susceptible in principle to integration within the still broader framework of physical law. But it had no necessary dependence upon divine, or even human, intent. Here was a dramatic case where the need for synthesis might be satisfied in essentially secular terms.

The distinctively human aspects of natural selection – central to controversies in religious and social thought to be considered later – were pursued hard throughout the 1860s by such Darwinists as Thomas Huxley and Herbert Spencer. But it was not until 1871, in *The Descent of Man*, that Darwin himself published his own extensive discussion of what his ideas might imply in this critical area. There he argued in detail that humans were descended from some less highly organized form and that it would now be savage to view man as the object of a separate act of creation. But about the deeper significance of these findings he was characteristically less decisive. With his customary moderation Darwin ended his book thus:

Man may be excused for feeling some pride at having risen, though not through his own exertions, to the very summit of the organic scale; and the fact of his having thus risen, instead of having been aboriginally placed there, may give him hope for a still higher destiny in the distant future . . . We must, however, acknowledge, as it seems to me, that man with all his noble qualities, with sympathy which feels for the most debased, with benevolence which extends not only to other men but to the humblest living creature, with his god-like intellect which has penetrated into the movements and constitution of the solar system – with all these exalted powers – man still bears in his bodily frame the indelible stamp of his lowly origin.

One could derive from this almost what one pleased. Whether it was taken to dignify rather than to debase man – to under-line the triumph of unaided human science rather than the necessity for human self-doubt – was a matter of choice and emphasis. A major dilemma of eighteenth-century Enlighten-ment was once more in centre-focus.

Among biologists themselves Darwin's influence was im-mense but not altogether even. For instance, in the case of the French it had to compete with a tradition of vitalist evolu-tionism heavily indebted to Lamarck which would come out strongly in the philosophical work of Henri Bergson at the end of the century. But especially in Britain and Germany, the leading centres of biological research, the main energies of a whole generation of scientists went into assimilating and testing further Darwin's generalizations. Even so, until 1900, these efforts produced no major extensions to the theory. The period was perhaps more notable for its distortions. Throughout his copious writings Darwin had employed a deceptively simple vocabulary that made his work especially vulnerable to vulgarization in scientific as well as general social terms. An excellent example of travesty comes from Ernst Haeckel, who spent most of his life at the University of Jena. Though he made some genuine contributions to its fame as a place of biological study, his particular attempts to make Darwin the catalyst in a transformation and sublimation of the German traditions of romantic idealism and organicist positivism were wholly retrograde. Unfortunately it was through Haeckel, more than any other scientist or publicist, that the German reading public gained its broad impressions of *Darwinismus*.

Haeckel believed it incontestable, after Darwin, that the world must be viewed in 'monistic' terms, with fundamental unity between the laws of nature and of human society, between organic and inorganic, matter and spirit, life and art, poetry and science. With this realization would come fulfilment of a certain positivistic quest for ultimate truths and final solutions. It was these that Haeckel unravelled in *The Riddle of the Universe* (1899), which proved immediately and immensely popular in Germany and far beyond. In 1906 he founded a league to propagate monism, which he defined as the belief that

a vast, uniform, uninterrupted, and eternal process of development obtains throughout all nature; and that all natural phenomena without exception, from the motion of the heavenly bodies and the fall of a rolling stone to the growth of plants and the consciousness of men, obey one and the same great law of causation; that all may be ultimately referred to the mechanics of atoms.

In support of this Haeckel produced a fantastical cosmology and founded a substitute religion. It was a pantheistic system equipped with its own intricate symbolism, and even with a formal catechism in which God had been replaced by Science.

Real progress in evolutionary biology was to come from altogether different quarters, and under doubly interesting

circumstances. Firstly, in the kind of coincidence not uncommon in the history of scientific advance, the same critical
breakthrough was made almost simultaneously in 1900 by
three investigators working separately. Secondly, it was soon
clear that in effect their achievements had been unconsciously a
replication of work published as early as 1866. In that year,
within the pages of a minor local journal devoted to natural
history, an Austrian monk, Gregor Mendel, had reported his
extensive experiments in plant hybridization. Even the
Munich authority Karl Nägeli, with whom he corresponded,
failed – partially because of a certain quite fashionable contempt for empiricism – to appreciate the significance of these
carefully quantified observations. In fact, Mendel's work offered the answer to the most important question left outstanding
by Darwin himself: how are variations inherited across
generations? Like nearly all his contemporaries, Darwin had
simply assumed that inheritance was a matter of blending:
that is, contrasting parental characteristics tended to merge
towards an intermediate equilibrium in the offspring. Such is
the tyranny of received ideas even in science that a challenge
in the 1860s to this seemingly self-evident truth stood little
chance of success or sustained notice – especially when it
emanated from a man of no previously acknowledged standing.

By 1900, however, other developments had increased the
receptivity to revision. August Weismann's pursuit of 'the
germ plasma', though it ended in more of a blind alley than
sometimes realized, was an important example of the greater
attention being paid to the cellular structure of heredity in the
1890s. In the same decade William Bateson was foremost
among those naturalists whose studies of hybridization suggested significant discontinuities in variation. It was while
working independently of each other on this topic that the
Dutchman Hugo De Vries, the German Carl Correns, and the
Austrian Erich Tschermak at last saw the relevance of Men-

del's monastery gardening. Their confirmation of his work on
the basic mechanism of heredity received relatively rapid
assent nearly everywhere. The blending thesis was replaced by
that of particulate inheritance, in terms of pairs of what were
soon called 'genes'. Though each parent contributed equally
to each pair, these factors controlling such traits as stature or
pigmentation retained their independence and operated in a
dialogue of 'dominance' and 'recessiveness' which produced
across generations statistically elegant ratios and yet remained
random in any particular manifestation. The supposition that
variations were averaged out in the very simplest way was
now conclusively refuted.

In large degree Mendelism complemented and clarified
the major hypotheses of Darwin. The latter had gone far
towards explaining change within the relative stability of
species, while Mendel had revealed the framework for the
persistence and recurrence of particular characteristics amidst
hybrid variations. 'Genetics' became speedily an established
branch of biological science, with claims even to be its very
focal point. By 1914 work on 'mutation theory' from De
Vries himself in Europe and T. H. Morgan in the United
States had drawn attention to spontaneous genetical deviations
and the role that these played in causing sudden evolutionary
leaps of a kind not envisaged by Darwin. Thus were revealed
new elements of discontinuity in evolution and further as yet
uncharted layers of complexity within the study of heredity
itself. Fifty years on, the most dramatic scientific revelations
of our own time would occur in the genetical field. But
already by the early twentieth century it was clear that Darwin and Mendel, as two of the last great naturalists of that old
school about to be replaced by the denizens of the biological
laboratory, had made major contributions towards raising
the life sciences to a new plane of maturity.

The prevalent conviction that such knowledge could be
used extensively as a practical instrument of biological control

had strengths and weaknesses. At worst, through no fault of their founders, Darwinism and Mendelism were invoked to support crude eugenicist cults. But, especially in medical areas; advance in biological understanding was altogether more effectively beneficial. There came of age a medicine based on relatively comprehensive scientific understanding rather than on chancy piecemeal inspirations. Weismann's angle of approach to heredity was symptomatic of an interest in the biology of cells which had intensified from the second quarter of the nineteenth century onwards. The study of micro-organisms reached a landmark when during the 1860s Louis Pasteur, in the greatest of his many biological achievements, enunciated the first rigorous germ theory of disease. In particular, he argued convincingly against the supposition that microscopic beings 'have come into the world without germs, without parents similar to themselves'. Thus he discredited current allegations about such spontaneous generation of life and provided orientations for the great twentieth-century science of biochemistry. More immediately, the germ theory was the foundation for the success of Pasteur and Joseph Lister in an often bitter battle to revolutionize modern surgery through antiseptic and aseptic techniques. It also allowed the new and soon highly internationalized science of bacteriology to identify and, from the mid-1870s, gradually to combat the causative organisms of such diseases as typhoid, tuberculosis, diphtheria, cholera, syphilis, plague, and dysentery. The foundation in 1888 of the Pasteur Institute at Paris was symbolic of new attitudes, of heightened expectations about the length and quality of life, and of confirmed faith in the direct efficacy of scientific knowledge.

Advance in the understanding of bodily processes was linked with developments in the scientific study of mind. Indeed, throughout the last third of the century, much psychology had a distinctively physiological basis. Eventually this tendency would be severely questioned – and the most contentious of these revisions, by Sigmund Freud, would constitute, through its extensive ramifications, one of the greatest intellectual revolutions of the early twentieth century. In the meantime it was psychological experimentation, related to the tradition of Gustav Fechner and Hermann von Helmholtz, that drew most attention. Animal behaviour under controlled conditions became a major field of investigation, especially after Darwin had underlined the connections between man and beast. By 1900 the experimental laboratory was becoming, pre-eminently in Germany and the United States, the established environment for psychological research. The way in which this was conducted, with stress on the relationship between stimulus and response and on the description of behaviour in terms of physical, chemical, and organic activity, reflected the general mechanistic assumptions of the time. Physiology, psychology, and physics were tightly enmeshed, often dealing with different aspects of the same phenomena. The first suggested how the brain and nervous system produced those elements of experience which, as consciousness, were the subject matter of psychology too. The task of physics was to investigate a realm of objects and events which had a real existence apart from consciousness but which were known only through consciousness and as the outcome of physiological activities. In its historical context such psychology was, as Carlton Hayes remarks, 'a whirling eddy in the merging stream of biology and physics'.

The foremost exemplar of this experimental psychology was Wilhelm Wundt, who in 1879 founded the Leipzig laboratory as a model of its kind. Being also a philosopher somewhat indebted to the British empiricist tradition he avoided the narrowness of some of his followers. His *Foundations of Physiological Psychology* (1873–4) was an original and systematic investigation of the physical bases of thought and behaviour in terms of organic stimulation and nervous impulse. The treatise of Hermann Ebbinghaus *On Memory* (1885)

was perhaps the most notable German attempt subsequently
to extend experimental techniques from the realm of the
sensations into that of the so-called 'higher mental processes'.
There came after the turn of the century a celebrated and still
influential Russian contribution to mechanistic psychology,
in the work of the physiologist Ivan Pavlov on conditioned
reflexes in the context of simple learning and habit formation.
His canine experiments, when projected into a general interpretation of animal and human behaviour, produced an oversimplified scheme of stimulus and response which threatened
to reduce all talk of consciousness to a rhetorical redundancy.
In France, with its own firm traditions of medical and metaphysical psychology, the experimental emphasis was weaker
than in Germany. Even so the Sorbonne laboratory was the
locus for an important advance in applied psychology, bearing
on age-old debates about nature and nurture. There around
1905 Alfred Binet was able to develop from his child studies
the first roughly effective age-related test-scale for measurement of normal intelligence. There was soon appreciation of
its implications for educational theory, and from it derived
that whole complex of aptitude testing which became such
an important feature of later psychology.

In the event, it was a quite different form of French psychological study which helped raise the curtain on one of the
great dramas of European intellectual history. The medical
contribution to the investigation of mind came not only from
physiology as such but also from experience in treating certain
types of mental disturbance that seemed especially difficult to
reduce to physiological terms. Nearly everywhere the nineteenth century had seen increasingly sensitive scientific and
even social attitudes towards such disorders. But after 1870
the French were here quite pre-eminent. Of special relevance
were the activities of Jean Charcot in isolating the phenomenon he termed 'hysteria', of Hippolyte Bernheim in seeking to develop hypnosis from a diagnostic into a therapeutic

instrument for such cases, and of Pierre Janet in exploring the cathartic possibilities of the hypnotic state for a range of disorders even outside the hysterical. This revival of the mesmeristic in an age of mechanistic materialism was a curiosity of the first order. It was also the starting point for Freud's sweeping challenge to complacency in every field of thought.

The founder of psychoanalysis cannot be pigeon-holed, and some would question his being treated at all as a scientist. Still, while certain aspects of his work and influence must be discussed elsewhere, it is convenient to sketch his pre-1914 development here because of its close relationship to clinical therapy. Born in Moravia in 1856, Freud was brought up in Vienna. There, as a young doctor, he developed special neurophysiological interests. In the 1880s he visited Charcot at Paris and Bernheim at Nancy. Back in Austria, and independently of Janet, he pursued with his mentor Josef Breuer investigation into patients' cathartic narration under hypnosis. Although their joint *Studies in Hysteria* (1895) aroused little interest, Freud followed up his conviction that there were powerful processes working in the mind beneath the level of rational consciousness and that under normal circumstances these were somehow stifled. Dropping hypnosis he concentrated on relaxed narration, as a means both of therapy and of understanding the depths of mind. Here he relied heavily on free-ranging verbal association, the interpretation of which material was fundamental to psychoanalytical procedure. Growing experience, including extensive self-analysis, suggested also the great relevance of dreams. Freud dismissed time-hallowed claims that they were prophetic of the future. But, as 'a disguised fulfilment of repressed wishes', they might provide keys to an individual's past. In that sense their interpretation could be 'the royal road to a knowledge of the unconscious activities of the mind'.

In his epochal *Interpretation of Dreams* (1900) and *The Psychopathology of Everyday Life* (1901) Freud had no support from

Breuer who had shown reluctance to accept another emerging emphasis – on sexuality, and childhood eroticism especially. Until the 1890s this whole area had been only rarely and perfunctorily treated. But that decade brought such more sustained studies as Richard Krafft-Ebing's *Psychopathia Sexualis* (1893) and Havelock Ellis's *The Psychology of Sex*, the first of whose seven volumes appeared in 1897. Every pioneer found this field mined with taboos. Certainly Freud's own growing insistence on the centrality of sexual matters agonized a most painful nerve in society. He came to view his female patients' tales of childhood seduction by their fathers as essentially recollections of fantasies based on wish or fear. He incorporated this conviction into a still broader theory of sexuality that included stress on every child's passion for the parent of opposite sex. Its thwarting, a major example of the universal phenomenon covered by Freud's use of the term 'neurosis', produced a guilt and anxiety all the greater because uncomprehended. The degree of success with which such shocks were assimilated by compulsive and unconscious processes of repression was a criterion of the hazy frontier between normality and abnormality in thought and behaviour. Where such adjustment had seriously failed, the technique of free association allied with the psychoanalyst's interpretative talent could have the immense therapeutic value of bringing the objects of repression into the light of consciousness. Most reaction to Freud's arguments was at first hostile. But he was fortified in his investigations by the formation in 1902 of a sympathetic circle, largely of fellow-physicians, which six years later became known as the Vienna Psychoanalytical Society. It acted as a focal point for growing international interest and four congresses were arranged before the outbreak of war. Unfortunately its dissensions became as notorious as Freud's own dogmatism, especially regarding the sexual basis of all neurosis. Principally over this issue, it became clear that the circle now contained not merely a father but also, most appropriately, a bevy of rebellious sons. There were notable defections by Alfred Adler in 1911 and by Carl Jung around 1912–13. Independently of the master, the former would pursue the symbiosis between aggression and feelings of inferiority, and the latter would explore in highly metaphysical vein the secrets of 'the collective unconscious'.

Such developments as Freud's theory of the whole personality in terms of conflict between Id, Ego, and Superego lay largely in the future. But the ideas already touched upon indicate that well before 1914 he was an intellectual revolutionary. In psychology itself, he had assailed the predominance of physical and mechanistic concerns. In his view, the fact that mind could not exist without brain did not justify simply equating the processes at work in each or describing their activities in a common mode. Mechanical psychology was irrelevant to the exploration of the deepest springs of human thought and action lying below the level of consciousness. The nature of the unconscious had been already a live topic of debate in Freud's youth. Yet none did more than he radically to transform its image. The unconscious seemed no longer a passive receptacle for trivial ideas and recollections. It was now depicted as an active and exigent force embracing concepts and memories literally too terrible to contemplate. But, as critics have repeatedly suggested, in Freud the exigencies of the unconscious were matched by those of the *Zeitgeist* itself – especially in so far as he left his theoretical expositions littered with figures of speech related to the mechanistic world-picture. Perhaps, after all, the problem of mental determinism had been merely shifted back one stage, from consciousness to a deeper realm where it was simply easier to cherish the illusion that will was free.

Whatever the outcome there, by 1914 Freud had laid many of the foundations for the revisions in man's self-image that would soon be so extensively influential. Over half a century later, in a culture suffused with that influence, it is difficult to

recapture adequately the force of his originality. In Wystan
Auden's wise words,

> If often he was wrong and at times absurd,
> To us he is no more a person
> Now but a whole climate of opinion.

Like Darwin whom he so admired, Freud produced theories
susceptible to crude interpretation within the context of an
animality and atavism that seemed to do much for the bes-
tiality and nothing for the dignity of man. Precisely because
of this it is essential to underline that he never intended to
vindicate irrationality. Freud did not always live up to the
demands of a critical positivism; but, most clearly during this
period of development at least, it was within such a tradition
that he sought to work. As Stuart Hughes remarks, 'Rather
than simply affirming that the unconscious did not follow the
usual rules of logic, he attempted to define the strange rules
by which such illogical logic operated.' With the map of mind
thus replotted, the domains of rationality were certainly much
reduced. But Freud believed that the chart, as a reflection of
reality, was now vastly more accurate. He was convinced, as
Hume and Kant before him, that only through the shedding
of pretentious illusions and the recognition of necessary limitations could the frail but indispensable instrument of reason be
used and dignified. But what seemed most emphatic to contemporaries was Freudianism's negative contribution – to the
dissolution of former certainties, and to the deflation of the
buoyant scientific optimism of the later nineteenth century.
Such a one-sided interpretation had always been likely, but
it was made virtually inevitable by developments in a wider
context. For, simultaneously but independently, Freud's
challenge to current conceptions of rationality and intellectual order was being paralleled still more conclusively in the
realm of physics. There too, in the very centre, the line of
scientific certainty had failed to hold.

For 200 years the influence of Newton had suffused physical science, even to the point of being invoked in ways and contexts that would surely have discomforted the incomparably subtle author of the *Principia*. In particular, he was much less willing than many of his successors to think of the unknown as merely the undiscovered and to assume a self-evident identity between scientific laws and objective forces. By the nineteenth century Newtonianism had developed in such a manner that its image of the universe was one of material bodies existing in separate spatial and temporal dimensions of the sort familiar to everyday experience. The basic units of matter were viewed usually as billiard-ball atoms of fixed weights, capable of being lumped together in many different ways. Explanation of their movements was structured in terms of a mechanistic dynamics. This described the forces operating between pieces of matter, and in all its mathematical neatness it conveyed the harmonies, regularities, and constancies innate within the external reality that science must portray. The objective existence of such logical order was most famously exemplified in that actual force of gravitation which Newton was thought to have revealed spreading from every piece of matter throughout all space. Under the aegis of this force the motions of all heavenly bodies had been brought within an almost totally coherent framework. Early in the nineteenth century it had been possible accurately to predict, merely from Newton's calculations and in advance of any telescopic observation, the existence and position of the planet Neptune. Through that achievement the forces and laws of gravitation seemed vividly confirmed in their scope and orderliness.

Qualities of universality were heightened also by other nineteenth-century developments that packaged together varied physical phenomena under unitary laws. The advancing study of atomic weights, integrating Newton's theory of motion and mass with Lavoisier's ideas on chemical elements, was one notable instance. Here the particular years under discussion were inaugurated with Dmitri Mendeleyev's periodic table of elements, logically expounded in 1869. It was upon these bases that by 1890 such new elements as germanium and helium had been discovered and some eighty forms had been recognized for those supposedly indivisible atoms whose motions were the object of the universal mechanical laws of the cosmos. But the century's pre-eminent example of physical unity and constancy came well before 1870, from achievements in thermodynamics that are associated with such names as Sadi Carnot, Rudolf Clausius, William Thomson (Lord Kelvin), and Helmholtz once more. The First Law propounded that sound, light, heat, electricity, magnetism, and the motion of matter itself are all measurable in terms of energy, the quantity of which is constant in the universe as a whole. The Second Law, embracing the concepts of entropy and 'heat death', stated that this very same energy was destined to become at some distant date unavailable for further use. Its sources were constantly running down towards a state of exhausted and tepid equilibrium; or, as Ludwig Boltzmann later reformulated the problem, atoms tended to assume an ever more disorderly state. Until the final years of the century most assessments of the general implications of all this tended to accord with the mood of buoyant confidence. In other words, much more attention was paid to the elegant universalism of both laws than to the possibly pessimistic features of the second alone.

A grasp of unifying law was, again, the hallmark of James Clerk Maxwell's *Electricity and Magnetism*, published in 1873. Over the last third of the century only the study of chemical structures rivalled work on electricity as a source for science-based technological advances to be exploited in large-scale industrial contexts. Though some applications of electrical power occurred before their bases were fully understood, fundamental work in laboratories such as Maxwell's own

Cavendish – founded five years before his death in 1879 – promised major theoretical and practical progress for the near future. Just as the development of Darwinian evolutionism consumed the effort of a subsequent generation of biologists, so during a comparable span did the exploration of Maxwell's principles remain the keynote of activity in physical science. With Faraday's more intuitive suggestions as a starting point, Maxwell had given rigorous mathematical support to a frame of synthesis where electromagnetism could be closely interwoven with current patterns of mechanics and thermodynamics. It now seemed that electricity was matter moving in waves and that light, together with radiant heat, consisted of 'the transverse undulations of the same medium which is the cause of electric and magnetic phenomena'. The accuracy of Maxwell's synthesis amongst all forms of energy appeared clinched by work undertaken at Karlsruhe in the mid-1880s. There, in the most remarkable feat of a tragically brief career, Heinrich Hertz confirmed experimentally that, except for their lower frequency, the electromagnetic waves were identical with those of light. This underlined that Maxwell had made a major advance within the tradition of classical physics. It would also be the last.

This finality, to the extent that it was perceived at all, was for a time ambiguous. Scientists wedded to uncritical positivism might be convinced of the conclusiveness principally in the sense that all which now remained to be done was a tidying of minor anomalies. But, in reality, classical physics had reached a terminus utterly different in significance. Indeed, the magnitude of Maxwell's achievement resided substantially in the fact that he had pushed this physics to a point where such problems of tidying became inescapably the centre of attention. Were there, after all, areas where scientific language had been placed under intolerable strain and where, in Einstein's terms, unbridgeable gaps remained between 'inner perfection' and 'external confirmation'? Mysterious properties in certain electrical discharges, inconsistencies in the qualities of the aether-medium for the transmission of light and heat, and doubts about the very integrity of atoms lent substance to such questions. Here were the telltale fault lines, too long perceived as local and temporary, that warned of volcanic eruptions beneath the very foundations of scientific certainty. But, since for two centuries the old assumptions had met the requirements of observation and practicality in most cases, it was unlikely that the overthrow would come in a single blow. Rapid as it was, this great revolution was spread over a generation and drew upon the combined talents of experimentalists, theoreticians, and philosophers of scientific method.

Chance too played a crucial part early on. At the end of 1895 Konrad Röntgen announced his discovery of X-rays, within a context scarcely at all indebted to the latest developments in electricity and magnetism. It had been known already that high-voltage current applied through an evacuated discharge tube produced a luminous glow. Now Röntgen described how during his work at Würzburg on such electrical conduction certain especially curious properties in this glow had become quite accidentally apparent. Its effects outside the tube included the penetration of opaque objects such as masked photographic plates. Röntgen's announcement, taken up by the scientific and popular press alike, proved immediately sensational. In medical circles the application of these rays to bone examination was promptly pursued. But much more fundamentally this discovery, so defiant of mechanistic interpretation, would trigger off experimental and theoretical work that transformed scientific discourse on matter and energy.

Within months it became clear that the properties which Röntgen had stumbled upon did not relate solely to the type of fluorescence created by the discharge tube. Henri Becquerel's investigation of uranium disclosed similar rays,

unstimulated by apparatus, emanating from seemingly inert
and permanent chemicals. In 1898 the Polish-born Marie
Curie, working with Becquerel and her own husband at Paris,
discovered two completely new elements – designated
polonium and radium – which exhibited these same qualities
and yet gave off altogether stronger radiation. By this time it
seemed likely, from Joseph John Thomson's Cambridge
experiments, that the vast amounts of energy involved in
these disturbingly spontaneous 'radioactive' transformations
of matter came from within the atom itself. Thomson had
announced that a beam of X-rays passed through any kind of
gas could produce negative particles or 'electrons': units of
matter which seemed to be the stuff of electricity itself and
whose qualities were moreover explicable only in sub-atomic
terms. All this certainly suggested that those, such as Wilhelm
Ostwald, who had been building up a quite influential opposition to any idea of atoms were wrong; but, equally, it indicated
just how mistaken was the particular atomic concept hitherto
maintained. In short, the atom – derived from the Greek for
'indivisible' – could no longer live up to its name. Indeed,
inquiry into the nature of disintegration within atoms was to
be a central theme of the new physics now emerging. Its early
study of atomic structure was dominated by Ernest Rutherford who, working at the University of Manchester from
1907 until his appointment as director of the Cavendish in
1919, developed J. J. Thomson's suggestions about the circulation of the negatively charged electrons around a positively
charged nucleus. But any analogies with the solar system and
Newtonian laws of orbit were dissolved by the atomic model
forthcoming in 1914 from Rutherford's Danish associate Niels
Bohr. He demonstrated that the revolving particles were
capable of making leaps between certain orbits and that it was
such electron jumps from an outer to an inner course which
gave off the radiant energy of light or X-rays.

Jerkiness of this sort had become already a basic characteristic of the new physics. Indeed, the work of Rutherford and Bohr in illustrating its symptoms within atomic structure derived partially from an earlier formulation of discontinuity by the Berlin physicist Max Planck. In its implications for the realm of ideas as such, his quantum theory – first made public at the end of 1900 – is of greater importance than any of the more experimentalist advances noted so far. In particular, it was a challenge to the truly fundamental assumption of classical physics that continuity must reign in all the causal relationships of nature. From his studies within the normal spectrum of radiant heat, Planck questioned the belief that energy must stream off continuously in infinitesimal amounts. Instead, he suggested that the emission of energy be seen in discontinuous terms – as the breaking off of units that had a definite magnitude within any particular wavelength. Each such 'quantum' represented an amount of energy (E) which when divided by the radiation frequency (v) must result in 'Planck's constant' (h), according to the formula $E = hv$. The way was open for energy, as well as matter, to be viewed as having a structure or graininess in terms of irreducible fundamental particles. Though understandably general assent was not immediate, some investigators quickly perceived the possible repercussions of these propositions even beyond the field of thermodynamics.. Most notably, in 1905 Albert Einstein, a German-born patent officer working in Switzerland, published a theoretical justification for extending the theory of individual energy particles to light itself. But even this achievement would be largely overshadowed by others from the same protean mind.

Einstein's special and general theories of relativity are the centrepieces of the early twentieth-century scientific revolution. Much of their relevant experimental and theoretical background has been sketched already. Still, their historical context must be enlarged to incorporate the contribution, from the philosophy of science itself, of a critical positivism.

The next chapter will mention some aspects of this in connection with neo-Kantianism and, more curiously, with the contemporary cult of philosophical intuitionism as well. But its impact on developments in physics is germane here. Although it fed upon certain anomalies in physical law already mentioned, some of its most interesting manifestations preceded the major experimental and theoretical advances of the time and sharpened the questioning of mechanistic assumptions about the structure of reality. A clear but not isolated instance is the work of Ernst Mach, whose influence Einstein readily acknowledged. In particular the latter admired *The Science of Mechanics*, which Mach published in 1883 while a professor at Prague. Its approach profited from nineteenth-century German achievements in the field of historical relativism, and its account of past developments in mechanics illustrated conclusively for Einstein the dangers of failing to keep assumptions under constant and close scrutiny. To him it was a source of philosophical consolation amidst the necessity of dissolving old illusions.

Mach allowed that scientific laws and concepts could be useful only so long as there was appreciation of their precise status: as mere instruments of economical selection and symbolization. It was wrong, for instance, to speak as though forces actually resided in matter as properties independent of measurement and of a preconceived frame of reference. Just as the idea of atoms need not directly reflect any corresponding reality so too must the concepts of space and time be seen essentially as means for communicating varieties of experience in a manner useful but imperfect. Once perverted into absolutes such concepts simply echoed 'the sham ideas of the old metaphysics'. The closeness of the links between Einstein's theories of relativity and Mach's critical positivism will become still clearer shortly. In Charles Gillispie's words, Mach had moved physics 'as close to its revolution into relativity as philosophy alone could carry it'. The particular philosophy at issue embodied, not least in its radical anti-atomism, important failings. Yet, as a solvent of received ideas, it could still prove valuable. Around the turn of the century strong currents of broadly similar criticism flowed also from the 'conventionalism' dominated by such Frenchmen as Pierre Duhem and Henri Poincaré. The latter was not only a polymath across the fields of physics, mathematics, and astronomy but also a talented publicist. This is demonstrable from the role played by his *Science and Hypothesis* (1902) in bringing before a wider audience the case for viewing scientific concepts as hypotheses that are dependent upon a framework of convention and are at best 'neither true, nor false, but useful'.

In the context of Einstein's achievement these insistent warnings against reifying abstract concepts had some special bearing on the question of 'the aether'. As the all-pervasive medium for the transmission of light and heat through space this was another central postulate of classical physics. But the developing study of electromagnetism in particular had elicited stubborn contradictions within the properties attributed to the aether. In 1887 the startling outcome of the American Michelson-Morley experiment complicated things still further. This suggested that the time taken for light to travel a given distance was not perceptibly different whatever relationship the beam had to the direction of the earth's motion. It seemed there was no way of detecting empirically movement through aether. Subsequently Hendrik Lorentz, a Dutch mathematician already much involved with problems in this area, developed a theory of 'transformations' in the hope of preserving the reality of a stationary aether and with it the seamless web spun between Newtonian and Maxwellian ideas. He suggested how the difficulty raised by Michelson and Morley might be attributed to limitations absolutely inherent within such observations. The immense and almost casuistical ingenuity of Lorentz's equations impressed Ein-

stein. But, most crucially, their impact produced in him a
realization that aether, having been so conveniently equipped
with the very properties which made its effects undetectable
in principle, was now manufacturing greater anomalies than
any it solved. Still more would be spawned by an alternative
supposition that it was undetectable merely because it moved
round with the earth. Einstein's conclusion was that aether,
like phlogiston before it, was ready to be deposited in the
museum of instructive scientific illusions.

The expression of this view, within what would soon be
known as the special theory of relativity, occurred in a paper
of 1905 entitled 'The Electrodynamics of Moving Bodies'. No
simplification can begin to do it proper justice. Nonetheless
its significance can be broadly appreciated in terms of three
interrelated features: the space-time continuum, the constant
and limiting velocity of light, and the mutual convertibility
of mass and energy. Pursuing Lorentz's point about inherent
observational blockages, Einstein had questioned how one
could ever establish the simultaneity of events. The necessary
signals between one observer and another themselves took
time to travel across intervening space, and their speed could
not be abstracted from the measurement. He concluded that
there was simply no escape from the relativity and interdependence of time and space. Each is part of a single reality
properly conceivable only as a fourth-dimensional continuum.
Connected with this was Einstein's contention that light had a
constant velocity whatever the movement of source or
observer – an argument which declared aether redundant and
managed to make sense of the Michelson-Morley findings.
Additionally, he viewed relativity of time and space as reflected
by that of mass and energy. Einstein stated that as particles
speeded up both their mass and their energy must increase.
Since acceleration became thus ever harder to sustain, it was
impossible for material bodies to exceed the velocity of light

itself. Further, because the increase in mass derived from a motion which was itself a form of kinetic energy, mass and energy could be regarded as mutually convertible and as distinguishable only through their differing ways of expressing a single process. In the epochal formula $E = mc^2$ Einstein conveyed that each particle of matter contained energy (E) equivalent to its mass (m) multiplied by the square of the velocity of light (c^2). This embodied the key theoretical expression of the vast energies contained within the atom.

This paper, together with his concurrent work on the particulate theory of light already mentioned, rescued Einstein from obscurity. He soon obtained chairs at Zurich and Prague. Then, through the good offices of Planck, he came to Berlin in 1913 – at the age of thirty-four only – with a joint appointment from the Kaiser Wilhelm Institute and the Prussian Academy. By now he was well advanced on a more general theory of relativity and was openly expressing the need for major reconsideration of Newtonian celestial mechanics. His line of argument was soon made clear, partially towards the end of 1915 and in full detail the following year. It allowed scientists to dispense with an occult force of gravitation operating at a distance. Instead any celestial motion had to be regarded as an expression of the qualities of space-time at successive points, allowing for distortions through the electromagnetic fields surrounding large bodies. As well as rejecting Newtonian mechanics, Einstein was here denying the universal applicability of Euclidean geometry. In 1919 some calculations derived from observation of Mercury during solar eclipse confirmed that Einstein's curvature of space could annihilate certain discrepancies that had defeated Newtonian solution. It was only then that the relativity theses began to make extensive impact upon ideas in non-scientific areas – a matter to be discussed later in the context of the 1920s. But among scientists it was generally clear by 1914, even before the formulation of Einstein's general theory, that within a single generation the emergence of the new physics had revolutionized a whole world-picture.

Much of the contrast with the nineteenth-century quest for scientific certainty is conveyed by the word 'relativity' itself. But, in the challenge to absolutes, this cannot be separated entirely from the concepts of discontinuity and indeterminacy. There had been drastic revision of long-standing beliefs about the workings of nature at various levels of generality. Amidst this it had become impossible to assume even that scientific laws must operate similarly across all levels between microcosm and macrocosm. It was evident that in at least some contexts, particularly of small-scale activity, discontinuity was a fundamental feature. In physics Planck's quanta and the work of Rutherford and Bohr on atomic structure and behaviour were instances of fundamental challenge to the assumption of continuous process in nature. From biology they could be supported by, for example, Mendelism and mutation theory. The cultivation of the absolute was no more readily reconcilable with indeterminacy. Within the framework of classical mechanistic assumptions it had been possible to aspire towards total predictive models. In principle at least, from a complete description of a system and of the forces operating on it all future states could be extrapolated. Uncertainty was here a factor of ignorance alone. However, even in similarly abstract terms, such conceptions of certitude were inapplicable to a world of leaping electrons and of matter and energy in discontinuity. In effect, of course, revolutionized science revealed great predictive capabilities. Yet these were actualized only after acknowledging the supremacy of chance and statistical probability. Scientists distinguished between predicting very accurately the disintegration period for a given quantity of radium and being nonetheless unable to comment at all about the order in which the constituent atoms would come apart. Predictions had to be surrounded by areas of inherent uncertainty which, though sometimes trivial in practice, still needed formulating with immense care. But it seemed that here the classical principle of causality – of nature proceeding from cause to effect through a strict chain of events each fully determining that which followed – was of limited applicability. How far this further axiom of earlier scientific thinking could be preserved at all was a matter still largely unclear by 1914.

Under all these circumstances it was scarcely possible still to maintain that, fundamentally, the pursuit of science was an impersonal activity. The supposition that scientific laws were the direct manifestation of divine or merely natural harmony was becoming increasingly implausible. They were not given but constructed – with the tools of that rationality whose subjective frailties Freud was currently revealing in his own distinctive way. Partially comparable with products of non-scientific activity, such laws were in the last resort feats of imagination. Through them the scientist sought, amidst the complexity of natural phenomena, to convey some conception of order such as would work equally conveniently whoever the observer. His success depended in part upon the degree to which he took account of the process by which facts themselves were obtained. As we have seen most acutely in physics, the act of observation wàs itself an element in measurement and a case of involvement more critical than hitherto appreciated. From this growing awareness of science as essentially 'operational' it was possible to derive a sceptical outlook even upon the one great regularity that seemed to have emerged within the new physics. Did the law of constancy and limitation in light velocity contain an element of circularity? Did it not defy guarantee while men remained ignorant as to how in principle any greater speed could ever be observed? Once by some means observed, would not this still higher velocity

then itself become no less insecure? In short, the revolution
initiated transformation in the status both of the scientist and
of his ideas.

The relationship too between science and everyday experience had been radically changed. In the past their reconciliation had been often difficult enough, but now in many contexts
the gulf became altogether unbridgeable. For instance, commonplace awareness provided no ready parallel to the strange
world of the electron. Again, men's perceptions and behaviour
continued still to be ordered as though space remained simply
a matter of three-dimensional plane geometry. As for the
relativity of time, there was even less chance of psychologically
assimilating this into forms of mundane experience. Newton's
gravitation had been dismissed as an occult force, but only to
be replaced by conceptions that to laymen might smack still
more strongly of the magical. The new physics could be
explained properly only in complex mathematical abstrac-
tions. To communicate in more generally comprehensible
form some idea of its features involved groping through
imperfect metaphor. Moreover, with Freud, the laws of
human as well as cosmic behaviour shifted farther than ever
before away from the realm of face values. Scientists, to the
extent that they still sought to reject concepts which could
not be defined in terms of discernible items of sense experience, might continue to claim that their activity was qualita-
tively distinct from theology or metaphysics. But for others
the breadth of this distinction could seem dubious, in a
context where the theoretical and observational means to
such experience had become so remote from the mundane.

Scientists and laymen alike would continue the attempt to
reduce incoherence through forms of synthesis. These characterized the aspirations of, for example, Einstein and Freud in
the years after the Great War. The inventor of relativity theory
was unwilling to conclude that the deity was a dice-player; and
the founder of psychoanalysis tried to render more coherent

and universal the laws of conflict in the mind. But no expert could expect to provide a synthesis as imminent and conclusive as that which had been in prospect at the beginning of our period – one offering at a stroke both complete unity within science and a sense of orientation for other activity as well. These years not only had produced rapid proliferation and realignment in the branches of science – the effects of which are still far from fully assimilated – but also had laid the foundations for a more critical questioning of science's claims to be the compass of intellect at large.

In magnitude this 'second scientific revolution" is truly comparable to that which more than two centuries before had culminated with Newton. It cannot however be argued that its impact on the popular mind was already great by 1914. Darwinism had lent itself to more immediate and flexible interpretation and had possessed certainly a more intimate and extensive appeal than the new physics. The delights of the specimen cabinet were much less esoteric than those of laboratory electronics or of mathematical notebooks. As a chasm opened between expert and non-expert, there was a popular willingness still to benefit from the applications of science – the certainties that counted – without troubling to go much beyond its 'wonders' to anything approaching understanding. The syndrome of science and progressive optimism was not easily dissolved. Only briefly, in the years following the bitter experience of general war, would features of scientific disillusionment impinge greatly on popular conceptions of a world in disarray. Before 1914 not even philosophers, social thinkers, and creative artists had appreciated in fullest measure the general intellectual implications of the new science. But that had not prevented them from developing over the same period their own analyses of a still more deeply textured crisis in European culture and civilization.

Chapter 3

PHILOSOPHICAL AND
RELIGIOUS THOUGHT

FROM the mid-nineteenth century onwards philosophers were well aware that their historic claims to be the pre-eminent interpreters of reality had been severely weakened by the dominance of natural science. It threatened theology with annihilation, and more secular philosophical speculation it menaced with thraldom at the very least. Comte's hierarchical 'law of three stages' provided a plausible explanation of what was happening. Though institutional religion was still an important social influence, the intellectual status of theology itself had been much devalued. Other forms of philosophy fared not much better. They seemed now less able to perform the previously prestigious function of providing a common language and conceptual structure that could unify the study of the natural and supernatural alike. In their own right the facts of science, even if still incomplete, had become more persuasive than any form of metaphysical deduction or affirmation. Many developments in philosophical and religious thought over the last century are in essence responses to, or evasions of, this chronic challenge from emancipated science.

Until at least the First World War many aspects of this debate in philosophy were much affected by the legacies of Kant and Hegel. German philosophical thinking towards the mid-nineteenth century, especially within the state-controlled Prussian universities, was dominated by 'idealism': broadly, the belief that the real resides in the sphere of thought and that the objects of external perception consist of ideas. In particular, contemporary German idealism was marked by

Hegelian images of reality as thought in motion and as the dialectical unfolding of the World Spirit or Absolute Idea. In the context of a buoyant natural science Hegelianism's cult of totalities was attractive enough. But it was highly questionable whether the dominance of scientific fact could be comfortably accommodated within such a cumbersome metaphysics, or indeed within any metaphysical framework at all. The most important form of response was to preserve Hegel's scope while conceiving the totality in terms mechanistic rather than organic and while also inverting the idealist hierarchy. Now matter must be considered the stuff of reality, and ideas as a mere projection of material being. Thoroughgoing materialism, exemplified influentially by Ludwig Feuerbach and Ludwig Büchner, reflected but weakly the creative powers of Hegel himself and produced most of its impact by a skilful use of currently fashionable scientific jargon. For all its popularity in an age of uncritical positivism, such an assault upon mind was unlikely to succeed in reconciling philosophy with science. Rather it implied the abasement of the former before the latter. Not surprisingly, Europe's most refreshing philosophical currents after 1870 would run through channels other than those of materialist synthesis; and in Germany especially the most suggestive work derived its inspiration from Kant rather than from an upright or even an inverted Hegel. It is however an ironical feature of late-nineteenth-century intellectual history that Hegelianism, even after its partial retreat in Germany, should have begun to enjoy a period of unprecedented influence amongst certain British and Italian philosophers engaged in further battles against materialistic modes of thought.

Britain had no idealist philosophical tradition comparable in depth to the German. But there were some precedents, as in the case of Berkeley, for invoking idealism against the adverse implications that philosophical materialism could have for religious belief. Though not primarily theological,

British idealism of the period received considerable impetus from religious concern. An example is Edward Caird's *Hegel* (1883) which set out an ingenious case for the ultimate spirituality of scientific law itself. While other leading idealist thinkers had to take serious account of Hegel they were more generally critical than Caird in their approach to him. For instance, the Oxford don T. H. Green drew upon Kant even more than upon Hegel in formulating his influential version of socially committed evangelical liberalism. It was however F. H. Bradley, best known for his *Appearance and Reality* (1893), who produced perhaps the most impressive philosophical work in the British idealist vein. He too was no simple Hegelian, not least in so far as he denied aspirations towards any ultimate fusing of the real with that which is thought. But his complex metaphysics, eliciting the imperfection of all arguments from relationship, did assail the status of the 'facts' as postulated by the materialists. Here Bradley sought rather to reveal in each empirical finding such contradictions as would suggest that it was merely 'a show of some fuller splendour' – that is, an appearance masking the Absolute as true reality. What guaranteed him a certain notoriety was the ease with which his argument about the imperfect status of the world described by science could be extended to suggest similar inadequacies in the man-related supernatural images purveyed by theologians. God too could be no more than an aspect, an appearance, of the Absolute. For many Bradley's version of idealism was scarcely more sympathetic to the proprieties of morality and religion than materialist philosophy itself.

Italian idealism, like British, tended to use Hegel mainly as a point of departure. In the newly unified peninsula the cult was closely associated with a spiritualized nationalist vision seeking to transcend the alleged materialistic pettiness of late nineteenth-century Italian liberalism and the concurrent predilection for philosophical positivism. Here the private Neapolitan scholar Benedetto Croce not merely led an idealist reaction but also came to assume a position of remarkable dominance in the larger cultural life of the country through much of the first half of the twentieth century. The primary organ of such influence was the literary, philosophical, and historical review *La Critica*. He founded this in 1903, jointly with his fellow-idealist Giovanni Gentile. The latter broke away in 1913, and soon became the leading philosopher of Italian Fascism. For this movement Croce showed some initial sympathy. Nonetheless, from the mid-1920s until the Second World War, he used *La Critica* to wage a vigorous battle not only against positivism and materialism on one hand but also against every form of superstitious mysticism – including Mussolini's – on the other. Also important was Croce's extended work on *The Philosophy of the Spirit*, under which general title he published four volumes between 1902 and 1917.

A brief period under the spell of Marx had helped prepare Croce for the wrangles with Hegel's legacy that bulked large in this treatise encompassing aesthetics, logic, 'practical' philosophy, and history. As its author recorded, from the turn of the century he could live neither with nor without the great Prussian idealist philosopher. Croce rejected Hegelian rhetoric about finality, but he did accept an image of the world in terms of flux and becoming. He believed that reality must reside within such forms of process and change, and therefore must be essentially provisional. It is historical study, allied with philosophy as a methodological guide, that deals most fully with these elements of the developmental. As the proper exhibitor of the workings of mind and as the sum of human knowledge, history constitutes the highest form of understanding. In such a context Croce dismissed as mere positivistic pretentiousness any case for the primacy of natural science. Neither in its analytical forms (purveying theoretical fictions according to criteria of practical adequacy) nor in its descriptive mode (having but rudimentary and scattered elements of the historical) did natural science escape the limitations of abstractness. Such questions about the relationship between humane studies and the natural sciences were also a prominent feature of the revival of Kantianism in Germany.

There positivistic modes of thought, though gaining ground as the status of science itself was enhanced, had never won the degree of support enjoyed in Britain, Italy, or France. Consequently the chief developments in German philosophy of the later nineteenth century took the form of modulation within a broadly idealist tradition. But this switch of emphasis, in so far as it was a shift from Hegelian to renewed Kantian inspiration, did indeed allow Germans to make significant contributions to the development of a critical positivism. Even as its own stock rose neo-Kantianism, drawing upon a philosophy and a legacy even subtler than the Hegelian, manifested itself in such a variety of ways as to reveal considerable divergences of opinion about the essential significance of its master's work. Two forms of interpretation were, however, predominant. In the first place, the Kantian spirit was held to be inimical to system-making whether of the Hegelian or of the uncritical positivist brand. Secondly, especially amongst those who regarded Kant's *Critique of Pure Reason* as the core work, it focused attention on problems in the theory of knowledge. Of special significance here was the Kantian distinction between the realm of phenomena, or appearances susceptible to empirical judgement, and that of noumena, or higher realities as the objects of purely non-sensuous intuition. In alliance, these forms of interpretation dictated that the essence of neo-Kantianism be an immensely heightened self-consciousness about the methods and aspirations proper to philosophy as the analysis of the logical conditions of knowing and willing.

This realization also necessitated moderating the pretensions of natural science itself. Here again some versions of neo-Kantianism offered aids to bridge-building between positivism and its opponents. For example, the critical positivism of the Austrian Ernst Mach, whose impact on Einstein we have noted already, owed much to Kant. Though he developed substantial disapproval of Kant's stubborn metaphysical addictions, Mach fully acknowledged the influence of the *Critique of Pure Reason* in moulding his view of science's limitations. In all these circumstances it was understandable that some other leading neo-Kantians, such as Friedrich Lange, should derive additional inspiration from the heavily epistemological strain in the established tradition of British philosophy – a fact which merely underlines the irony of the simultaneous development in Britain of a novel taste for the less critical forms of German idealism. As we have seen in Croce's case, the assault on any autonomous primacy claimed for the natural sciences could be further fortified by sceptical examination of their relationship to other fields of study. In this still more radical undertaking the Italian was indeed preceded by a number of German neo-Kantians, amongst whom Wilhelm Windelband, Heinrich Rickert, and Wilhelm Dilthey are the most notable.

The debt to Kant was demonstrated principally in their concern properly to distinguish categories of thought. The boundary between the phenomenal and the noumenal world was also to be that between the modes of study appropriate to the natural sciences on the one hand and those suited to the *Geisteswissenschaften* ('sciences of the mind') on the other. These two roads to knowledge, though different, were deemed equal in status. Windelband's famed Strassburg rectorial address of 1894 on 'History and Natural Science' directly challenged those aiming to establish a hierarchy which might in any way devalue the study of the social and cultural. In order to explain how the humane might be grasped independently of borrowings from natural science these neo-Kantians resorted to the often fruitful but also vulnerable concept of *Verstehen*, a form of inner understanding or even sympathetic intuition. It was employed most centrally in regard to the study of history as the basis of humane reality. There it conveyed how the historian, though circumscribed by his own time and culture, could evoke the past through in some sense 'experiencing' it. Problems arose, however, in so far as such experience was inseparable from the historian's own system of values. When Windelband's pupil Rickert, fearful of relativism, sought to bestow on these values an absolute validity this was for the positivists mere confirmation of the neo-Kantian inability to achieve independence from a superfluous metaphysic.

Dilthey, however, was somewhat more emancipated. He boldly accepted the relativity of values and sought to banish metaphysics from the humane as well as the natural sciences. He wished also to establish through the processes of *Verstehen* a case for the autonomy of history and for the dignity of humane studies without resort to those frameworks of rigid and universal law that he considered inappropriate to the *Geisteswissenschaften*. His *Introduction to the Sciences of the Mind* (1883) was conceived originally as merely the first part of a still more substantial critique of historical reason. This was never filled out. Until his death in 1911 Dilthey toiled over further fragments and was agonized by the incompleteness of his achievement. The stature and influence of his work nonetheless grew with time. Still, in the last resort, Dilthey was scarcely more likely than Rickert to effect an acceptable compromise with positivism. His assertion of cultural science's equality with and independence from natural science went so deep as to suggest conflict rather than condominium. How near, for instance, was *Verstehen* to a relativism of an essentially irrationalistic kind? Commenting on the general relationship between humane studies and the natural sciences from this time onwards, Gerhard Masur writes: 'The two halves of man's cognitive effort were divorced from each other, neither half paying great heed to the labours of the other. It was the first time in the history of Western civilization that such a separation had occurred.' Dilthey had made especially subtle contributions not only to this schism but also to a still more general debate about the role of the non-rational. Indeed it was this latter development which constituted perhaps the most distinctive feature of philosophical activity in the two or three decades before 1914.

The responsibility was, of course, far from being Dilthey's alone. The growing cult of the irrational must be set in a much wider context embracing, for instance, vulgarized Darwinism and the first real stirrings of doubt about the plausibility of mechanistic physics. Even the Kantian contribution itself must be seen in terms broader than those relating simply to Dilthey. As I. M. Bochenski says, 'Kant's teaching that metaphysical problems are not accessible to reason directly inspired one aspect of irrationalism, while his own rationalism was responsible for its other aspect by the opposition which it provoked.' Reactions against positivism, if they were sufficiently exaggerated, could amount to flights from rationality as well as merely from science. This was truest among certain philosophers who identified positivistic rationalism as being simply the ally of bourgeois materialism and mass mediocrity and who then packaged all of these together as objects for denunciation within diatribes against the spiritual desiccation of modern society. In doing so they not only set a gulf between science and non-science but also opposed the widely accepted assumption that the primary criterion of philosophical probity was to accept as true only what commended itself to reason. Contrary to this rule, the thirty years or so before the First World War saw a vigorously intensified assertion of philosophies of the Will. The main tendency of this voluntarism, which contemporaries sometimes dubbed 'the new spiritualism', was a subordination of conscious reasoning to the products of unconscious instinct and vitalistic intuition. As with the contemporaneous but largely independent case of Freud, it cannot be assumed that the aim here was straightforwardly to annihilate rationality. Often such philosophies sought merely to establish the complementarity between reason and will. Yet they might do so in such a manner as to risk diminishing severely the respect due to sober reflection.

The full pedigree of this philosophical irrationalism cannot be traced here. However, there was certainly a great debt to the romanticism of the earlier nineteenth century; and in that context some reference must be made to the influence of Arthur Schopenhauer at least. When he died in 1860 his writings were only beginning to be well known. But his most seminal work, *The World as Will and Idea*, had been published as early as 1819 when he was thirty-one. The starting point was, again, the Kantian distinction between phenomena and noumena. Schopenhauer argued that reason was incapable of providing a passport from the former, the world merely 'as Idea', to the deeper realities of the latter. These could not be reached without recognition that it is will alone which lends to our thoughts any significance they might possess. Yet Schopenhauer also believed this same will to be essentially evil. As an urge to life it was continually evolving – but blindly, without goal. The individual might be redeemed from purposelessness only to the extent that he could escape temporarily into the realms of art or of religious asceticism – most especially into the state of nirvana where all human will and desires are negated. Both in· its ethical nihilism and in its pessimistic premonitions of civilizational disaster Schopenhauer's philosophy was deeply disturbing. But its pleas for moral revaluation and for an ascendancy of will over reason proved increasingly alluring as the century went on.

Most particularly, his work impressed not only Søren Kierkegaard (whose own posthumous renown will be noted later, in the context of twentieth-century existentialism) but also Friedrich Nietzsche. It was the latter who towards the end of the nineteenth century emerged as the most powerful and notorious exponent of the philosophy of will. However, this fame arrived too late for Nietzsche himself to appreciate it. Personal tragedy had intervened. Born in Saxony in 1844, he had been made Professor of Classical Philology at Basel during his mid-twenties; but in 1879 ill health led him to resign, and from 1889 until his death in 1900 he was totally incapacitated by mental derangement. Thus his deserved reputation as a figure of the first order in the history of the modern European mind derives from an outburst of creative energy which occupied only the relatively brief span from around 1870 to 1888. In the earlier part of that period he developed a revolutionary conception of culture, reliant upon the intoxicated and chaotic 'Dionysian' spirit which alone could assail successfully the chimerical truths offered by specious rationalism. At this stage Nietzsche, like many lesser contemporaries, was partially under the spell of Richard Wagner. The latter's operas were by now widely acclaimed, and the composer had also written at tedious length on the subject of heroic redemption through will. By 1878, however, Nietzsche had come rightly to discern in the Master of Bayreuth deep vulgarity of mind, which an undoubtedly great musical talent might conceal but not cure. Henceforth Nietzsche asserted his independence of one who had become a mouthpiece for chauvinism in the Second Reich. The Nietzschean attack upon contemporary values would brook no such compromise with the fashions of the day.

Like Schopenhauer, Nietzsche was concerned principally with levels of feeling and understanding more profound than any he thought attainable through merely rationalist philosophy – which, in his opinion, had reached its arid nadir in British empiricism. Reason was powerless so long as it was isolated from passion. Expressing a view which would gain ground in certain circles during the twentieth century,

Nietzsche declared that the philosopher must be essentially the committed critic of culture and modes of life. Windelband perceived something of this involvement in his contemporary assessment of Nietzsche as a man 'who expresses all the tendencies of the time, and suffers from the same unsolved contradictions by which the time itself is out of joint'. Of course Nietzsche himself preferred to be seen as transcending them. However, in the role of cultural critic he did become one of the most important prophets of the realization that advances in literacy and the diffusion of ideas, in reason and supposed intellectual refinement, might have little or no bearing upon the quality of human behaviour. For Nietzsche the 'progressive' ideas of the nineteenth century amounted simply to a capitulation before herd values. He believed that history, if conceived as linear progress, was meaningless. Instead it needed to be grasped as a cyclical process of 'eternal return'. It pointed neither towards relentless secular progress nor towards redemption in terms of religious fulfilment. From *The Gay Science* (1882), uttered significantly through the character of the madman, came Nietzsche's now famous words: 'God is dead! God remains dead! And we have killed him! How shall we comfort ourselves – we who are the greatest murderers of all?' The profoundest challenge which Nietzsche set his contemporaries was that of accepting, and then benefiting from, the loss of illusion in the realms of the secular and sacred alike.

The response that Nietzsche himself proposed was couched in terms perilously susceptible to distortion. Rejecting the pity-ethic of Christianity and its more secular reflections, he advocated the exercise of a masterful 'Will to Power' within a context of continual struggle. This required an ethical revolution of the kind indicated in the aptly-titled work of 1886, *Beyond Good and Evil*. Here Nietzsche proclaimed that virtue had meaning only within the context of what was useful for survival and domination. The *Übermensch* (easily, if somewhat unfairly, transformed later by others into Aryan 'superman') was he who thus survived, through organizing the chaos of his own passions and freeing himself for a life of creative activity. Only in him could the Will to Power be praised; only he had transcended successfully the mediocre morality of bourgeois and mass society; only he had passed beyond a superficial conception of Good and Evil. In him even falsehood must be cherished, for there its renunciation would be a negation of life itself. Nietzsche, by glorifying an élite made up of such *Übermenschen*, was indulging what Bertrand Russell termed 'aristocratic anarchism'. Against the background of most previous European intellectual history it seemed that the Nietzschean 'transvaluation of values' in favour of those 'over-rich in will' was essentially perversity erected into a philosophy.

In Nietzsche content and style were utterly at one. Both were products of mind at the end of its tether. It was soon possible to speculate upon just how terrifyingly symbolic might be the very fact of a mad philosopher. The increasingly frenetic torrents of aphorism left many hostages to fortune, and of them Nazism especially would take advantage. Although he left no 'school' of thinkers behind him, Nietzsche through his energetic assault on previously accepted values made a deep impact upon twentieth-century European culture at large. To age-old debates on Fall and Redemption, secularized as conceptions of decadence and regeneration, his contribution was of central relevance. By 1900, particularly through the efforts of the Danish critic Georg Brandes, Nietzsche's importance within a literary context was already established; and by 1910 he was a focal point of cult and controversy amongst academic and popular moralists everywhere. In the last resort, what mattered most was not the extent of their agreement or disagreement with him. Rather it was their experience of catalytic confrontation. In the task of excoriating the complacency of the epoch he stood, with Freud, supreme.

Nietzsche's influence was indeed the more quickly felt; but his achievement, unlike that of Freud, was almost entirely negative in essence.

In the early years of the twentieth century Nietzsche's fame as a philosopher of will was rivalled only by that of Henri Bergson. The latter, though he lived until 1941, accomplished his most notorious work before 1914. A whole generation testified to Bergson's compelling personality and brilliant teaching, and to an influence radiating afar from the Collège de France where he held a chair from 1900 onwards. While offering yet another intuitivist reaction to pretentious positivism, his thinking had developed without any substantial reference to Nietzsche and exhibited the greater sympathy for rationalist values. Bergson wished to accommodate scientific progress, but also to transcend it in a manner worthy of metaphysical philosophy's highest traditional aspirations. Scientific endeavour and all forms of rational inquiry relied upon the analysis and dissection of phenomena. However useful, this activity obscured that sense of continuum, especially of time not as discrete particles but as ongoing 'duration', which was a fundamental feature of reality as actually experienced. As Bergson suggested for example, aggregations of musical notes do not correspond with our experience of music itself. Such deeper understanding derived from 'the immediate data of consciousness', which were logically prior to conceptualization and could be appreciated only through that mode of sublimated instinct or inner reflection (in some ways comparable with *Verstehen*) which for him constituted 'intuition'. These were the themes that Bergson explored in his first major work, the *Essai sur les données immédiates de la conscience*, which was published in 1889 and later issued in English translation as *Time and Free Will*.

It was, however, the instantly successful *Creative Evolution* (1907) which guaranteed Bergson's fame. Here the principles of time-as-duration and reality-as-actually-experienced were applied to biological development and thence to questions of social evaluation. As scientific fantasy the book rivalled Haeckel's *Riddle of the Universe*. Bergson was viewing evolution as the expression of an *élan vital* or 'life force', which moulded and dominated all that was merely material. Hence the process was essentially creative rather than mechanistic, needing to be apprehended in terms that were intuitively aesthetic rather than analytically rational. Within a human context such evolution, ceaseless but blind, brought a progressive liberation of consciousness – a cumulative awareness of the seamlessness of reality, a growing recognition of the implications of this continuity for the enlargement of will and choice. As Bergson sought to explain:

Thus, intuition may bring the intellect to realize that life does not quite go into the category of the many nor yet into that of the one; that neither mechanical causality nor finality can give a sufficient interpretation of the vital process. Then, by the sympathetic communication which it establishes between us and the rest of the living, by the expansion of our consciousness which it brings about, it introduces us into life's own domain, which is reciprocal interpenetration, endlessly continued creation.

That Bergson was a magnificent rhetorician in the worst sense did his immediate reputation no harm. He delivered the right unctions. He was less irrationalistic than Nietzsche, yet also the more truly uncritical. Even as he smote arid materialism and unbridled positivism, Bergson was purveying his own brand of scientific mysticism. Couched in terms of evolutionary vitalism, his vision of an inexorably progressive cosmic urge – accommodating or not accommodating God according to choice – proved immensely alluring to many contemporaries in France and beyond.

This malaise is no less clearly shown by the serious attention simultaneously devoted to 'pragmatism' especially in Britain and France. It was Europe's first significant philosophical importation from the United States, and its transatlantic

impact was due mainly to William James of Harvard. Having
made distinguished contributions to psychology, he became
unfortunately no less celebrated for the weakest aspects of his
later activity as a philosopher. He rejected both the absolutes of
idealism and the system-building of monistic positivism. He
accepted with Bergson that reality, in flux, was beyond the
compass of intellect and that will must be viewed as the
dominant factor in our experience. Yet in James its exercise
had distinctively opportunistic implications. For him conventional assumptions about the way in which truth 'agreed'
with reality were generally unhelpful. He argued rather that an
idea, or an action, might be validated only by reference to its
usefulness in life. This was the brand of reality which defined
truth. In baldest terms, 'the true . . . is only the expedient in
our way of thinking'. James himself was no cynic, and certainly he intended that his conception of utility be interpreted
in a more than material sense – rather, as whatever was conducive to improved behaviour and therefore to better evolution in man and society at large. Still, this did not rescue his
philosophy from flabbiness. For example, his justification of
religious beliefs was, in the last resort, tantamount to the
assertion that they were unlikely to be counter-productive in
this world and were an admirable insurance regarding any
hereafter. James's pragmatism, whatever its intentions, could
not avoid encouraging an intellectual debasement whereby,
as Bertrand Russell remarked acidly, 'theories become instruments not answers to enigmas'. But, in all its flaccid flexibility,
this reduction of truth to a matter of practicality could accord
just as well with the dissolution of scientific certainties as with
the facile optimism still being engendered by the technical
triumphs of the pre-1914 world.

   The European vogue for pragmatism, with its protean
timeliness, helped the reception of a still more radical critique
of the status of philosophical truth. Though largely completed
by 1877, *The Philosophy of 'As If'* by Hans Vaihinger appeared

only in 1911. By then the view that fictions were useful, indeed essential, within scientific investigation was no longer startlingly novel. It had been prominent in neo-Kantianism and in French conventionalism. But Vaihinger, although starting from the former and eventually being indebted also to the latter, pushed farther than either. Mach and Poincaré had tended to conflate fiction and useful hypothesis. Vaihinger however argued for a clear separation which suggested that 'what is untenable as a hypothesis can often render excellent service as a fiction'. Conventionalism had treated hypothesis as 'neither true, nor false, but useful'; pragmatism had defined truth in terms of usefulness; now, in the service of a similar principle of expediency, Vaihinger's 'fictionalism' seemed to be habilitating even what was demonstrably false. His influence remained small compared with that of Nietzsche, Bergson, or even James. Still, Vaihinger's mode of thought remained relevant to the explicit glorification of myth and artifice in certain irrationalist philosophies of the Fascist decades. Though he intended to promote a refined empiricism, it was not from his quarter that substantial advances in critical positivism would come.

Instead we need to focus on the philosophical axis starting to form between Cambridge and Vienna. The Viennese contribution to this (as well as to the contemporaneous development of a contrasting 'phenomenology' through Edmund Husserl) can be best dealt with in the post-1920 context. But it is proper to mention at once the work accomplished soon after the turn of the century within a broad tradition of British empiricism embracing such earlier figures as Locke, Hume, and J. S. Mill. Its new leaders were Bertrand Russell and his Cambridge associate G. E. Moore. In their conviction that philosophical progress must reside in the detailed analysis of particular concepts and problems these two derived some assistance from pragmatism, particularly from what Leszek Kolakowski calls 'its empirical alertness, pedantic nominalism, and its ostracism of metaphysical dogma'. On the other hand, they were intolerant of the elements of rampant subjectivism manifested in this and all other forms of voluntarism or intuitionism. They were no less unsympathetic towards the system-building that characterized the mainstreams both of idealism and of positivism. It was principally against the idealist rhetoric of absolutes, especially in Bradley, that Moore exercised his magnificent dissecting talent. Meanwhile Russell's more variegated genius was occupied mainly in refuting uncritical positivism's arrogant misjudgement of the nature of scientific knowledge.

In Russell's view philosophy, to be defensibly empirical, needed to be brought into the closest association with logic and mathematics. His talents had been displayed already in a book of 1900 dealing with the methodological virtues in Leibniz's account two centuries earlier of the possible relationships between mathematics, logic, and a theory of human consciousness. With such interests Russell could scarcely fail to be affected also by the mathematical revolution – not so easily pin-pointed as that in physics, but certainly dramatically apparent in regard to non-Euclidean geometry and set theory – which was gaining ground towards the end of the nineteenth century. It implied chiefly that the proper role of mathematics was not to demonstrate the true in any sense concordant with nature, but rather to analyse formal relationships strictly within the realm of logic. Within this context Russell benefited especially from the ideas of the Italian Giuseppe Peano and the German Gottlob Frege. The former was proposing a logical symbolism appropriate to the tendencies of the mathematical revolution, while the latter was suggesting particularly the light which all this might shed upon the errant ways of ordinary language and syntax. On these foundations Russell produced his *Principles of Mathematics* (1903) and then, jointly with A. N. Whitehead, the three-volume *Principia Mathematica* (1910–13) which sought to detail the arguments for regarding all mathematics as a formal expression of logical relations. This collaborative work was the first major landmark in twentieth-century empiricism's characteristic concern to demonstrate that the expression of thought, whether through number or language, involves the use of a symbolism requiring more subtle analysis than hitherto developed.

This was the period of Russell's most impressive work as a technical philosopher; but his later career revealed considerable talents also as a popularizer. Both facets are reflected in Russell's own assessment of his earlier aims and achievements as contained in the pages of the highly partisan *History of Western Philosophy* which appeared first in 1946. There he argues that, within the empiricist tradition as a whole, twentieth-century analysis derived its distinctive advantages from the incorporation of mathematics and the strengthening of logical technique. He continues:

It is thus able, in regard to certain problems, to achieve definite answers, which have the quality of science rather than of philosophy. It has the advantage, as compared with the philosophies of the system-builders, of being able to tackle its problems one at a time, instead of having to invent at one stroke a block theory of the whole universe. Its methods, in this respect, resemble those of science. I have no doubt that, in so far as philosophical knowledge is possible, it is by such methods that it must be sought ... There remains, however, a vast field, traditionally included in philosophy, where scientific methods are inadequate. This field includes ultimate questions of value ... Philosophers who make logical analysis the main business of philosophy ... confess frankly that the human intellect is unable to find conclusive answers to many questions of profound importance to mankind, but they refuse to believe that there is some 'higher' way of knowing, by which we can discover truths hidden from science and the intellect.

There is no clearer statement of the broad lines along which twentieth-century critical positivism would develop. Like the mid-nineteenth-century positivists, its proponents pleaded for the reliance of philosophy upon science; but, as Russell's greater tentativeness revealed, the meaning and substance of this relationship was being revolutionized. Not least, as we have seen, the idea of science was itself in flux. To the potentially vast implications of this situation Russell and his school were earlier and more sensitively aware than most philosophers.

By 1914 the state of philosophy resembled that of science in its fragmentation and heightened scepticism about aspirations towards synthesis. Especially in logical analysis, traditional attitudes to the role of philosophy as a guide to values had been shaken. Russell might argue that, in pursuing this version of scientific truthfulness to the point of abandoning much of the prescriptive-dogmatic function, 'philosophy does not cease to suggest and inspire a way of life'. But already opponents were suggesting that this customarily essential purpose of philosophical activity was being annihilated through a pedantic obsession with the scrutiny of propositions from the methodological standpoint. Some believed that, in the last resort, logical analysis was just as amoral as the Nietzschean cult of will. Of course these were but two contributors to the ethos of doubt pervading the pre-war philosophical scene. Deep uncertainty affected even areas that requirements of brevity have forced us to neglect. It is, for instance, far from accidental that this was reflected in the greatest monument to Spanish philosophy of the period. The trauma of imperial defeat in 1898 proved a stimulus to cultural revival. This had among its most notable contributors Miguel de Unamuno. He argued eloquently that Spain needed to re-establish substantial contact with the mainstream of European intellectual life. His own efforts to this end culminated in *The Tragic Sense of Life* (1913) – and the 'tragedy' of the title centred on his feelings of uncertainty amidst the eddies of reason and anti-reason. For all its distinctively Spanish timbre, this book curiously epitomizes European philosophical doubt on the eve of the Great War. Bearing in mind that it was also the work of a mystical moralist and an unorthodox Catholic, we may now turn back to consider how theology – the brand of philosophy traditionally most committed to the formation of life-values – and religious thinking at large had been coping with the challenges of the period.

Here too there was a crisis of authority. Our present stress on its intellectual aspect must not hide the links with its social and institutional facets, especially as forged in the simultaneity of two general developments. For Christianity was being questioned on an unprecedentedly extensive scale within sophisticated circles at the very time when the Churches, in their work within society at large, were undergoing also a great organizational strain: that of adapting to an increasingly urban and materialistic environment, wherein the state was rapidly enlarging its own functions and secularist ideologies such as Marxism were gaining ground. Without renewed emphasis upon the social content of the Christian message might not the defection of élite minorities contribute all the more readily to the acknowledged acceleration in popular religious indifference? Then, for how much longer could Christianity maintain its still quite pervasive influence over European morals and mores? Would mass society develop a new morality, on Nietzschean or other lines, or merely devise novel and non-religious justifications for the old? Such broad questions had of course been pursued since the age of Enlightenment. But by the later nineteenth century, with further general advance in secularization, they were lending to theological debate an ever more urgent relevance for spheres far beyond the narrowly religious.

Yet again the greatest intellectual pressures were produced by the advance of science. Here actual discoveries were matched in importance by the model of scientific method and technique behind them, and by its potential for application far beyond the physical and biological realms. Science seemed increasingly capable of emancipating itself from theology; but it was more doubtful whether theology dared stand so independently of science. Though thinkers in other disciplines might face similar pressure, the theologians were the most vulnerably placed by virtue of the traditional approach to their subject matter. They claimed to be purveying statements about reality. But many of these were steeped in metaphysics and scarcely fell within the ambit of ordinary scientific validation. It was now easier than ever to dismiss discourse on such topics as divine creation, the human soul, the after-life, and the miraculous suspension of natural laws as mere rhetorical flourishing. The staple characteristic of theological 'revealed truth' had long been a brand of revelation which, according to the criteria of science, denoted precisely what was *not* revealed in any controllable sense. More than ever before this was being taken adversely to matter.

The most important elements in the scientific challenge were already apparent well before 1870. In particular, even before mid-century geologists and palaeontologists such as Georges Cuvier and Charles Lyell were indicating a need to enlarge the universal time scale in a manner dismissive of any rigidly literal interpretations of the Bible. The limited chronologies of Archbishop Ussher and others would have to be replaced by a scale which, though it might be roughly conveyed in mathematical terms, could no longer be in all its vastness humanly imagined. Only within the context of this more leisurely beat of time could the Darwinian evolutionary theory itself be sustained. As John Burrow confesses, it is tempting to view the circumstances of Darwin's switch of career aspirations from the clerical to the natural-historical as 'sent by providence in a fit of self-destructiveness'. His *Origin of Species* did indeed strike the finally devastating blows against literal constructions of the Genesis account of creation. It not only confirmed the ruin of traditional dating but also threw into doubt – for some, even into absurdity – the doctrine that man had his origin as the object of a special act of divine creativity. The cousinship between man and ape implied by the book made it notorious even before the *Descent of Man* discussed this delicate topic explicitly. Moreover, regarding the natural order at large, the stress in both volumes upon blind and impersonal struggle was an invitation to view as redundant all broadly animistic approaches and in particular the concept of divine purpose.

The pressure of scientific method on theological orthodoxies was evident across still wider fields. The development of more rigorous standards in general textual and historical investigation bore directly upon biblical scholarship and gave rise well before 1870 to schools of 'higher criticism'. Again, studies in anthropology and comparative religion – their popularity enhanced by Darwinistic debates – tended to diminish the uniqueness and even the dignity of Christianity through exploring its close kinship with pagan and savage practice and its place within a wider context of symbolism and mythology. Influential exemplars of such work around 1900 were Salomon Reinach in France and James Frazer in Britain. In *The Golden Bough*, which began to appear in 1890, Frazer developed the study of a particular antique rite into a vast comparative treatment of the evolutionary associations between magic and religion. His devaluation of Christianity, though oblique, was unmistakable. The subtlest response to these and other threats emanated from theological 'modernism'. Exploring the extent to which the struggle between science and theology might be a mock battle, it became the most significant positive development in the religious thought of the period. Under somewhat differing forms it manifested itself within both the Protestant and Catholic traditions, in each case meeting with lively internal opposition. Those later dubbed as 'fundamentalists', associated principally but not exclusively with some brands of Protestant evangelicalism, maintained blind yet often immensely ingenious adherence to biblical literalism. Granted that the Bible had long been a cultural as well as theological centrepiece, the popularity of this attitude is understandable. But such extremism represented less a dialogue with than a jamming of the voice of scientific criticism, whether destructive or constructive. On the other hand, the line taken at the start of the period by official Catholicism – despite a rationale differing especially in its lesser reliance upon the biblical text – is susceptible to the same harsh judgement.

The papal *Syllabus of Errors*, issued in 1864 together with the encyclical *Quanta Cura*, stands supreme as a blanket denunciation of social and intellectual modernity. This codified the principal pronouncements of Pius IX, whose mild and brief flirtation with liberalism had ended amidst the revolutions of 1848-9. The document was a thoroughgoing assault on the pretensions of civil powers, on secular education, on all vaguely progressive political doctrines, and upon freedom of thought and conscience in general. It anathematized throughout the spectrum from atheism to liberal Catholicism. Pope Pius, scandalized especially by the activities of Charles de Montalembert and by Ernest Renan's naturalistic *Life of Jesus* (1863), denounced the belief that 'the method and principles by which the old scholastic doctors cultivated theology are no longer suitable to the demands of our times and to the progress of the sciences'. The *Syllabus* concluded with a shudder against the thought that 'the Roman Pontiff can, and ought to, reconcile himself, and come to terms with progress, liberalism, and modern civilization'. This same mode of hollow and almost desperate assertiveness characterized the decision to convert into dogma the idea of papal infallibility in questions of faith and morals. The relevant Vatican Council decree of July 1870 met with uncompromising opposition from a minority of distinguished Catholic scholars, led by Ignaz Döllinger of Munich, who regarded it as further retrogression from a truly critical approach to theology. But the declaration was generally welcomed throughout a Church now increasingly threatened both in its remaining temporal power and in its spiritual and intellectual prestige by pressures towards secularization. During the autumn of 1870 political sovereignty, except over the Vatican City, was indeed extinguished by the newly united Italian state. It remained to be seen what bearing this development might have for better or worse upon the other and deeper form of authority.

Towards the close of his pontificate in 1878 Pius seems to have appreciated something of the futility of thorough intransigence. Still, a less rigid attitude towards modernity in society and even in scholarship became apparent only with Leo XIII who, though elected rather as a stop-gap successor, survived until 1903. While relations with the civil powers in France and Italy continued difficult, Leo achieved some early success in defusing the *Kulturkampf* between the Catholic Church and the new German Reich. The encyclicals *Immortale Dei* and *Libertas*, dating from the 1880s, confirmed the emergence of a more flexible approach to contemporary social issues. It was clearer still in *Rerum Novarum* (1891), concerned especially with the condition of the working classes as 'the pressing question of the hour'. By the standards of the various movements of Christian socialism developing roughly simultaneously among Protestants these documents were still very conservative. But within the Catholic context they did suggest an unprecedented willingness to respond positively to the human problems of mass society. Leo's vigorous defence of private property as a natural right was balanced by his strictures against the injustices unleashed upon the weak within the setting of unfettered capitalism. He knew that the tide of secularist socialism was less likely to be stemmed by anathemas than through the formation of rival Catholic workers' organizations dedicated to the fulfilment of an authentic Christian quest for social justice untainted with crude materialism.

Under Leo there also began some halting dialogue with
modernity in the field of critical scholarship. Yet gestures such
as the appointment of John Henry Newman to the cardinalate
and the opening of much of the Vatican Archive to historical
researchers promised more than was to be fulfilled. In Leo's
view, any necessary degree of *rapprochement* with science could
be achieved best through renewed attention to the lasting
implications of Aquinas' philosophy. This was the message of
the encyclical *Aeterni Patris* (1879). Although purging many of
the weaknesses of post-Reformation scholasticism, such neo-
Thomism still circumscribed tightly the extent of any official
theological revisionism. On the other hand, the papal recognition that there was a challenge demanding of careful critical
response encouraged willy nilly an intensification, most
notably in France, of modernist thinking within an already
existing liberal Catholic tradition. The proponents of Catholic
modernism advocated a thorough scrutiny of all traditional
beliefs in the light of the latest scientific, historical, and biblical
scholarship. Particularly critical of scholastic metaphysics in
general, they refused to assume that of all philosophies
Thomism could be alone consistent with Christianity. They
tended to deny the absoluteness of doctrinal statements and to
suggest rather that these be viewed as instruments, mutable in
principle, for expressing the living experience of the Church.
From this standpoint dogma becomes, in Alec Vidler's words,
'a direct and unsophisticated guide to revelation and the
classical religious experience, which theology attempts to
rationalize, but in a manner that is always susceptible to
improvement and development'.

The most distinguished representative of these views was
Alfred Loisy, dismissed in 1893 from his teaching post at the
Parisian Institut Catholique on account of unorthodoxy. His
continued responsiveness to the higher criticism led him to
publish in 1902 a brief but brilliant work on *The Gospel and
the Church*. Outflanking the liberal Protestants he used what

were broadly their own techniques of radical criticism regarding Christian origins and development in order to substantiate the claims of the Roman Church to be the authentic vehicle and interpreter of the Gospel message. In Vatican eyes Loisy and his sympathizers were wielding not torches of illumination but firebrands. During the pontificate of Pius X, from 1903 to 1914, the basic intransigence of the official line was confirmed. In 1907 the decree *Lamentabili* and the encyclical *Pascendi* denounced modernism as heresy and left its convinced supporters with the choice of silence or secession. Loisy was among those actually excommunicated in the following year, and by 1910 an anti-modernist oath had been imposed upon the clergy everywhere but in Germany. Had modernism been the tightly organized intellectual conspiracy that Pius perceived with such paranoid clarity it might have survived the assault in some substantial form. In fact, Pius prevailed over it all too thoroughly. His imprint really began to be erased only in the later 1950s, ironically just after he had become the first canonized Pope of modern times. One of his salient achievements had been to postpone for half a century the kind of intelligent dialogue with Protestant theology that has featured prominently in recent ecumenicalism.

In this earlier period Protestants certainly enjoyed a freer atmosphere of theological debate. Catholic modernism was itself often a reflection of their more radical questioning. The Protestant churches, though being in many countries partners to the secular authority, normally allowed to their theologians a degree of independence not experienced by Catholic thinkers and thus accommodated a marked diversity of views. At one extreme fundamentalist assertions remained prominent, but Protestantism's traditionally close attention to the Bible could be preserved in altogether more flexible forms by underlining the respect due to private judgement in interpretation. Throughout the nineteenth century the Germanic world remained the primary locus for such diversity within liberal

Protestant theology. Again the relevance of Kant and Hegel was great, amidst debate on the significance of their competing brands of idealism for distinguishing and reconciling the natural and supernatural as objects of discourse. Here the argument tended to run eventually against the Hegelian attachment to a directly metaphysical knowledge of God. Much more was derived from Kantian suggestions that God be spoken of in terms not of 'pure' reason but of that 'practical' reason sufficient to meet the demands of the moral life. This was, broadly, the point of departure for the liberal Protestant understanding of God. Analysis in the mode of metaphysical rationalism was inappropriate to the context. Rather, resort must be had to those forms of essentially religious and moral experience innate within the personal impact made by God on men.

Against scientific, philosophical, and other forms of external criticism such argument promised a certain autonomy and immunity for theology. But this was achieved without hindering its ability to benefit selectively from compatible intellectual developments in spheres of the profane. Critical history, for example, had made a creative impact on liberal Protestant theology as early as David Strauss's *Life of Jesus* (1835). It was now exemplified by Julius Wellhausen, whose *History of Israel* (1878) put the Pentateuch in a new light and whose later work suggested revisions of approach towards the New Testament too. The requirement that historical naturalism should not, however, spawn new illusions – especially anachronistic ones – was much emphasized by Albert Schweitzer. His critique *The Quest of the Historical Jesus* (1906) appears, with hindsight, a landmark for the development of much Protestant thinking in the inter-war years. But before 1914 the most pervasive influence remained that of Albrecht Ritschl of Bonn, whose *Christian Doctrine of Justification and Redemption* appeared between 1870 and 1889, the year of his death. He had linked historical sensitivity and the Kantian insistence upon non-metaphysical theology in such a way as to concentrate attention on the progressive establishment through time of 'the Kingdom of God'. Seen not in terms of ecclesiastical institutions but as the community of Christians, this represented 'the association of mankind . . . through the reciprocal moral action of its members' in the light of the example provided by the historic Christ. Ritschl's most distinguished follower was Adolf von Harnack. Principally in his *History of Dogma* (1886–9), Harnack developed the arguments against both doctrinal and institutional encrustation into an appeal for an altogether simpler faith based on 'the fatherhood of God and the brotherhood of men'. This faith was to be regarded, in Vidler's phrase, as 'the religion *of* Jesus rather than the religion *about* Jesus'. Of all contemporary Protestant theologians it was Harnack whom Catholic modernists found most profitably challenging.

The social and intellectual ferment we have been glimpsing had least impact on religious life and thought in Eastern Europe. There any creative vitality within the Orthodox tradition of Christianity was stifled, especially by a thorough subordination of religion to the needs of conservative secular authorities. There was, for instance, official hostility to Vladimir Solovyov's attempt at synthesizing religious philosophy, science, and ethics in a way that pointed towards *rapprochement* with Roman Catholicism. Nor was the growing hostility of these same authorities towards Jews likely to induce within the faith of the latter anything but a fortification of traditionalism. In Western and Central Europe however the Jewish populations faced more varied, though still largely painful, dilemmas. These rendered meaningful the continuing debates between Jews of orthodox, reformist, and outright secularist persuasion. Such confrontations were analogous to those traced within and even between Catholicism and Protestantism, at least in so far as all had some relationship to the challenge from science and fashions of intellectual modernity. But when viewed also within a social setting such similarities are altogether weaker. By the turn of the century political anti-semitism was growing in many western as well as most eastern parts of Europe. Not least, the great number of Jews that fled westwards from persecution on one side of the continent served to heighten fears on the other. Thus the Jew, even where he had become theoretically the beneficiary of formal political emancipation, was being widely regarded as still the denizen of a moral ghetto. Under these circumstances debates on the future of Judaism continued to be in unique degree inseparable from discussion about how and whether belief should engender a sense of community no less social than spiritual.

Every field of theology and religious thinking here surveyed has revealed a certain defensiveness. But we must keep this in proper perspective. As George Santayana elaborated on the eve of the Great War, the civilization characteristic of Christendom had far from disappeared even though another one had begun to take its place. The Churches' great effectiveness in exploiting the many missionary opportunities created by the wave of imperial expansion did much to compensate for their sense of encirclement at home. Nor, within Europe itself, were they yet facing intellectual and organizational hostility on the scale applicable to the confrontations, with Marxism and Fascism especially, of the inter-war years. Undeniably there had been in the half-century before 1914 an enlargement of religious indifference among the masses, a growth in the extent and respectability of agnosticism among the intellectuals, and – at every level of sophistication – an acceleration of the tendency to put secular loyalties before spiritual ones. Even so, throughout all strata within each European society, examples of Christianity being explicitly and thoroughly rejected were still the exception rather than the rule.

Scientific advance had certainly taken heavy toll. Yet it had been far from completely successful in accomplishing that rout of religion implied, intentionally or otherwise, by the aspirations of the uncritical positivism so respectable at the start of our period. In the early twentieth century science, no less than secular philosophy, was characterized by fragmentation and doubt. With dawning awareness of the implications of the new physics especially, convincing scientific synthesis seemed farther off than ever. Indeed, it might be possible – even essential – to incorporate principles of uncertainty and indeterminacy into the very fundamentals of scientific thinking and procedure. In many ways contemporary knowledge of the physical and biological world still left room for that sense of profound mystery upon which religious sentiment had long flourished. In this context the rising stock of such cults as spiritualism and Madame Blavatsky's theosophy is a minor but instructive feature of religious fashion in these years. Moreover, through the application of its positive discoveries, science was changing the everyday circumstances of life so speedily and extensively as partially to sustain those very feelings of bewilderment for which religion had traditionally provided solace. On the other hand, the task of ministering to the bewildered was felt by many theologians, particularly of modernist persuasion, to be unprecedently complex. Their thinking tended to reflect much contemporary development in philosophy at large, through its shift of emphasis from matters of content towards those of method, from statements of dogma towards explorations of the diverse modes of living religious experience. It was no longer easily acceptable that theology, any more than philosophy, could fulfil the straightforward prescriptive-dogmatic functions hitherto conventionally associated with it. The reluctance of so many philosophers and theologians to dictate the content of values may have been quite proper. Still, it could only further accentuate the sense of profound disorientation that pervaded much of European life and thought at the opening of the twentieth century. This same crisis of intellectual authority and its mass consequences bore heavily on the concerns of those social and political thinkers to whom we now turn.

Chapter 4

SOCIAL AND
POLITICAL THOUGHT

AROUND 1870 European liberalism reached a peak of self-confidence. Its critics discerned easily enough this high morale, but they found the creed's content more obscure. Liberalism meant many different things to different men. It risked classification as a political invertebrate, a spineless specimen of middle-class capacity for self-interested compromise. At worst it appeared a merely negative expression, of impatience with traditional conservatism on one hand and of anxiety about more thoroughgoing change on the other. This judgement seemed confirmed, for instance, by the way that liberals were just as bold in opposing radical socio-economic egalitarianism as they were in asserting equality before the law. Or, again, it might be substantiated from their attitude to democracy. Here, while supporting a strengthened sovereignty for parliamentary institutions and insisting that government should serve the interests of the whole community, most liberals hesitated about pursuing that unlimited adult suffrage which was the precondition for any sovereignty of the people itself. Moderation is, however, never self-evidently a mere negative quality. There was indeed in the liberal compromises a core of very real conviction: the belief that individual and collective happiness could be maximized progressively through the natural development of free institutions directly representative of the many who had some sure, and usually propertied, stake in society.

This expectation was certainly simplistic. But it had then rather more plausibility than ever before or since. Though still weak in Eastern and even in much of Central Europe, liberalism had enjoyed a progress in the West that seemed to herald eventual conquest over minds and institutions elsewhere. Enlarged freedom in belief and expression, fuller education and greater literacy, moderately broadened franchise, and more responsible government were welcomed as auspicious omens. Few liberal oracles appreciated, however, the much greater complexity of the real future. Perhaps even Tocqueville and Mill had been insufficiently sceptical. Certainly most liberals, though wary of universal suffrage, did not foresee the full extent of the chasm between wider and wiser electorates. Still deeper insight was required to appreciate, for example, the weak correlation between material progress and civilized behaviour, or between more literacy and less gullibility, more schooling and less social discontent. But by the mid-1880s liberalism had suffered some unexpected and sobering reverses. They gave rise to more doubt about the accuracy of the liberal vision of progress than had been current in the previous generation.

Some of the most notable reverses were inflicted by traditionally conservative opponents. There was something of a revival in political Catholicism and, in a different context, the manipulative talents of an authoritarian Bismarck appeared all too relevant to an era of popular politics. Yet towards the end of the century it was also becoming clearer, from developments in events and ideas alike, that there were altogether different forms of major hindrance to the arrival of the liberal millennium. Classical liberalism found inimical many newer features of that rapidly changing environment described earlier. The situation of mass socialization that liberals had helped to encourage could work against the moderation at the heart of their political practice. Prominent among the threats to liberal individualism were the conditions of anonymity and standardization accentuated in mass society, and the increased powers being assumed by the state in order to cope with new social complexities. Anti-individualistic too were the repercussions from nationalist hysteria and racist stereotyping. But, in liberal eyes, the most extensive menace would soon be a broadly organized and increasingly popular socialism. This sought to dominate, or otherwise to destroy, many of the institutions that liberals had fought hard to mould as instruments of their own imminent triumph.

Then, as now, the more explicit challenges to liberalism were categorized quite commonly in terms of 'Right' and 'Left'. However, in a history of ideas, it is useful to superimpose another pattern of distinction. This relates to the polarization already established between critical and uncritical positivism. Their interaction was a major characteristic of nineteenth-century liberalism. Even at the peak of its naïve optimism it had proponents, such as the mature Mill, who sought to strengthen its capacity for fundamental self-scrutiny. Within this framework the intellectual assault on liberal beliefs in the last decades of the century can be viewed as emanating from two separable but related sources: from those who indulged mutually antagonistic versions of uncritical positivistic pretentiousness about natural progress and, conversely, also from those who doubted the wisdom of such arrogance under any label at all. While some forms of scrutiny in the latter vein themselves suggested only irrational alternatives, others embodied fruitful insights from which liberals could benefit greatly. Liberalism, transmuted thus by intellectual criticism and steeled too by harsh realities from the realm of events, would continue among the main currents of twentieth-century European social and political thought. But the first price for this survival amounted to the loss of many illusions.

The more realistic self-assessment that helped liberalism in the longer run was not necessarily conducive to its immediate popularity. The age of mass society was hardly likely to forge some automatic link, hitherto unattained, between the possession of greater philosophical rigour and the acquisition of larger influence. As usual, the vagaries of political fashion were affected by many factors besides intellectual ones. Furthermore, even where supposedly sophisticated argument had some real purchase over patterns of influence, assertions of that which was the case remained often subordinate to assertions of what one wished the case to be. This was perhaps the chief characteristic of political arguments that had made them, eventually, so vulnerable to seduction by uncritical positivism. If immediate influence alone mattered, it might be said that late nineteenth-century liberalism was remiss in not yielding more completely to this particular temptation. Important rivals were less restrained, and they benefited accordingly. Despite each having some areas of sympathetic contact with liberalism, both socialism and nationalism prospered in these years at its expense – and they did so not least because they derived much greater impetus from uncritical positivism. Racism, which burgeoned in a still more fundamentally anti-liberal manner during the same epoch, reflected this derivation with even greater clarity. It constituted the most thorough adaptation to the contemporary taste for creeds panoplied in 'science'. How racism, in its wishful thinking, drew just as eagerly from the wells of irrationalism is something that can be treated best in the later context of Nazism.

There were further factors conditioning liberalism's relatively weak response to what the age most required by way of political doctrines. As often before, these needed to appear purposive – lending meaning to history at large. The liberal attachment to progress via the development of free institutions, especially when it was expressed in terms of secular rather than divine providence, did partially answer this requirement. Yet the belief tended to be expounded in a manner insufficiently systematic to qualify as 'ideology' proper. Its allure was thus lessened, while rivals developed more readily the truly ideological programme of revealing what Isaiah

Berlin calls 'a unitary pattern in which the whole of experience, past, present, and future, actual, possible, and unfulfilled, is symmetrically ordered'. Much nationalism, most socialism, and all racism found such monolithic synthesis a more natural mode of theoretical expression than did liberalism. But perhaps more damaging still was the inability of liberals to meet as surely as these competitors the requirement that a political idea should channel and concentrate group loyalties. From the unpromising material of bourgeois man liberalism never managed to design any adequate magnet for such allegiance. Meanwhile the destiny of the rival proletarian class, or of a particular race or nation, proved more powerfully attractive. The need itself was old enough. Unprecedented, however, was the sheer urgency now marking the quest for focus, identity, belonging. Mass socialization was, even in itself, highly disruptive of established patterns of group loyalty and social discipline. Coupled with the contemporary crisis in religious authority it was doubly disorientating. The large ambitions of much social theorizing in the later nineteenth century are explicable largely in terms of the quasi-religious functions it had to assume. The concepts of class, nation, and race seemed to provide the age with increasingly effective instruments both for social identification and for moral orientation – with cadres both for the conduct of present strife and for the pursuit of future secular redemption.

Within this setting no feats of synthesis were invoked more readily than those of Darwin and of Karl Marx. The former died in 1882, the latter in 1883; and the greatest intellectual achievements of each were accomplished before 1870. It is chiefly their legacies, often distorted, that concern us here. What Darwin's work suffered through misinterpretation by natural scientists was venial compared with its fate at the hands of more general pundits, and of social theorists especially. Haeckel's travesty was one example that covered this whole spectrum. It was widely ignored that Darwin had sought to write neutrally of adaptation not of progress, to deal in terms of contexts not absolutes. No less wrongly, he was taken to be pronouncing upon virtually everything. The writings of Darwin were indeed more easily and, until the 1917 Revolution, more widely read than those of Marx. During this period the impact of the latter was narrower, but amongst social and political thinkers no less profound. Their dialogue with Marx (or what they took to be Marx) was continuous, and has remained so. In these years its conduct was affected significantly by recognition of similarities between Marxism and much of 'social' Darwinism. Each was, for instance, at odds with prevailing religious orthodoxy. Each embraced a form of materialism. Each claimed to expound a fundamental and unifying law of social development that was not only scientific but also evolutionary. Within such evolution each raised doubts about the status of individual freedom and choice, about the balance between blind conflict and rational effort. Moreover, each had as its evolutionary dynamic a form of unremitting group struggle. If class were taken as the operative unit for competition then it was easy enough to bring Darwinism into direct alliance with the Marxist dialectic itself. The desire to forge such a union was exemplified in two famous incidents. At his partner's graveside Engels declared: 'Just as Darwin discovered the law of development of organic nature so Marx discovered the law of development of human history.' Earlier, Marx himself had wished to dedicate to Darwin an English edition of *Capital*.

Most political doctrines, old or new, could gain in plausibility through being presented in the jargon of social Darwinism. By this means almost any expression of opinion, however arbitrary or platitudinous, about rivalry and struggle was sanctified with science. Such malleability was of social Darwinism's essence. Its implications varied especially according to the chosen unit of competition; and then, again, according to whether the immediate stress was on struggle within or between such units. Britain provided outstanding examples of liberals using Darwin just as enthusiastically as socialists might. In 1872 Walter Bagehot published, in vindication of individual initiative, his *Physics and Politics: Thoughts on the Application of the Principles of Natural Selection and Inheritance to Political Society*. Similarly, the already influential Herbert Spencer used Darwinistic language to underpin his 'Synthetic Philosophy'. This was expressed in a number of volumes between 1862 and 1893, and embraced sociology, psychology, biology, epistemology, and ethics. Its politics centred on laissez-faire aspirations towards maximizing personal liberty, for the fit at least, by demonstrating that the laws of social evolution must operate with minimal state interference. Even so, it was not in connection with the competition of individuals that Darwinistic modes of argument were most extensively used. Their greatest success was reserved, rather, for those arenas of rivalry between nations or races outlined in an earlier chapter.

In the earlier half of the century nationalism had tended to consort with liberalism. After 1848–9 it was clearer that the marriage was one of temporary convenience. The ideological liaison between nationalism and racism in the later nineteenth century was much closer, but even it was ultimately dissoluble. Amidst the uncertainties of rapid social change theorists of national and racial fulfilment shared a quest for organic belonging and for objectifying their essentially subjective group-identifications. There, together, they could derive from social Darwinism many new insights, or assistance in reformulating old ones. But racism, with its unequivocal commitment to a scientific and indeed biologized conception of politics, was the more deeply affected. Social Darwinism fortified the tendency to judge morality only in terms of its contribution towards improving the chances of survival. And racism was the very purest statement of association between physical fitness and a wholeness of moral, intellectual, and cultural capacity. In its depiction of the criteria for group formation it was more dogmatic than nationalism. Racism asserted the more readily a monolithic determinism over all social and political processes. In considering relationships between groups, nationalists might dispense with the deduction of inequality from difference; but for racists this illogical procedure was fundamental. The former were surrounded by foreigners, the latter by half-men. When structuring dealings with what was alien, the nationalist might choose between hatred and indifference. The racist, confronting the innately inferior as potential agents of biological degeneration, had much less choice. He tended to manifest both hatred and contempt – and indifference only in the sense of carelessness about whether those who thus endangered his race were treated like men at all. Nationalism might serve, according to circumstance, the purposes either of freedom or of bondage. But racism idealized always an epitomization of illiberal society. It was necessarily, and not merely contingently, aggressive and anti-individualistic. It was the most rigid expression of belief in an almost divine finality – a predestination by blood. At its apogee, in the Hitlerian New Order, it would seek to transcend and annihilate even the concept of nation itself.

From the mid-nineteenth century until 1945 racism was an increasingly important theme in European thinking about society and politics. It developed in the context of confrontations not only between men of different colour but also within the ranks of Europeans themselves. It was not, as often thought, a mere temporary aberration from some profoundly more beneficent 'Western tradition' of political ideas and practice. Rather, as David Thomson suggests, it must be treated as 'a modern counterpart or variant of those principles of exclusion, intolerance, absolutism and claims to élitism which have been persistent throughout the experience of European civilization'. The first major systematic and genuinely ideological accounts of racial distinctions as the fundamental key to socio-political explanation come from the years around 1850. Most notable is the *Essay on the Inequality of the Human Races* (1853-5) by the Frenchman Arthur de Gobineau. This was an ambitious and idiosyncratic attempt at effecting synthesis between earlier studies of physical phenomena on one side and of cultural phenomena on the other. Like most who wrote earlier in the century about 'Aryan' dignity, Gobineau gave some particular weight to linguistic evidence. Just when many philologists were, however, recanting previous expressions of simple equation between language and race, Aryan or otherwise, Darwinism came into vogue. Racists then tended to rearrange their priorities of evidence. By adopting and developing for their own purposes such phrases as 'struggle for existence' they could emerge with an aura no less scientific than before.

In the last decades of the century 'anthroposociology' became a veritable craze. From complex physical measurements a host of racial and social deductions were made. The most famous manifestation was craniometry, which commended itself to any who might mistake statistical panoply for something more substantial. Debates on such topics as the relative social merits of 'brachycephaly' and 'dolichocephaly' engaged many of the most intelligent men of the time. The career of Paul Broca, a leading founder of the Anthropological Society of Paris in the very year that *The Origin of Species* appeared, provides a typical example of broadly racist assumptions colonizing some of the most reputable science of the age. His operations on the brain made a valuable pioneering contribution to modern neurosurgery; but he was no less active on the surface of skulls, revelling in every variation of size or shape and using his intricate patterns of measurement to support bold correlations between physique and cultural capacities. In such an atmosphere many had ceased to question the basic premises of racism. Throughout Europe argument

often centred instead on the particular details of the conclusion –
whether Celt rather than Anglo-Saxon, whether Teuton
rather than Slav was the appropriate blood-hero of the hour.
It did not greatly matter that relatively few writers elaborated
systematized racial interpretations of past, present, and future.
In terms of repercussions, much was to come from little. The
language of racial thinking, the idiom of eugenic engineering,
the jargon of the calliper, all penetrated to a wider public.
There they mingled, sometimes indistinguishably, with the
no less pervasive rhetoric of nationalistic identification and
assertion.

Within the intelligentsia of every European country there
were men who found such a mixture attractive. The combination was, however, clearest in the new Germany. This
was dominated by a Prussia that had long enjoyed doctrines
of freedom distinguishable usually by their capacity for ready
reconciliation with state dominance. Increasingly in the Reich
at large authoritarian nationalism would free itself from any
residual restraint that even this special form of liberalism
might have managed to exercise. With population booming
on an exceptional scale, the Second Reich was buoyant. But
it was also fearful of an encirclement as much cultural as
political and military. A similar fear, though not a similar
buoyancy, possessed Austrians seeking to hold together a
multi-national Empire. Despite the simultaneously intensified
assertions elsewhere of Celtic and Slavonic genius, there was
during the two generations after 1870 (and especially after
Bismarck's withdrawal in 1890) no real rival to the sheer
stridency of Teutonism in its various forms. In the political
uses of tribal history, for example, what Numa-Denis Fustel
de Coulanges did to vindicate the Gallic tradition was far
surpassed in boldness and influence by the thunderings of the
ex-liberal Heinrich von Treitschke on behalf of an opposing
cause. Treitschke misused his genuine historical talent to assert
that the Hohenzollern crown was not only the noblest but

also the oldest in the world and that the Bismarckian Reich was the realization of Divine Reason. In Berlin he used both his Reichstag seat and his university chair to preach such wonders to the city and the world.

Another influential example of dogmatic Teutonism in action was the Wagner cult, sedulously fostered from Bayreuth both within and beyond the lifetime of the composer. Not least, it was responsible for Germanizing Gobineau's ideology and for converting its pessimistic acceptance of inexorable ethnic degeneration into a messianic creed of racial redemption. Under the spell of the Bayreuth Circle the Englishman Houston Stewart Chamberlain published, in German, his version of the racially determined past under the title *Foundations of the Nineteenth Century* (1899). Hitler later described it, with partial accuracy, as 'the gospel of the Volkish movement'. At the same time, the Nietzschean canon was starting to be used in the service of a Second Reich that its author detested. After the turn of the century there were such further contributions to the chauvinistic ethos as Ludwig Woltmann's *Political Anthropology* (1903) and General Friedrich von Bernhardi's *Germany and the Next War* (1912). The latter's best-selling statement of his nation's pretensions in an age of geopolitics was expressed in the kind of Darwinistic terms that were now common currency among the leaders of Europe.

A salient feature of contemporary chauvinism, both in Germany and elsewhere, was the intensification of intellectualized anti-semitism. The accentuation of national self-consciousness throughout Europe was a threat to Jewish communities that were everywhere a minority and nowhere fully assimilated. In Tsar Alexander III's programme of 'Russification', for instance, they had no place. Indeed, his vicious pogroms of the 1880s caused many Eastern Jews to migrate westwards. Thus they came into societies which, horrified by the great influx, were themselves already recon-

ditioning older instruments of anti-semitic diatribe, and
fashioning new ones – especially from the concepts of racial
biology. The image of the Jew as enemy was protean and
flexible. He could epitomize warmongering as well as
cowardly pacifism, the forces of entrenched finance capital
as well as of social revolution. From whatever part of the
political spectrum the hostility was expressed it tended to
relate to anxiety about the march of modernity, about the
insecurity and moral disorientation of societies undergoing
massive transformation. This helps to explain the willingness
of the Churches to continue condoning or actively promoting
anti-semitic movements. Some, such as that of the Protestant
Adolf Stöcker in Berlin or of the Catholic Karl Lueger in
Vienna, combined Jew-baiting with programmes of social
reform designed to attract particularly the lower middle class.
It is hardly surprising that the Habsburg capital, seat of a
regime so distrustful of modernity, should have been considered Europe's most anti-semitic city. Amongst many Austrians hatred of the Jews had taken on the quality of a fundamental political principle. In Germany Eugen Dühring's *The
Jewish Question* (1881), which even envisaged exterminatory
solutions, was a notable assault from the socialist flank. Its
picture of a financiers' conspiracy was also prominent in
Édouard Drumont's *Jewish France* (1886), which evoked
rather the fears and nostalgia of the French bourgeoisie. His
daily paper *La Libre Parole*, founded in 1892, was soon influential in building up the semitic aspects of the Dreyfus case. The
great *affaire* seemed to catch the Jewish enemy in his most
odious role, as conspiratorial traitor against the pillars of
order and stability. The theme of his national rootlessness was
exploited from 1899 by Charles Maurras' Action Française
movement, which was Catholic and royalist as well as anti-
semitic. The contemporaneous growth of Zionist aspirations,
formulated most clearly by Theodor Herzl in *The Jewish
State* (1896), was readily interpreted as confirming that the

tribe was both arrogant and inimical to any project of national fulfilment besides its own.

Many of the assertions of national and racial superiority made in these years were marked also by their close relationship, sketched earlier, to the environment of colonial expansion. The pursuit of empire was ancient enough; more modern was the appreciation by Europe's ruling classes that it now required fuller ideological justification within the setting of mass politics. In popular and serious literature alike, what resulted was normally pervaded by Darwinistic modes of argument. These stressed the superior fitness of particular European nations or indeed the manifest destiny of the white races as a whole. The accuracy of this reading of the global map of life was not doubted by great entrepreneurs of empire such as Hubert Lyautey, Carl Peters, and Cecil Rhodes. They were typical in having an idea of dominance that embraced, particularly, axiomatic assumptions about Europe's cultural and intellectual pre-eminence. 'In the average European dependency', writes A. P. Thornton, 'the native races were never admitted to the mental life of their masters . . . This was the true barrier. All other forms of segregation were flimsy compared to it.' Still, there were also Europeans in whom the imperial explosion provoked deeper questioning, and even anxiety. After the turn of the century speculation on 'the yellow peril' became commoner in Europe and in the United States too. When Rudyard Kipling, Britain's poet and tale-teller of empire, referred to the coloured native as 'half devil and half child' he revealed elements of fear as well as paternalism. In 1902 his compatriot John Hobson published *Imperialism*, a classic of liberal economic criticism. Believing in racial hierarchization, Hobson did not deny the need for a form of European dominance. But he argued that this should be structured around a purified concept of 'trusteeship' rather than of empire – the latter having shown contemporary capitalism at its most exploitative and inhuman. John Maynard Keynes was one whose ideas benefited from this critique. Another was Lenin, whose own *Imperialism: the Highest Stage of Capitalism* (1916) was an uncompromising assault on the new European colonial ventures as symptoms of a divided capitalist system that was bidding to avoid social revolution at home by transferring the main burden of exploitation to a proletariat overseas.

Lenin's tract exemplified the manner in which the legacy of Marx, like that of Darwin, needed continuous adaptation in order to survive under rapidly changing circumstances. *Imperialism* was written, amidst war, partly to show how so many European proletarians had been duped into behaving as nationalists and jingoists. But it also needed to demonstrate how, with expectations having been raised to unprecedented pitch and urgency, even that behaviour would contribute still to revolutionary fulfilment. Over the preceding two generations such problems of adaptation had encompassed many issues alongside those of war and chauvinism. State-sponsored welfare schemes and other forms of capitalist self-protection against social crisis, stronger trade unionism, suffrage extension, and the new conditions of political organization and propaganda were prominent among the further stimulants to rethinking. Not surprisingly, the socialist ideas of this time tended to emanate from those who were activists first and thinkers second. Though their intellectual wrangling was incessant, they were unable to match Marx in theoretical depth. Nor was that the quality in him which they most cherished. Throughout this period the most sophisticated parts of his writing were still closed books to all but a few. He was known, rather, for his pithier and more simply polemical pieces. Above all, his importance derived from what he was taken to symbolize – as the engineer of bridges between the theory and practice of proletarian revolution. Around 1870 Marx's influence was rivalled by that of Pierre Proudhon, Auguste Blanqui, Mikhail Bakunin, and Ferdinand Lassalle.

By 1914 there was a more marked recognition of his pre-eminence, even if his meaning remained disputable. Within and without the socialist ranks, Marx's work was well on the way to providing a common frame of reference. It might be accepted or rejected, in greater or lesser degree, yet, as a stimulus to social thought and action, it could scarcely be ignored. Upon this process the Bolshevik Revolution of 1917 set the seal.

To revolutionary possibilities in Russia Marx gave some attention in his last years. But his perceptions of them were fragmentary, his conclusions indecisive. More generally, hindered by illness Marx produced after 1870 little of importance apart from the *Address on the Civil War in France*, published immediately after the bloody extinction of the Paris Commune in 1871, and the *Critique of the Gotha Programme*, concerning the orientation of the new German Socialist Party. Composed in 1875, this appeared only in 1891. Among other posthumous publications were the second and third volumes of *Capital* (1885; 1894). These were all elements in Friedrich Engels' task, lasting until his own death in 1895, of tidying and systematizing the legacy. This development had been heralded in 1878 by his *Anti-Dühring*, to which Marx himself contributed a chapter. Over the next generation or so this polemic of Engels was to be perhaps the most influential text associated with Marxism. Increasingly, however, Marx's partner purchased tidiness at the expense of subtlety. By 1895 Engels had given to the canon of orthodox Marxism a distinctive bias. It now embodied, more markedly and unequivocally than before, an overwhelming determinism, a pervasive materialism, and a capitulation to uncritical scientism.

It was in Germany that socialism at large became strongest. Bismarck's Anti-Socialist Law (1878–90) proved a failure. From the German Social Democrats a lead was eventually expected on a continental scale. They grew to enjoy a stature within the Second International, founded in 1889, far greater than that possessed by their countrymen in the First, split by 1872 and finally dissolved in 1876. But they also displayed most clearly the great tensions within socialist thinking. Their party was born of liaison between the Marxist inspirations of Wilhelm Liebknecht and the non-Marxist ones associated with the tradition of Lassalle. From its very beginning, in the Gotha Programme of 1875, the German Socialist Party was unable to escape problems derived from this mixed parentage. Marx's *Critique* was directed against the compromises with the 'old familiar democratic litany'. Yet the German socialists maintained a certain moderation in practice, even after adopting in 1891 the theoretically more radical Erfurt Programme. Indeed Engels, who had a hand in its drafting and who certainly never renounced force as a continuing option, seemed finally willing also to explore the possibility of revolution via the ballot box. Thereafter this rather fragile liaison between Marxist orthodoxy and some form of democracy was sustained most notably by Karl Kautsky, the main architect of the Erfurt platform and editor of the chief party organ from 1883 to 1917. That he was a disciple of Engels was clear from his taste for a scientism expressed dogmatically in terms of materialistic evolution.

Those in Germany who interpreted evolution in politically more moderate fashion, as being the very opposite of revolution, had as their leading spokesman Eduard Bernstein. The formulation of his 'revisionism' was aided by contact with the Fabian Society, a British intellectual pressure group for reformist socialism. It was founded in 1883 and counted among its earliest members Sidney and Beatrice Webb, William Morris, and Bernard Shaw. In Britain, where revolutionary Marxism itself remained weak, the Fabians enjoyed an environment particularly favourable to gradualism. They could relax enough to show some sympathy for T. H. Green's idealist revamping of the liberal philosophy. Nowhere was it easier to believe that such gradualist instruments as parlia-

mentary government and enlarged suffrage could be expro-
priated from the liberals and turned to more distinctively
socialist ends. Bernstein contended that this line of argument
had increasing relevance also to the situation of Europe at
large, where Marxist prophecy about dramatically worsening
conditions remained unfulfilled. He jotted in a note: 'Peasants
do not sink; middle class does not disappear; crises do not
grow ever larger; misery and serfdom do not increase.' The
development of these perceptions involved a more fundamental revision of Marxist assumptions and conclusions than
anything undertaken by Engels and Kautsky. Bernstein shared
their positivism; where he, and the Fabians, differed from
them was in giving it more critical formulation. George
Lichtheim has commented as follows on the case presented in
Bernstein's *Voraussetzungen des Sozialismus* (1899; translated as
Evolutionary Socialism): 'If he was right, the gradual establishment of socialism signified no more than a broadening of the
area of freedom already attained under liberal democracy.
This . . . was precisely what Marx had regarded as nonsense.
On this issue no compromise was possible.' In a sense, orthodox German socialism did manage some compromise – but
only by thinking one way and acting another. At successive
party congresses in the years around 1900 Bernstein, while
continuing to regard himself as a supporter of Marxism,
attempted unsuccessfully to bring theory into closer alignment
with more moderate practice.

At the 1904 congress of the International itself a similar defeat was inflicted upon Bernstein's foreign sympathizers, such
as Victor Adler of Austria and Émile Vandervelde of Belgium.
Among the triumphant were the German delegation and that
part of the French socialist movement led by Jules Guesde.
He had long carried the banner of Marxist orthodoxy in a
country where socialism lacked even the broad organizational
unity enjoyed in Germany and where anarcho-syndicalists,
Proudhonists, Blanquists, and others claimed separate atten-

tion. Yet, in regard to the important issue of gradualism, the German pattern was roughly repeated. The clash between Kautsky and Bernstein was paralleled by Guesde's confrontation not only with Paul Brousse and his 'Possibilists' but also later with 'Independents' such as Alexandre Millerand and Jean Jaurès. In 1899 Millerand had become the first socialist to accept ministerial office in a coalition, and this concrete instance of reformist compromise loomed large in the International's discussions thereafter. Its 1904 condemnation of all such 'opportunism' was accepted by Jaurès loyally but reluctantly, and only after he had eloquently justified socialist collaboration in the general pro-Dreyfus campaign. Under his leadership, and virtually upon orders from the International, the French in 1905 at last forged a United Socialist Party formally dedicated to Marxist-Guesdist ideas. But this was at the cost of excluding some of the ablest socialists, such as Millerand, who believed that the International, by forbidding compromise, had prepared a recipe for impotence.

The most rigorous assaults on the kinds of position taken by Millerand and Bernstein came from a small but significant collection of 'radical' Marxists. They were younger than Kautsky and far less vulnerable to the accusation of having practised more moderation than they preached. Their dismissal of gradualism was linked, however, to a wider range of intellectual activity. Among the radicals based on Vienna were Max Adler, whose philosophical bent allowed him to add to his other refutations a timely neo-Kantian critique of Engels' scientific materialism, and Rudolf Hilferding, whose *Finance Capital* (1910) was the first major treatise of a distinctively Marxist character concerning the economic substructure beneath imperialism. Prominent in a German-Polish group was Rosa Luxemburg. Something of her view of imperialism is indicated by the very title she gave to a work on this subject published in 1913, *The Accumulation of Capital*. Her belief that this process was utterly doomed to self-destruction – once the world no longer had any significant non-capitalist areas left for exploitation – lacked those insights into the unpleasant possibility of its self-perpetuation shown by Hilferding and Lenin. Another and still deeper difference between Luxemburg and Lenin can be appreciated best within the more general setting of the Russian contributions to radical Marxism and of the varying interpretations put upon its relevance to the Russian situation.

Here, with parliamentary institutions absent before the abortive revolution of 1905 and only feebly present thereafter, much of the German socialist debate was irrelevant. Amongst Russian tacticians (many of whom were, significantly, in exile from Tsarist repression) there was general agreement that pursuit of even a minimum programme would involve some degree of violent action. The revolutionary intelligentsia disputed, rather, matters concerned with the location, leadership, and timing of the great eruption. The populist Narodniks, distrustful of 'Western' modernity, contended that it was for the peasants to hew out a new order by utilizing those elements of collective harmony already present in the *mir*, or traditional village community. Conversely the Marxists, guided first by Georgi Plekhanov, stressed that revolutionary hopes must be focused on Russia's rapidly enlarging proletariat. By the 1890s battle between these groups was fully joined. Refutation of the Narodnik position marked Lenin's first major work, *The Development of Capitalism in Russia*, written pseudonymously in Siberian exile but published legally at St Petersburg in 1899. Within each camp, however, disagreement existed about whether the initial phase of revolution would be a matter of spontaneous mass uprising or essentially the product of conspiratorial activity by an élite composed of the intellectually aware. Once the Russian Marxists had in 1898 followed current fashion by organizing themselves into a Social Democratic Labour Party – soon the object of official repression – their need to settle this question internally became pressing indeed. From 1900 Lenin, now editing in the West the party's aptly-named periodical *Iskra* ('The Spark'), devoted his practical and theoretical energies to achieving a solution in the élitist vein.

Its justification was expressed clearest in Lenin's *What Is To Be Done?* (1902). This stressed that even the industrial proletariat needed an injection of revolutionary consciousness from outside – that is, from a tightly organized party of professional revolutionaries charged intellectually to enlighten and politically to command the wider masses. Lenin believed this to be the recipe for success under conditions not only of Russian autocracy but also of parliamentary institutions and broad suffrage. By seeking to demonstrate that improvements in the political and economic situation made militant and conspiratorial preparations for revolution more rather than less necessary he was undertaking, in effect, the most fundamental of all refutations of Bernstein. This is not to suggest, however, that as yet Lenin's thesis met with general acceptance among other radical Marxists. Over these doctrines of organizational élitism he was very widely criticized, despite his own denials, for having forsaken Marx to flirt with Blanqui. Revision of the Russian party's constitution along élitist lines was the issue that produced in 1903 the split between the 'Bolsheviks' of Lenin and the 'Mensheviks' led by Lev Martov and supported here by Lev Trotsky. By 1912 these had become, in practice, separate parties; and their disputes not only over organization but also over the timing of a distinctively socialist (as opposed to bourgeois-democratic) revolution would be central during 1917 itself. However, of all Marxist radicals, Luxemburg was the most trenchant in criticism. She continued to trust in the spontaneous revolutionary capacities of the masses. Thus she saw in Lenin's ideas on organization only a charter for enslavement to a bureaucratic dictatorship likely to expropriate the proletariat's distinctive political destiny. Events – in Russia during the Great War and in Germany immediately after it –

would soon test their competing interpretations of how Marxist revolutionary doctrine could be adapted best to the demands of their own time.

Luxemburg's fears about the authoritarian implications of Bolshevism in particular were reflected at certain points by another brand of criticism directed throughout the period against Marxism as a whole. This came from the anarchists. The First International foundered, indeed, upon conflict between Marx and Bakunin over what the latter viewed as contemporary socialism's devaluation of spontaneity and its readiness to use rather than destroy state structures. After Bakunin's death in 1876, another Russian aristocrat, Peter Kropotkin, emerged as the leading figure among anarchist intellectuals. The classic exposition of his ideas, *Mutual Aid: a Factor in Evolution* (1902), claimed to rescue Darwin from Huxley by demonstrating that, for beast and man alike, the most fundamental natural law was one of cooperation not relentless struggle. It elaborated the worn theme that man's natural goodness had been corrupted only by vicious environment. The proper goal of social evolution was the attainment of a morality derived from what was good within man rather than from the external restraints and compulsions epitomized especially by the state itself. However, only when conditions of common possession and absolute equality had been already attained could this 'morality without obligation or sanction' come into existence – necessarily and spontaneously. Until then men would need violence as the instrument of their release from the oppressions of capitalism and representative democracy in the present and, possibly, from those of authoritarian socialism in the near future. In refusing to condone violence that was merely indiscriminate and in welcoming the age of the machine, Kropotkin differed from many other anarchist intellectuals of his day. Nonetheless he was utterly typical in being much better at destructive negation than constructive affirmation.

This was, in thought and deed alike, the heyday of European anarchism. Its uncompromising political posture made it especially attractive in areas such as Russia, Spain, and southern Italy that had only weak reform traditions. But nearly everywhere anarchism, though lacking much by way of doctrinal rigour and organizational coherence, had considerable cultural impact as a general attitude of mind. The future French premier Léon Blum, for instance, testified: 'The whole literary generation to which I belonged was impregnated with anarchist thought.' Far beyond the narrow circle of those who actively embraced it, anarchism attracted such wider sympathies both because of the objects and because of the mode of its aggression. The anarchist revolt, even more radically than the Marxist one, was directed against bourgeois-dominated mass society's capacities for moral suffocation. In having these as the chief target of its alienation it was, most literally, timely. Yet it was no less timely in advocating also that the revolt be conducted through a mode of seemingly irrational violence which would constitute the true precondition for liberation of the individual. As the expression of his unique spontaneity, this violence could restore his sense both of dignity and of identity. Anarchism, once appreciated as a philosophy of will given political application, can be seen in all its relevance to the strange new worlds being variously explored by Nietzsche, Bergson, and Freud.

Still more complex patterns of connection emerge in the work of Georges Sorel, a French engineer who turned to social philosophy in his middle years and who for the rest of his days reflected perhaps more richly than anyone its state of complexity and confusion. From liberal conservatism he moved during the mid-1890s into a phase of Marxist allegiance that coincided with Croce's own and led Sorel to collaborate in preaching the creed to Italians. By the end of the decade he was in greater sympathy with Bernstein's revisionism. Though he counted himself among the supporters of Dreyfus, Sorel was so deeply disgusted by the manner in which other sympathizers exploited the great affair for immediate political advantage that he never returned again to any advocacy of parliamentary democracy. His interests shifted towards revolutionary syndicalism which, especially in France and Italy, linked anarchist inspirations with the organizational potential of the trade unions. By 1910, disillusioned by the way in which even the syndicalists showed compromising reformist tendencies, he was coming to prefer certain elements in the nationalist mysticism represented by Maurice Barrès' rhetoric of *la terre et les morts* and by the Action Française generally. After the struggles of 1914–18 he felt able not only to praise the new Bolshevik regime but also to show sympathy for the nascent Italian Fascist movement which then attained power shortly after his death. Though ignored by Lenin, Sorel was plucked by Mussolini for use as an intellectual fig-leaf. Even mere summary of such a career indicates that this was a mind refusing to be constrained by conventional categories of political thought and allegiance. But beneath the superficial eddies of inconsistency flowed steadier currents. In particular, like anarchism itself, Sorelian thought maintained consistently a revolt against the bourgeois world, a dialogue with Marx's legacy, and an exploration of the realms of creatively violent energy.

These themes were clearest during Sorel's phase of association with French syndicalism. His immediate influence on the movement was small. But its journal provided during 1906 the organ for the most stimulating of his essays, the *Reflections on Violence* which were collected into a volume two years later. There Sorel praised Bergson's deflation of rationalistic presumptuousness and regarded the *élan vital* as a conception concordant with his own belief that human fulfilment depended upon an energetic creativity which had to be appreciated emotionally rather than scientifically. The bourgeois world could be overthrown only by a form of socialism

founded not upon scientism but upon 'social poetry' – by a
Marxism transcending into an élite-inspired 'myth'. Its
efficacy as an instrument of social change was not to be correlated with the extent of its accuracy as a representation of
reality. The ability of myth to generate activity and thereby
to mould the future was related, rather, to its capacity for
mobilizing the will and channelling the emotions. At the time
of the *Reflections*, Sorel believed that the anarcho-syndicalist
weapon of a totally uncompromising general strike provided
the most promising basis for a myth of this kind. Even when
he shifted towards mystical nationalism, he was consistent in
searching still for whatever would foster an epic state of mind
as precondition for moral and social regeneration. 'Violence',
Sorel declared, 'is an intellectual doctrine, the will of powerful
minds who know what they are doing.' Although he wished
with Kropotkin to distinguish this creative violence from
mere force, it is not difficult to see what hostages he left to
Fascist fortune. In the end he must be added to the swelling
ranks of those whose achievement was more impressive in its
negative than in its positive aspects. Yet, like Nietzsche, he
cannot be dismissed simply on that account. Not least, Sorel
is worth attention because his corrosive criticism touched
upon so many of the major points of agenda already confronting those who were then laying the foundations for the
academic social sciences of the twentieth century.

The case of sociology demonstrates this most clearly.
During these years its leading figures shared with Sorel the
desire to bring speculations about the hollowness within liberal
democratic society or about the validity of Marxist social
analysis into the closest association with a grasp of the hitherto
undervalued role in human behaviour of myth and violence,
emotion and unreason. Already pioneers such as Vico and
Montesquieu in the eighteenth and Comte and Marx in the
mid-nineteenth century had contributed greatly to developing
the sociological imagination. But it was, above all, the appre-

ciation of even more complex and disturbing springs to human action than were assumed by the older classics that enabled sociology to come of age around the turn of the century. In concentrating upon this area of social science we need to keep in mind two tightly related points. Before 1914 the bulk of work on what now would be termed sociological topics was still conducted as an offshoot from activity in other fields; and, largely in consequence, sociology during these years derived very direct benefit from contemporaneous developments in other disciplines.

A prime example was the debate with Marx's ghost being conducted by the neo-classical economists, headed by Alfred Marshall in Cambridge and Eugen von Böhm-Bawerk in Vienna. Their concern with the functioning of the market system in the allocation of resources involved substantial treatment of the nature and limitations of rational choice as applied to a basic sector of human life. Those areas of contemporary anthropology that were relatively free from racist assumptions also provided important stimuli. In particular, it was becoming more apparent that there were dangers in seeking to derive from purely European experience adequate judgements about the quality or desirability of particular social and cultural phenomena. Anthropologists were even depicting supposedly 'primitive' societies which managed to satisfy complex needs and to sustain harmony on a basis that was seemingly instinctual and certainly remote from the conscious procedures hallowed by Western rationalism. Both the retreat from mechanistic psychology and the changes of diagnostic and therapeutic approach towards mental illness must be counted as additional factors in provoking sociological investigation. In Jacques Barzun's words,

Phenomena formerly lumped together as madness were now distinguished and related to their antecedent conditions, most of them not physical but social, emotional, sexual; and this in turn led the inquiring student to investigate the workings of contemporary society, of the family, marriage, the legal and economic systems, and the dictates of religion.

Indeed, the formulations of Freud himself can be savoured fully only within the context of the social nuances and conventions of contemporary Vienna. Again, and more generally still, the heightened concern both of natural scientists and of philosophers with matters of method began to have some appreciable impact upon the manner in which society too was investigated. The work of Dilthey and Croce, noted earlier, exemplifies attempts to inculcate greater awareness of methodological problems not only in historical scholarship but also throughout a wider range of social studies.

Some such disentanglement from the trammels of uncritical positivism was one major precondition for sociological maturity. Another was some adequacy of response to the challenging conditions of mass society. Amidst its turmoil, especially in the cities, custom and tradition had been progressively debased both as guides to action and as keys to the explanation of behaviour. Could sociology evolve any concepts, however tentative, that might contribute to understanding and orientation? This was the problem to which Tönnies' model of transition from *Gemeinschaft* to *Gesellschaft* was addressed. It was also central to the pioneering studies by the Frenchmen Gustave Le Bon and Gabriel Tarde in the field of mass behaviour. Their findings did not encourage complacency. Le Bon's *Psychologie des Foules* (1895; translated as *The Crowd*) treated the transformation in conduct that occurred once the seemingly rational individual was herded together with his fellows. It argued that in this crowd setting whatever was reasonable suffered through the triumph of more emotional processes of 'mental contagion' that worked towards credulous unanimity. Le Bon believed, moreover, that these processes could be fortified greatly by leaders skilled in manipulating the collective will. The criminologist Tarde issued a similar warning, particularly about 'imitation' of superior by inferior, in his widely-read *Opinion and the Crowd* (1901) which investigated the impact of the various media of mass communication. From Graham Wallas of the new London School of Economics came *Human Nature in Politics* (1908), exploring the extent to which 'impulse and instinct' diminished the rationality of political man. Studies of this kind made it necessary to question more carefully whether democracy – in liberal, socialist, or any other form – could ever be more than a cloak concealing from the collectively gullible the perennial triumph of calculating élites.

In earlier times assertions about the inevitability of oligarchy seemed merely platitudinous. But, at the end of a century in which the rhetoric of egalitarian and democratic fulfilment had been freely indulged, the very same assertions now appeared disruptive of ideas widely accepted. Three outstanding students of élitism, and of its socio-psychological preconditions, were Vilfredo Pareto, Gaetano Mosca, and Robert Michels. The first two were Italians; and the last, despite Franco-German origins, regarded Italy as his spiritual home. To large degree each was provoked into questioning by the manner in which the heady aspirations of *Risorgimento*, or national regeneration, had failed to be sustained. As a Sicilian, Mosca felt deepest the hollowness of the peninsula's recent 'unification' under northern dominance. His *Elementi di Scienza Politica* (1896; translated as *The Ruling Class*) was the work of a political moderate, who advocated a pluralist balance of social forces within a system of parliamentary representative government. It suggested, however, not only that every state must possess some political élite but also that the élite of the moment could maintain its ascendancy over rivals only through the purveyance of 'political formulas' adapted to 'the consciousness of the more populous and less well educated strata of society'. It was the congruence of such formulas with this general psychological and cultural condition, rather than with truth, that gave the capacity to stabilize power and thereby to convert it into acknowledged authority. Thus they appeared disturbingly similar to what Marx had called 'the ideology of the ruling class' and to what Sorel envisaged as 'myth'. The main contribution of Michels is indicated in the very title to his book of 1911, *Political Parties: a Sociological Study of the Oligarchical Tendencies of Modern Democracy*. It contended that even those parties most dedicated to implementing equality could not escape from 'the iron law of oligarchy'. In every setting the price to be paid for more efficient organization was a professionalization of leadership. Michels believed that this could not fail to confer upon an élite certain prerogatives of expertise, and therefore of dominance. Under conditions of mass socialization this law was indeed likely to be at its most inexorable.

Linkages between the authority of the élite and the psychology of the mass were explored still more systematically by Pareto, who, having been first like Sorel an engineer, eventually became an economics professor at Lausanne. He published his *Socialist Systems* in 1902 – the year, significantly, of *What Is To Be Done?* He accepted the reality of class struggles but dissented from the Marxist view that the triumph of the proletariat would mark their conclusion. Instead, one élite would be replaced by another – and this would merely claim to speak in the workers' name. For Pareto such 'circulation of élites' was the inescapable and often violent outcome of differences in natural ability. But, yet again, so long as a particular élite survived it did so by virtue of its talents for political manipulation. The relationship between these and the realm of the non-rational was the central theme of Pareto's *Trattato di Sociologia Generale* (translated as *The Mind and Society*) which quickly brought him fame when it finally began to appear in 1916. Success came despite intractable prose, strained vocabulary, and insufficient awareness of the difference between exhaustive description and adequate explanation. Some readers were certainly impressed by an ambitiousness of

scope and assertion which partly discredited the outcome of
Pareto's expressed determination to avoid the insufficiently
critical scientism of Comte and Spencer. Essentially, the treatise explored the distinction between 'logical' and 'non-
logical' (rational and non-rational) elements in behaviour. To
do so it surveyed patterns of relationship between 'sentiments'
(characteristics of the mind that are permanent but not
directly observable), 'residues' (observable actions that relate
to the sentiments and take the form of conduct which is, in
part at least, something other than rational), and 'derivations'
(rhetorical structures, comparable to Mosca's formulas, that
rationalize and interact with the residues). For Pareto the
ability to use derivations as means of controlling the residues
of the populace at large was the chief criterion of a governing
élite's success. Here was, potentially, the foundation for a
doctrine of power and propaganda divorced from any consideration beyond that of oligarchical self-preservation. Not
surprisingly Pareto, shortly before his death in 1923, accepted
nomination as a senator in Italy's new Fascist order.

The justification of a more moderate brand of political conservatism occupied France's leading sociologist, Émile Durkheim. Having forsaken a philosophical career precisely because
of its supposed remoteness from practical issues, he inaugurated the first French chair of social science established
in 1896 at Bordeaux. Six years later he moved to a Sorbonne
professorship in education and sociology, and also founded
L'Année Sociologique, which was to play a distinguished part
in the periodical literature of his subject. Though more subtle
in method and less addicted to over-systematization than
Comte, Durkheim never relinquished completely some uncritical positivist conviction that sociology could provide truly
scientific bases for identifying the best political and social
morality concordant with the conditions of a mass civilization
which was rightly rejecting Christianity. His varied interests
were all linked by the search for means of realizing this newer

morality. It would need to foster in particular that social solidarity which previously, under less stressful conditions, had permitted readier harmonization of conflicting elements. Believing that contemporary France still possessed much of the institutional framework which was also required, Durkheim became the chief unofficial ideologue of the Third Republic. Until his death in 1917 he sought to preserve the régime – and especially its crucial educational structures – from extremists of right and left alike. Their activity was symptomatic of what he termed 'anomie'. He accounted for this absence or confusion of norms in a manner typical of his general approach to patterns of behavioural causation. It was the product, first, of a disorganization in society which, only thereafter, impacted to disrupt behaviour in the individual. Such a view of social conditioning invited some comparison with Marx's own. Nonetheless Durkheim, while certainly alert both to the reality of class conflict and to the dangers of general upheaval, disagreed with any contention that conditions were now nurturing inevitable revolution.

Durkheim's *Division of Labour in Society* (1893) took issue with the view that specialization of economic and social functions was necessarily disruptive of a sense of community. He believed that, in principle, real moral benefit could be derived from reciprocity of obligations, exchange of services, and genuinely mutual interdependence. These were the means by which society moved from 'mechanical' solidarity to a more satisfying state of 'organic' solidarity. If each man occupied his proper functional position within an organically co-ordinated whole, the various forms of social differentiation could themselves be productive of a sense of individual fulfilment capable of banishing anomie. Conflict existed at present principally because of the lack of accord between the division of labour and the distribution of natural talent. So long as this situation prevailed it was unavoidable that functions be allocated coercively and that social jealousies be boundless.

Harmony could be restored, however, through a new brand of moral regulation. In somewhat conservative vein, Durkheim argued that this must inculcate a sense of social duty and discipline capable of limiting mass desires, especially within the sphere of material acquisitiveness. In *The Rules of Sociological Method* (1895) he discussed some of the procedures that might enable social science better to illuminate the kind of morality now appropriate. Two years later he published *Suicide*, a pioneering empirical study suggesting how extensively conditioned by social dysfunctions was a type of behaviour commonly regarded as supremely individualistic. This work reflected already his conviction that modern society, in order to cohere, must develop the functional equivalent of a religious system. In *The Elementary Forms of Religious Life* (1912), which helped forge what became a characteristically French closeness of alliance between sociology and anthropology, Durkheim investigated through Australian totemism the basic sentiments that give rise to religion. For him the accuracy, or otherwise, of the now quasi-religious pronouncements relevant to the contemporary world mattered little. What was really significant was their symbolization of social interests and their response to felt needs. Thus he was describing, in the last resort, a form of moral regulation that replaced coercion by a mere illusion of free acceptance. Just as Sorel believed in the great utility of myth so too, despite his positivist leanings, did Durkheim. Within the France of their day, the mythical was for one a spur to violent action and for the other an instrument of peaceful stabilization.

With Max Weber the immediate political context shifts to the Second Reich. He was born in Prussia, but lived mainly farther south in that 'cultural province of the Upper Rhine' which self-consciously maintained a certain distance from Berlin values. His academic career, rooted first in law and then in economics, was complicated by bouts of nervous illness. Yet sympathetic consideration from Heidelberg University sustained Weber through his most remarkable phase of work, in the decade before 1914. It embraced much of his lastingly significant contribution to the methodology of the social sciences. In essence, he aspired to span the divide between a philosophical idealism that was lapsing into unmitigated relativism or intuitionism and a positivism that was frequently uncritical in its pursuit of supposedly hard facts. Weber, educated within the first of these traditions, had found the debates of Rickert and Dilthey stimulating but ultimately unsatisfactory. Without sharing Durkheim's complete dismissal of intuitive method, he himself contended that the procedure of *Verstehen* must be complemented by more empirical and quasi-positivist discussions of causation. He was not daunted by his realization that in the social sphere especially even this latter mode of explanation must also remain severely incomplete. Further, he saw no essential conflict between pleading that society be studied with as much scientific neutrality as possible and agreeing with Dilthey's stress on the relativity of value judgements. Weber thought that harmony could be preserved here so long as Durkheim's muddle of prescriptive and descriptive functions was avoided. On the other hand, he was no less concerned than the Frenchman that sociology be useful. Weber, at least, did not believe that it could dictate how men should live. Rather, its role was to clarify the issues and conditions pertaining to social choices that would be settled, ultimately, as expressions of subjective value preference. Weber's point was that, without scrupulous discrimination between categories of 'is' and 'ought', sociology would not attain the objectivity necessary to serve this task. Upon these foundations he developed what Stuart Hughes calls 'an infinitely complex view of human affairs in which pluralism was as inevitable philosophically as a succession of unilateral approaches was a practical necessity'.

These subtleties were elaborated in essays contributed to the *Archiv für Sozialwissenschaft und Sozialpolitik*, a periodical which Weber co-edited from 1904. Most notably, its pages carried during 1904-5 the articles comprising *The Protestant Ethic and the Spirit of Capitalism*. Although flawed by excessive selectivity of evidence, this description of the positive contribution made by Protestantism, and Calvinism especially, to capitalist development has remained a landmark in historical and sociological scholarship. Weber's starting point was the unique extent to which Western capitalism had succeeded in the pursuit of gain. He decided that this outstanding proficiency was related to the practice of substantial capital reinvestment. And this was the very feature that, at a crucial period, had been fortified into habit by the appearance of a new religious ethos which, though devised for essentially other-worldly purposes, could serve marvellously well the quest for secular profit. To encourage the believer to view in worldly success the signs of his eventual salvation and yet also to discourage him from spending luxuriously the products of that success was, in combination, the recipe for capitalist consolidation. The Weberian thesis thus assailed Marxism, especially as made canonical by Engels, through describing how religious factors might rival economic ones as dynamic· influences upon social development. But, more fundamentally still, Weber denied that he was substituting any narrowly spiritualistic interpretation of causation for a restrictively materialistic one. His main achievement, here and elsewhere, was indeed to suggest the limitations of monistic explanation in any form. Until his death in 1920 a series of wide-ranging studies – particularly in the social psychology of the great world religions, and including the unfinished *Economy and Society* – argued for an interpretation of human behaviour within a more richly textured conception of existence than Marxism envisaged. Above all, he was seeking to establish a much more pluralistic and balanced view of the interpenetration between ideas, religious or otherwise, and society itself.

In capitalism and Calvinism alike Weber had discerned forms of discipline that were part of Western civilization's characteristic 'rationalization'. This process was not without its drawbacks. Another of its important manifestations, in contemporary Europe generally and in the Reich especially, was the growth of bureaucratic control. Weber, since he was both aware of modern social complexities and alert to the need for orderly administration, never sought to dismiss completely this particular development. Yet he appreciated the extent to which it endangered the ends of government through excessive concentration upon rendering efficient the means. Like Michels, he was concerned about preserving individual liberty in settings where expertise and power were bracketed ever closer together. Weber offered no simple solution to the dilemma. It was however the chief stimulus for his speculations on 'charismatic leadership', a possible countervailing force about which he had similarly mixed feelings. He defined charisma as 'a certain quality of an individual personality by which he is considered extraordinary and treated as endowed with supernatural, superhuman, or at least specifically exceptional powers or qualities'. This, Weber argued, could give rise to forms of political authority which were 'based upon belief in magical powers, revelations, and hero worship' and were therefore, properly speaking, irrational. Could attachment to such élite figures rescue individuals from bureaucratic domination? More generally still, could such loyalty provide some psychological compensation for what seemed, under increasingly secularized conditions, a diminished sense of purpose? Was reason's march destined, otherwise, to produce only soulless demoralization?

Weber's response is best understood by appreciating that the process of rationalization is also one of *Entzauberung*, or 'disenchantment'. This suggests a liberation from the magical which is accompanied by a feeling of real loss – indeed, by 'disillusionment' as commonly conceived. Once more the ebbing of traditional belief, the situation of disorientation, and the value of some functional substitute for religion are central issues. In effect, Weber was querying – as Freud would continue to do – just how much reality humankind could bear. He never advocated charismatic authority outside the context of parliamentary government. Still, over this matter at least, his naïvety seems to have rivalled his caution. Though repelled in youth by Treitschke's Berlin lectures and though destined in his final years to assist the birth of the Weimar Republic, Weber was in his own value preferences still enough of a 'national' liberal to share some of the chauvinistic simplicities of many far less intelligent Germans. He appears to have erred in supposing that, through communion with the world of charismatic fictions, the masses could be rescued from over-bureaucratization without falling necessarily beneath the tyranny of something else. But such criticisms are indebted to hindsight. They must not obscure the fact that in these years no European grappled more persistently and honestly than Weber with so many problems both of method and of substance that were fundamental to a better understanding of society.

On the eve of war European social and political thinking was still influenced heavily by uncritical positivism. This underlay the conceptions of those masses who were still generally faithful to expectations of inexorable progress. Its respectability among intellectuals, though weaker, also remained considerable. But there was no denying that its arrogance had come under severe and sustained challenge. Many ideas about society now shared with speculations upon much else a growing sensitivity to dissolving certainties. Even though the wider intellectual repercussions of the revolution in physical science were as yet scarcely felt, the modesty increasingly apparent in much contemporary philosophical development was already becoming appreciated by a number of social theorists. Weber particularly, in refusing to dignify personal value preferences with any quality of absoluteness or universality, stood alongside many of the philosophers and theologians previously noted. Moreover, at a different level the extent and pace of mass socialization had been themselves sources for a dissolution of certainty. Yet, here as elsewhere, it is necessary to question at which point scepticism ceased to be healthy and became instead corrosive, to ask at which stage the elucidation of reason's limitations might be perverted into a glorification of irrationality itself. It was easy to fudge the distinction between knowing less and devaluing all knowledge; between charting, with the aid of reason, the domains of the irrational and supposing, thereafter, the emotional or the unconscious to be omnipotent. From many directions doubt had been cast on that image of social and political man nurtured by much progressive thinking over the preceding two centuries. The worlds now postulated – whether of Darwinian biological conditioning, of Marxist economic conditioning, of Durkheimian social conditioning, or of Freudian psychological conditioning – made it more difficult than before to assume that in any large degree men were free to choose, were conscious of their own motivations, were susceptible to rational argument. But, again, it was one thing to show a greater sensitivity to such limitations for the purpose of activating more efficiently whatever liberty and awareness could remain; it was another to dispense altogether with concepts of rational freedom. Men such as Freud and Weber were not alone in encouraging their contemporaries to make, for the defence of reason, the right kinds of discrimination. Nor would they be alone in suffering misrepresentation.

Amidst these potential confusions those who strove to maintain the legacy of constructive criticism associated with the best in the *philosophe* tradition would be opposed not merely by the many survivals of uncritical positivism but also, increasingly, by forces prepared to raze rather than to refurbish the Enlightenment's house of intellect. By 1914 liberalism and socialism were still so mutually hostile as to be largely neglectful of newer threats, nurtured by dissolving certainty, becoming directed against the human and rationalistic assumptions they had in common. For liberals and socialists alike the outbreak of general war and the crude chauvinism that accompanied it were bitter blows. On balance liberalism, being already upon the defensive, was in intellectual terms perhaps the less inadequately prepared. Socialism, however, had abruptly to reconsider its interpretation of those major tenets of internationalism and pacifism that had been long debated in the abstract but not fully tested hitherto. In the event, the International fell apart and it was confirmed that, for the bulk of the European proletariat, the war of the nations must take priority over the war of the classes during the immediate future at least. More broadly, there were throughout the whole political spectrum many beliefs and assumptions whose validity had to be questioned very deeply in the midst of the horrors now unleashed. Nonetheless, even before the guns fired, most of the important doubts had started to be expressed.

Chapter 5

LITERATURE
AND THE ARTS

IN the intellectual turmoil of these years none participated
more perceptively than the creators of imaginative literature
and art. They were being challenged to accept, willingly or
otherwise, a major responsibility for the proclamation of
values. This was the task that religion and philosophy, defen-
sively confronting the march of scientific certainty, had
seemed increasingly unable or hesitant to undertake. At the
beginning of the period it was common even for writers and
other artists themselves to seek much of the validation for
their activity in an association with, or an imitation of, scientific procedure. But by the early twentieth century they
tended to adopt more richly textured forms of self-justifica-
tion. As we have seen in every sphere of intellect so far discussed, there was then growing awareness – derived partly
from the emergent anomalies and indeterminacies within
natural science itself and partly from simple rejections of the
scientific as such – of the necessity for a still more complex
world picture. In it the place accorded to will and emotion,
to instinct and immediate experience, to the unconscious and
the irrational would have to be vastly enlarged. Literature and
the Arts could be regarded readily enough as the most appropriate vehicles for their expression. The creative artist might
yet, in Victor Hugo's terms, fulfil his destiny as magus. More
decisively than ever before, his talents gave him an opportunity of assuming a guiding significance that would be both
autonomous and dominating. But whether he would indeed
serve or spurn the social was an altogether different matter.

Already by 1870 improvements in literacy and general education were well on the way to creating for writers their first truly mass audience. The rapidly rising sale of newspapers towards the end of the century was one powerful testimony to this enlarging public appetite. Another was the boom in popular fiction, whether found in magazines or in volume form. Such authors as Karl May, Pierre Loti, and Rudyard Kipling succeeded in responding to the widespread taste for tales of exotic places. The equally strong attraction of what was distant in time underlay the international triumph of *Quo Vadis* (1896), a novel about Neronic Rome by the otherwise rather neglected Pole Henryk Sienkiewicz. In 1912 his book suffered its first adaptation for the cinema, a cultural medium which had not yet supplanted the kind of popular live entertainment offered by vaudeville and music hall and whose potential had still to be properly realized. On another front, the detective story pioneered by Émile Gaboriau came of age during the 1890s with the success of Arthur Conan Doyle's creation, Sherlock Holmes. The public also bought by the thousand the scientific fantasies of Jules Verne and H. G. Wells. As the case of Wells suggests, the boundaries between popular and serious literature were frequently unclear and arbitrary. But it is indisputable that beyond the tales of explorers, legionaries, sleuths, and inventors lay writing of deeper significance. This had a value that could not be measured according to the size of any immediate audience. Here was the literature, especially in the form of novel and drama, that best exposed and communicated the vast anxieties of the epoch.

Early on these were expressed chiefly through 'naturalism' – which, like many other cultural 'isms', was a well-established label for something whose contents were far less tidy than any single term suggests. Broadly, it reflected in literature the contemporary prestige of science. Indeed, for a time, the novel and drama stood in peril of being regarded as mere

auxiliaries to scientific investigation. At its purest, work in the
naturalistic mode was suffused with philosophical materialism
and with the desire to reproduce nature through methods
imitative of the laboratory. The author thus became a
'moralist-experimenter'. It was disputable, however, whether
there remained much room for morally assessing characters
whose actions and fate were so conditioned by powerful
physical or quasi-physical laws. The chief determinants on
which naturalism focused were heredity and environment.
Their inter-relationship, especially absorbing for a public
excited by Darwinistic controversy, was a dominant theme
in such literary-philosophical critics as Hippolyte Taine.
Naturalism commonly found in the story of a family and its
changing situation across generations the best clinical setting
for the study of such interaction. This approach was often
stultifyingly rigid, but it had value in developing more awareness of the linkages between the social and the psychological.
Such realization was aided further by the fact that naturalism
diminished reliance on violent action and convoluted plot. It
expressed, rather, the conviction that many of the most
important facets of human character are explored best
through the medium of men's response to the relative tedium
and uneventfulness of their everyday lives. Many felt that, in
consequence, naturalism overplayed the squalid aspects of
existence. But this was a bias that brought important advantages, social and artistic alike. Naturalism not only helped in
publicizing hideous conditions; it also insisted upon the kind
of detailed observation that later, when no longer so readily
regarded for literary purposes as an end in itself, would constitute a precondition for still greater creative achievements.

The firmest monument to naturalism in literature was
erected by the French novelist Émile Zola. *Les Rougon-Macquart*, his twenty-volume *roman-fleuve*, appeared between 1871
and 1893. Inspired partly by Claude Bernard's writing on
experimental medicine, it was sub-titled significantly 'A

Natural and Social History of a Family'. The hereditary weaknesses of the Rougon-Macquart clan reflect, in microcosm, the features of a society much more generally diseased. Paris of the Second Empire – its slums and brothels, its stores and finance-houses – is here the chief, and painstakingly observed, environment with which heredity must interact. Yet there is also excursion into provincial life. Indeed, the most famous volume within the whole series – *Germinal* (1885) – explores, with uncompromising coarseness, the miseries of the mining communities near the Belgian border. Whatever the setting, Zola presents figures ensnared in the trammels of heredity and environment. Each man seems to be the passive product of conditioning rather than any kind of active moral agent. The common charge that the outcome is weakness of characterization indicates merely the gulf between Zola's view of character and that of his critics. On the other hand, even he failed to banish entirely from his novels some important issues of choice and moral evaluation. These were, moreover, eminently present in his own experience. His famous intervention on behalf of Dreyfus was, in every sense, decisive. Indeed, for many reasons, genuine relief can be derived from the fact that his practice of naturalism was less dogmatic than his preaching. John Cruickshank goes to the point of suggesting that 'Zola's failure as a scientist is the source of his artistic strength. By temperament he was a poet and visionary, and if the tension between romance and science encouraged some ill-judged melodramatic writing it also created some of the most powerfully imagined scenes in his work.' French sympathizers included Guy de Maupassant, notable for the application of naturalism to the shorter story, and Edmond de Goncourt, who with his brother had earlier pioneered the documentary novel and who after 1870 continued alone their remarkable *Journal*. On the wider European scene too the reputation of Zola was assured by the time of his death in 1902.

The foremost figure in naturalistic drama was the Norwegian Henrik Ibsen. Though impatient of his fellow-countrymen, he played a leading role in the general Scandinavian cultural efflorescence over this period. His was a theatre of mental anxiety rather than of physical action, and one in which problems were stated much more clearly than solutions. He had a far deeper poetic sense than Zola and an altogether more provisional attachment to naturalism itself. But there is irony in the fact that he felt the Frenchman had overstressed the sordid. For whatever international renown Ibsen himself enjoyed by 1900 had been won in the face of much bitter public resentment at his own 'filth'. Typical, both in his passion and in his idiom, was the critic who dismissed *Ghosts* (1881) as 'an open drain, a loathsome sore unbandaged, a dirty act done publicly'. This, the most harrowing of Ibsen's plays, treated the common enough naturalistic theme of a family enshackled by physical legacy from the past. That the legacy was expressed as congenital syphilis blinded many to a sensitivity of treatment unmatched by any contemporary. Ibsen, like Freud, realized that bourgeois toleration of criticism was least generous when sexuality was at issue. On the other hand, his depiction of the professional and commercial classes in Norway – and, by inference, in Europe generally – derived from a consideration of bourgeois hypocrisy in a host of further forms.

Those who did greet Ibsen as a liberating force tended to concentrate unduly upon the more immediately social aspects of his message. Certainly such plays as *Pillars of Society* (1877), *A Doll's House* (1879), and *An Enemy of the People* (1882) had much to say about the conduct of public life, or about the conventions of marriage and the position of women in general. Less fully appreciated in Ibsen's own time was the quality of the psychological, or even spiritual, exploration present both in these works and especially in such concluding masterpieces as *Hedda Gabler* (1890), *John Gabriel Borkmann* (1896), and *When We Dead Awaken* (1899). The destructiveness of dogmatic ideals, suggested through Gregers Werle in *The Wild Duck* (1884), and the association of choice and responsibility, asserted by Ellida Wangel in *The Lady from the Sea* (1888), exemplify recurrent themes that Ibsen treated with consummate skill. In the final resort, he was asserting that individual fulfilment depended upon deciding for oneself – and, if necessary, deciding in defiance of every established social norm. The resulting ethic might be regarded as relativistic, even anarchical; but it had the supreme merit of being unquestionably one's own. Ibsen as dramatist, but also as poet and moralist, expresses himself in the final triumphant line of the supposed 'public enemy', Doctor Stockmann: 'The strongest man in the world is the man who stands most alone.' The congruence with the Nietzschean ethic is clear. A form of naturalistic social criticism was manifestly one of Ibsen's concerns, but it is this distinctively moral dimension to his castigation of received ideas and conventional behaviour that constitutes the essential core of his achievement.

The Swedish playwright and novelist August Strindberg had, like Ibsen, talents that were not entirely circumscribed by naturalism. Nonetheless it was dramas in that mode, especially *The Father* (1887) and *Miss Julie* (1888), which eventually brought him international recognition. Strindberg illuminated, even more boldly than the Norwegian, the borderlands between sanity and insanity. Prominent too was his exploration of the links between sexual conflict and social hypocrisy. This was undertaken most maturely in *The Dance of Death* (1900), a play deeply permeated by Strindberg's own bitter experience of hollow marriage. In Britain a leading proponent of dramatic naturalism was Bernard Shaw, the Dublin-born polemicist whose notoriety was firmly established by the early years of the twentieth century. Inspired by Fabian socialism, he became engaged in a running war against conventional social values and self-deceptions. His essay *The Quintessence of Ibsenism* (1891), though a brave attempt at habilitating the new drama before angered London audiences, was rather a mixed blessing. By depicting Ibsen too exclusively as a social reformer it intimated the manner in which Shaw would soon be turning his own plays into lectures. Not even a coruscating wit could succeed always in redeeming the tedium of his sheer didacticism. Subtler but less generally optimistic than Shaw's was the naturalistic comedy of Anton Chekhov, for whom Ibsen's plays were the object of respect rather than of liking. Chekhov's accomplishment, both in story-writing and in a great bout of dramatic creativity around the turn of the century, was to lay bare the foibles of Russian society. The disorientation of the provincial gentry, numbed and confused, was captured for all time in *The Cherry Orchard* (1904) which, staged in the year of his premature ·death at the age of forty-four, constituted his final masterpiece. Chekhov's plays, particularly as interpreted at the Moscow Arts Theatre under Konstantin Stanislavsky, forced audiences to contemplate upon the stage those same elements of the random, the drifting, the inconsequential, and the inarticulate so familiar to them as the very stuff of everyday life. In these dramas of anomie even silence became creative.

A generation before Chekhov the Russian novel had reached an apogee in the work of three formidable social critics. The first to attain international renown was Ivan Turgenev, whose most important book *Fathers and Children* (1862) appeared shortly before his withdrawal to live in Western Europe. The significance of Leo Tolstoy too was also soon recognized far beyond Russia. His great stories of family tribulation, *War and Peace* (1863–9) and *Anna Karenina* (1873–7), brought a European fame that was not diminished by a subsequent spiritual crisis which made him an arch-critic both of artistic modernity and of conventional religion. The confusion in contemporary values, which absorbed Turgenev, Tolstoy, and Chekhov alike, was stated even more vividly by Fyodor

Dostoyevsky. He pursued this theme in a series of major novels running from *Crime and Punishment* (1866) through to *The Brothers Karamazov* (1879–80). The latter contained, in the parable of the Grand Inquisitor, one of the epoch's most challenging statements of the transformation of values. For Dostoyevsky at least, naturalism had little to do with the everyday. He claimed to be asserting realism 'on a higher level', where the melodramatic and the macabre might be used freely not to provide cheap thrills but to illuminate 'phenomena in which the elements of real life intermingle, displace, and outbid each other in a fantastic way'. The conviction that reality could be best investigated at the depths of men's souls drove him into describing and even vindicating behaviour conventionally regarded as abnormal or depraved. To this task he brought great psychological insight and the passion of a man who had himself once been condemned to death for fomenting resistance to Tsarist iniquity. It is true that, especially during the final decade before his death in 1881, Dostoyevsky attained a certain social respectability. Even so, his work continued to exemplify well how, under a regime committed to the repression of all overt hostility, literature might still provide channels for oblique commentary in a spirit of dissent.

In contrast, such a literature of protest was less essentially characteristic of the new Germany. Her writers' handling of contemporary social and political questions proved often to be acquiescent in, or equivocal about, the values of the Reich. Muted and ambivalent was, for instance, the social commentary contained in the naturalistic novels of Theodor Fontane. *Effi Briest* (1895), the last of them, shows this while delicately studying the adulterous heroine's confrontation with the established code of honour. In other respects, however, it was precisely his refusal to simplify issues that strengthened Fontane's position as the most sensitive chronicler of Berlin and Prussian attitudes during the first decades in

which Germany had to face up to new responsibility and
enlarged temptation on the national and international scenes
alike. In Berlin's theatres around 1890 the dramatist and
theorist Arno Holz sought to surpass Zola and other French
pioneers by advocating a more rigorous naturalism based on a
'second-by-second style' of writing and performance. Though
achieving little in itself, this did provide valuable inspiration
for the crucial naturalistic phase in Gerhart Hauptmann's
development. Uproar greeted his first play *Before Dawn* (1889),
in which the congenital repercussions of alcoholism made a
leading theme. Nonetheless, his next work was assured of a
better reception once it was known that official efforts towards
censoring its performance had failed. Here in *The Weavers*
(1892), about the Silesian troubles of the 1840s, he dramatized
the miseries suffered by a whole community, workers and
owners alike, during the industrialization process. Still,
despite the stir they caused, these plays did not suggest that
Hauptmann, any more than Fontane, was committed tren-
chantly to reform. Indeed these dramas, through so clearly
depicting men's impotence before fateful circumstance,
might well be considered as fortifying amongst Germans a
social spirit not so much of protest as of passive acceptance or
disengagement.

Many of the tensions within contemporary German literature were crystallized in the disagreements of the brothers
Mann. Even while both were contributing substantially to
some form of naturalism in the novel, they were developing
very different assessments of the society that nurtured them.
The elder, Heinrich, favoured a literature harnessed to
political, indeed socialist, transformation. For him Wilhel-
mine Germany's greatest defect was the uncritical worship of
authority. This he satirized in *Professor Unrat* (1905), a novel
about the classroom tyrant whose downfall at the hands of a
cabaret girl brings him universal ridicule. The author's fears
were expressed more impressively still in *Man of Straw*, whose

anti-hero Diederich Hessling aspires to social success through demanding from every inferior that same total abasement which he himself exhibits before his own betters. This work began to appear between 1911 and 1914, but so subversive was it of the very values for which Germans were soon fighting that its publication could not be resumed and completed until 1918. In that same year Thomas Mann issued a fraternal rebuke to one who seemed lacking in patriotism and especially in appreciation of the superiority of German *Kultur* over mere French *civilisation*. The *Reflections of an Unpolitical Man* registered his failure to grasp the broad accuracy of the indictment mounted by Heinrich. This might have vitiated severely the achievement of a less talented author than Thomas himself. But *Buddenbrooks* (1902), his own major undertaking of the pre-war years, had demonstrated that, in these hands, even a novel nostalgically indulgent towards the values of traditional *Bürgertum* might properly aspire to be a masterpiece.

Already Thomas Mann was, in important respects, an ambiguous and pivotal figure. Not least, he shared with many of the authors already mentioned – and, eminently, with Ibsen, Strindberg, and Hauptmann – an increasing dissatisfaction with the constraints imposed by naturalism. From certain viewpoints, and especially as a treatment of family history, *Buddenbrooks* seemed to belong to the mainstream of the genre – indeed, 'naturalistic' was the epithet that Mann himself applied to the work. Yet he was also pursuing themes typical of much of the literature that was now rivalling and even superseding naturalism. Most crucially, he participated in fundamental reformulation of questions about the relationship between the artist and bourgeois society. Mann, like his fictional dynasty, came of Hanseatic merchant stock. His novel, describing how over the generations the solid practical morality of the Buddenbrooks had been eroded by their fascination with things artistic and reflective, became a deeply personal study of his own ambivalent affection for two seemingly hostile worlds. The issue of their relationship is equally salient in the story *Tonio Kröger* (1903). It is precisely the equivocal response, the refusal to simplify, that makes these works of Mann valuable points of entry into any study of the new aestheticism. Around the turn of the century Germans led this vogue for *Künstlerromane*, novels wherein treatment of the nature and value of personal creativity took precedence over concern with more straightforwardly social issues. They posed the problem of the artist's role within a civilization geared to the demands of the practical and the material. If the artist was powerless to respond to these, or possibly to any social requirement at all, was there some other destiny for him to fulfil?

Significantly, even before the name of Freud was common currency, the ensuing debates often dealt with an impotence that was not merely social but also physical and sexual. The wilting Hanno Buddenbrook epitomized the linkage which Mann made between art and sickness. *Death in Venice* (1911) stated this matter even more poignantly through the character of Aschenbach. The great author expires obsessed still with the distant figure of the boy Tadzio. Especially in his futile cos-meticized rejuvenation Aschenbach becomes emblematic of all who, in art and life alike, search for a beauty that is corrupt and corrupting. This novella's delicate handling of the theme of homo-eroticism must be seen within the context of a whole generation struggling for greater frankness in the literary treatment of sexuality. To take Britain alone, contributions were made during this period by writers as varied as Wells, Algernon Swinburne, Samuel Butler, and, towards the eve of war, D. H. Lawrence. In considering sexual feelings that threatened to transgress the official conventions of bourgeois society Mann had managed to show understanding; but many other authors, in their lives as well as their writings, would go further and even commend the freer indulgence of these passions.

The realm of sexuality was that in which the bourgeoisie was most readily shocked and its hypocrisies most easily punctured. In effect, all its doctrines of respectability sought to restrain spontaneous and irrational forces that otherwise might prove dangerously uncontrollable. Naturalism, through its manner of treating such subjects as adultery and prostitution, had helped to advocate increased candour from one angle. But other approaches to its promotion were possible. Here a landmark was *The Awakening of Spring* (1891, but denied performance until 1906), by the leading Munich playwright Frank Wedekind. Without primary resort to naturalistic imitation, he dramatized the process whereby the purity of adolescent sexual self-discovery might be corrupted and deformed by prudish convention. The play assailed the bourgeois world on behalf not of the social downtrodden but of those who cherished natural instinct and the spontaneity of art itself. Such works could imply an even more fundamental social critique than naturalism itself had mounted. They might even reach the point of renouncing any kind of social engagement at all. Advancing was a literature of liberation from bourgeois convention in which the artist might assert himself as the supreme custodian of values, but in which the values themselves might scorn the social altogether and pertain to some realm of pure art alone.

The image of the creative artist as rebel had been nurtured in the romantic movement. It was developed further during the mid-nineteenth century by figures who hallowed drugs and drunkenness, debauchery and vagabondage, as appropriate stimulants to inspiration. Amongst their principals had been Baudelaire whose reputation, especially after his death in 1867, grew progressively more significant. He presented, in Arnold Hauser's words, a model of 'how to reconcile the new

mysticism with the old fanatical devotion to art'. By the end
of the century alienation from bourgeois society had become,
to an unprecedented degree, typical of artistic attitudes. It also
went deeper and was elaborated more systematically than ever
before. Its fullest expression was found in doctrines about 'art
for art's sake'. The upshot might be the evolution of morali-
ties running completely counter to those of the bourgeois
world; or – more drastically, and in ways that writers of
Zola's ilk found puzzling – it might result in the renunciation
of any social and moral commentary whatsoever. In the latter
case, there was withdrawal – sometimes literally as well as
metaphorically – from the world of crude factuality, of
surging masses in society and of cold scientism in intellect.
Concentration was focused instead upon an inner and more
private world of symbolic expression and pure form, and any
audience that might be presupposed was unlikely to extend
beyond the narrow circle of the artist's peers.

Only at one level, however, did such narcissistic self-
contemplation and self-enchantment constitute a retreat. At
another, it revealed similarities with something encountered
already in Nietzsche – a brand of almost superhuman assertiveness. This was clearest in the conviction that one's own life
might be moulded into a work of art. The fundamental tenet
of aestheticism was that whoever desired entry into the élite
of sensitivity and refinement must have the capacity, and
acknowledge the duty, to surround himself with beauty and
to express it in every facet of his existence. However, the
beautiful would be found not in raw nature but in artifice.
The artist's chief task was, indeed, to improve and transcend
the natural. He must develop a mode of life characterized by
the extravagant, the useless, and the effete. Pursuing novel
sensations for their own sake, he must seek out the exotic, the
occult, the mystical. He might well be stimulated by religious
or quasi-religious experiences, but often these would be ones
in which Catholicism and Satanism jostled uncomfortably

together. In an earlier generation the artist had affronted bourgeois conventions by fostering a style of tavern boorishness. Now this tended to be exchanged for a dandyism which was subtler but no less alarming.

From this new setting emerged some startling fictional heroes. The most seminal was created by Joris-Karl Huysmans. This French novelist of Dutch descent had written his first works under the influence of Zola's naturalistic circle. Nonetheless *À Rebours* (1884; known in English as *Against Nature*, or *Against the Grain*) marked an important break. Its frail protagonist, Jean des Esseintes, expresses the essence of neurotic hypersensitivity. Release from boredom is his deepest desire. What stimulates vulgar imaginations does not, however, provide any solace for him. Instead, his attempts at dispelling *ennui* take the form of retreat into an exquisitely private world – of delicate perfumes and rich textures, of exotic experiences and perverse pleasures. But even these prove futile. Nor is there any indication that as yet Huysmans thought the realm of religious sentiment, upon which the story touches in conclusion, was capable of giving lasting relief from the afflictions of lassitude. Contemporaries were struck particularly by the wantonness of the hero's concern to construct, in defiance of conventional values, a paradise so elaborately artificial. Even so, in Philippe Villiers de l'Isle-Adam's play *Axël* (first published in 1890, a year after its author's death) the themes of *taedium vitae* and of the quest for perfect illusion were further developed. Here the hero and heroine prefer to die before their passion has attained complete sexual fulfilment, lest the physical reality fall below their sublime expectations. Living, Count Axël suggests, is something that can be left to servants. Soon a novel by the Dublin-born iconoclast Oscar Wilde was making a vivid addition to the gallery of perverse heroes. *The Portrait of Dorian Gray* (1891) established his reputation as an author enchanted by the perilous delights of an immoral hedonism. Three years later Wilde published, with provocative illustrations by Aubrey Beardsley, his play *Salome*. But in 1895 Oscar – in his own life-style a dandy hero – was gaoled upon conviction for homosexual practices. Polite society had obtained a modicum of revenge.

That same year saw the appearance of Max Nordau's *Degeneration*. This broad indictment of artistic modernity, in which the new aestheticism was regarded as only the latest manifestation of general cultural decay, became an international best-seller. In 1897 Tolstoy, whom Nordau had actually numbered amongst the corrupt, published *What Is Art?*, his own assault on the current condition of European culture. The denunciation, though again wide-sweeping, gave some special attention to the mistaken view of art nurtured by the contemporary aesthetic movement. By this time Tolstoy had rejected much of his own earlier writing and was devoting the rest of his life and work to the peasantry of his estate at Yasnaya Polyana, and to all whom in their unsophisticated goodness those peasants symbolized. Accordingly, he now advocated an art that communicated simply and directly to the mass of men. With Nordau he believed the practice of an élitist, hermetic, and escapist conception of art to be a sign of decadence. That Huysmans and company should attract such criticism is easily understood; but more surprising is the extent to which many of them had already adopted 'decadent' as a label of approbation. Increasingly, for them at least, the idea of progress was losing its plausibility and even its allure. Instead, they felt possessed by a growing awareness of being the leading spirits of a civilization whose ripeness was passing irremediably into decay.

The cults of aestheticism and decadence were part of a more general mood of dissatisfaction with naturalistic assumptions that found clearest expression in the literary movement known as 'symbolism'. This, though limited to no single country or genre, had a focal point in French poetry and reflected once more the general indebtedness to Baudelaire. Symbolism's first really distinctive achievements were recorded during the early 1870s – the period of the brief and tempestuous love affair between Arthur Rimbaud and Paul Verlaine. During the remainder of the century its influence was consolidated by such poets as Stéphane Mallarmé (whom Des Esseintes is said to have read devotedly) and the Belgian Émile Verhaeren. The latter's countryman Maurice Maeterlinck developed symbolism in drama, after a manner suggested already by Villiers de l'Isle-Adam's *Axël*. The movement embodied the convictions that art is concerned principally with expressing its creator's own state of mind and that this expression is least imperfect when symbolized through the imagery of the poet. Naturalism had used prose as the main vehicle for its quasi-scientific description of reality. But symbolists, more romantically inspired, preferred poetry as the basis for an evocation of reality. They relied not upon the models of science but upon what Rimbaud strikingly called a 'disordering of all the senses'.

The symbolists believed that only through such means could the artist free himself from the imperfections of the everyday world and attain deeper levels of reality. This position made them, implicitly or more directly still, the allies of much contemporary philosophical idealism. More particularly, their concern to evoke atmosphere and effect contributed to that rehabilitation of the mystical and the intuitional which we have met in other contexts of the time. The symbolists resembled Bergson in their reliance upon an immediacy of experience that transcended conceptual thinking. They immersed themselves in the flow of language. They conjured with the magical properties and associations of words. Yet through seeking thus to convey intensity of feeling they found themselves confronted, in their own way, with questions that were to become increasingly pressing for philosophers over succeeding generations. Théophile Gautier had written earlier of 'the ultimate utterance of the Word, summoned to final expression and driven to its last hiding place'. Now in the hermetic poetry of Mallarmé – contorted in grammar and syntax, experimental in typography – the pursuit of an artistic privacy from philistinism had reached the point where language was all too clearly bending, and even breaking, under strain.

Among those writing in German Stefan George, who had associated in Paris with Verlaine and Mallarmé, was the leading exponent of a lyricism directed similarly not towards the external world but inward for the purposes of artistic self-contemplation. He spurned the values of the Kaiser's Reich and aspired to establish an 'empire of the spirit'. George believed that within it the poet must, in Nietzschean terms, transcend conventional morality. He himself became the high priest of a mystical élitism that was concerned particularly with the cult of youth. He lived withdrawn, surrounded only by the 'George Circle' which was composed of intimates willing to model their existences upon the ideal of beauty glimpsed in his own life and work. His influence was at its most interesting in regard to two Austrians. Rainer Maria Rilke, though never a member of the Circle, developed very intensely George's quasi-religious conception of poetic meditation. He too enjoyed an existence tending towards seclusion, and it culminated by the early 1920s in withdrawal to a tower-hermitage. In Rilke's art and life alike, the objects of the external world were relevant only as stimuli for processes of aesthetic transformation. Similar ideas were prominent in the early career of the Viennese Hugo von Hofmannsthal as well. Even while still in his teens, he was the object of George's encouragement and had some loose contact with the Circle. The early poems and prose-poetry show, indeed, precocious facility in handling the tones and themes dear to the contemporary aesthetic sensibility. Yet, without ever losing awareness of its residual virtues, Hofmannsthal became no less remarkable for the manner in which soon he was illuminating aestheticism's vices. Around the turn of the century his work ceased to be characterized fundamentally by poetic form. Even the famous collaboration as operatic librettist with the composer Richard Strauss stemmed from Hofmannsthal's rejection of any lyricism that was merely private. He had, as Gerhard Masur suggests, 'found the way from the temple to the street'. There he sought to preserve some healthy link between the artist and everyday society. No other product of the aesthetic movement perceived more clearly than Hofmannsthal that its own values, when assimilated into the forces of self-enchantment, risked becoming thoroughly corruptive.

The early twentieth century abounded with specimens of such pathological transformation, wherein the renewed attempts at applying art to the world took a diseased – and, most commonly, a chauvinistic – form. In Germany and Austria the growing literature of aggressive racial assertion found within the mystical aesthetic of the George Circle one source of inspiration. The literary expression of Italian nationalistic frenzy attained apogee in Gabriele D'Annunzio, whose poems, plays, and novels reflected all the worst aspects of Nietzsche's homage to instinct. Prominent among French cases was that of Barrès, especially bitter at the German conquest of his native Lorraine. Much of his writing dealt, quite explicitly, with the manner in which individual fulfilment depended upon an awareness of rootedness in nation, race, and soil. Significantly, he had titled one trilogy (1888–91) *The Cult of Self* and another (1897–1902) *The Novel of National Energy*. However unsatisfactory in themselves, these works of Barrès were indicative of a more general and stimulating awareness that, even in prose narrative, classical naturalism suffered from severe limitations of expression. On the eve of the Great War there were already intimations that the European novel was capable of profiting from certain aspects of Zola's approach while also transcending it in a fruitfully new manner. Some assessment of this achievement – in writers such as Joyce and Lawrence, Gide and the later Thomas Mann – is reserved for the years beyond 1914, when its impact was fully felt. Nonetheless the significance of its germination within this earlier environment can be conveyed by touching here upon the one great novelist whose contribution had been most substantially prepared even before the outbreak of war.

It is true that Marcel Proust continued work on *Remembrance of Things Past* until his death in 1922 and that a complete, though still imperfect, text was not available until 1927. But already by 1913, when he issued the opening volume *Swann's Way*, he had been contemplating the cycle for nearly twenty years and had finished a rough draft of the whole. Its unifying themes and tones were established. Proust's account of decaying French high society around 1900 revealed, especially in minuteness of observation, a debt to naturalistic technique. Yet his full achievement rested upon a willingness and capacity to go much further. Naturalism had been developing to the point where it stressed psychological even more than social observation; now, outstandingly, Proust combined the benefits of this with the insights that could be derived from deeper revolts against naturalism itself. After all, *Remembrance of Things Past* was written by one who, following his mother's death, withdrew to work in a cork-lined room amidst torments of neurosis about asthma and homosexuality. And upon the masterpiece of this latter-day Des Esseintes the influence of the aesthetic movement was patent. In the treatment of love, the ideal is once more threatened by the actual presence of its object; in the exquisitely tendrilous sentences there is renewed awareness of fragile language under strain; in the narrative by and about the sensitive 'Marcel' there is, however ambiguously, the familiar and characteristic investigation of self.

Proust was making a distinctively literary contribution to

the discussion of consciousness. He explored it independently of Freud, but confronted similar problems: Marcel's earliest memory is of a maternal kiss withheld. Between Bergson and Proust there was more awareness of congruent interests. The latter too was focusing on the relationship between consciousness and the flow of time. Like Bergson, Proust was intimating the difficulties of truly isolating any single experience from a more complex web of memories. Within this nexus he illuminated especially the evocative power of casual sense-association – the faculty famously exemplified by that taste of madeleine dipped in lime-blossom tea which allows Marcel suddenly to remember childhood experiences at Combray. Recollection through such intuitive and involuntary processes is an active, not passive, force. It gives us our sense of identity. It releases from the prison of the subconscious something of our own past. Once recaptured, this forms the basis for the only present that really matters to us. Indeed, our sole contentment stems from the remembrance of time gone, from the contemplation of paradises that are lost. This is a world where memory is not a derivative from some external reality but rather the substance of reality itself. The interpenetrations and refractions of past and present within Proust's cycle are such that the work lacks chronology in any conventional sense. Characters, events, and places appear differently according to shifts of temporal and spatial perspective – even though, ultimately, the shifts themselves merge within the overall continuum of memory and actuality. Moreover, the identity of he who registers the appearances is constantly in question: Marcel as the object of the narration, Marcel as narrator, Proust as novelist, even the reader himself, all maintain relevance as receptors upon their different planes. Vertiginous and disorientating in its evocations of memory and consciousness, Proust's work, like Einstein's, heralds an age of relativity. Between his *Remembrance of Things Past* and Zola's earlier *Germinal* lies a gulf whose significance is limited neither to France nor to the novel nor even to literature generally. It indicates nothing less than a major upheaval in European ideas and sensibility.

Over the same period transformation in visual art too was startling. Though except by way of commentary words were absent, ideas were not. Indeed, amidst the crisis of the word intimated by Mallarmé the significance of non-verbal means of communicating ideas was potentially enhanced. The painter's vision is related to feeling, and feeling itself to thought. During these years ways of thinking, of feeling, and of seeing were, alike, in flux. Artists made their own distinctive response to the forces of social change; they maintained dialogue with literary figures; and often their work reflected, with varying degrees of self-awareness, something of the scientific and philosophical concerns of the day. The upshot was a rage of artistic experimentation. Most of the lastingly important work was done by associates of various movements of tacit or explicit 'secession' from the orthodoxies of the academies. Many of these artists of the avant-garde certainly starved, but eventually the fashionable cult of the unfashionable brought to some a considerable acclaim, acceptance, and security. Though innovatory vitality was quite widespread, it is clear that in these decades most European artists regarded Paris as their major spiritual capital. From there in 1874 an epoch in the history of art was inaugurated by an exhibition featuring prominently names such as Claude Monet and Auguste Renoir.

The fact that 'impressionism' began as a term of abuse symbolizes the hostile reception which first greeted the work of their group. Some critics regarded the impressionists' degree of enthusiasm for everyday urban topics, such as the bustling bars and boulevards, as indicating insufficient appreciation of what was artistically dignified. Eventually the bourgeois buying public adapted more easily to such timely and far from unflattering subject matter than to the new techniques of presentation. Despite earlier hints from Turner or Corot, the first spectators tended to view impressionism as an art of blob and smudge. They remained to be educated in nothing less than a new manner of seeing. For us it is the way in which this vision related to contemporary views about the status and nature of science that constitutes much of impressionism's intellectual fascination. Concordant with the positivism of the time, the impressionists became associated with attempts to improve upon the realism both of Gustave Courbet and of the camera. In short, they aspired to establish a truly scientific art.

Zola, a friend to many of these painters, readily applauded impressionism as an ally of literary naturalism in the search for quasi-scientific procedures. The impressionists, for their part, certainly felt the challenge of conveying accurately the complexity of optical experience. They responded by analysing each seeming visual whole into its component elements. Shadows assumed hues that offended the orthodox, and colour in general was treated independently of its associations with particular material objects. Above all, impressionism became, as Zola remarked, 'the study of light in its thousand decompositions and recompositions'. Monet believed it important to explore such subjects as the west front of Rouen cathedral and the lily-pond at Giverny in as many conditions of light as possible. For him and his associates studio studies seemed generally less challenging than work in the open air, where from minute to minute tones and values vibrated and transformed. Attending to the ephemeral chromatics of sun and snow, of showers and steam, these artists hoped to capture movements of time and vision about to be lost. Edgar Degas' paintings of horses and dancers were still more explicitly addressed to the problem of simultaneously freezing and expressing movement and change. The grandiose scientific pretensions originally embraced by, or thrust upon, the impressionists were of course doomed to failure. Paradoxically, the movement's success resided not in any ability to complete an experiment but in the capacity to suggest mood and atmosphere. It became increasingly clear that, in terms already applied to the literary movements then transcending naturalism, their talent was less for objective description than for subjective evocation. The manner in which the impressionists intimated that perceptions of the flux of reality were temporally and spatially personal inspired all who followed in every field of artistic innovation whatsoever. Nor was their achievement without some relevance to the imminent revolution in scientific ideas. For, in the very process of escaping the influence of the old science, impressionism was stressing the uniqueness of each single observation. It was thus anticipating, however unconsciously, the central relativistic postulates of the science to come.

This was further emphasized by the manner in which later impressionist art developed. For instance, Georges Seurat's 'neo-impressionism' featured juxtaposed points of pure colour which fused into comprehensible images not on the canvas but only within the eye. More significant still was the so-called post-impressionism of Paul Cézanne, even though his stature only began to be appreciated shortly before his death in 1906. The analytic approach was extended by him from light to shape. Just as there was in Seurat active inter-relationship between pure colours, so in Cézanne there developed an altogether more dynamic interaction between pure forms than previous theories of composition had allowed. He preferred increasingly the simple geometry of cylinder, sphere, and cone. But in his maturest work these forms were left fragmented and broken upon the canvas. In effect, Cézanne placed himself in the vanguard of those wanting the role of the imagination to match and complement that of raw vision. This was also true of the Dutchman Vincent van Gogh, whose public recognition was posthumous. He felt the full force of the impressionists' work only upon reaching Paris in 1886, but the four years that remained before his suicide –

years in which Nietzsche too was succumbing to dementia – were ones of intense activity as he strove to deepen and transform their insights. Through distorted colours and tortured lines he was helping to lessen painting's concern with the phenomenal aspects of reality and, conversely, was strengthening its claim to be, essentially and even entirely, a record of personal experience and emotion. In 1901, when a Paris memorial exhibition at last did Van Gogh justice, Hofmannsthal commented aptly that here was an artist 'whose vision answered the spasms of his own most dreadful doubts'.

The elements of primitivism in Van Gogh's art had important appeal for Paul Gauguin, whom, at one point in their tumultuous friendship, the deranged Dutchman had tried to murder. Gauguin's abandonment of a stockbroking career was one of the marks of his cult of natural simplicity. His painting was relatively little concerned with the detailed imitation of objects. The concentration was, rather, upon the decorative qualities possessed by interrelated areas of flat colour. Understandably, he sought inspiration from the art of Egypt and the Orient. Moreover, while still directing himself to the European art market, he did his own finest work in self-imposed exile amidst the savageries and beauties of Tahiti. This enhanced interest in the art of other cultures, paralleled amongst anthropologists especially, was typical of Gauguin's whole generation. Still, its full significance is appreciated only when we also realize that these were the very years in which for the first time sustained attention was paid to the art of children and of the insane. What all such productions shared, when contrasted with 'orthodox' art, was the capacity to suggest fresh and uninhibited uses of line, colour, or perspective – to suggest, in effect, that the hitherto fashionable ways of seeing were simply some among many. Sophisticated primitivism reached new heights when in 1905 the Paris Autumn Salon included pictures, by Henri Matisse and others, that in their contempt for conventional form and their bril-

liant but arbitrary colours seemed to be the pictorial embodiment of an instinctual, almost Bergsonian, self-expression. A
critic dubbed the group 'les fauves' ('the wild beasts'). As
Anthony Blunt writes, 'For them a painting was simply a
painting; content was of quite secondary importance. In fact
the fauves applied in practice, and ruthlessly, what their predecessors had proclaimed in theory but had only carried out
timidly.' By doing so they helped to inaugurate the most
hectic decade in the history of modern art – the decade in
which were launched, most particularly, cubism, exp·ess-
sionism, and futurism.

The cubist vision was evolved jointly by the Spaniard
Pablo Picasso and the Frenchman Georges Braque. They met
in the autumn of 1907 and became thereafter, as the latter put
it, 'two mountaineers roped together'. Though at first slow
publicly to exhibit the resulting pictures, they found that their
studios in Paris were soon on the visiting list of every avant-
garde artist of note. Moreover the poet Guillaume Apollinaire, whose essays on cubism were collected in 1913 as
Aesthetic Meditations, proved an enthusiastic and influential
publicist for their art. The point of departure was a Picasso
painting, completed early in 1907 but not placed on general
display until thirty years later, known now as Les Demoiselles
d'Avignon. The mask-like faces, revealing indebtedness to
African and other exotic art, contributed only partially to the
general and timely atmosphere of anonymity surrounding the
subject matter. The depersonalization of the figures derived
more deeply still from the angular and fragmented manner of
their presentation. The multiplicity of viewpoints fortified,
as in the literature of Proust, an uncertainty of identity. Pursuing further Cézanne's intimations of splintered form,
Picasso and Braque were soon breaking repeatedly with the
tradition of single-point perspective that had dominated
European art for nearly half a millennium. Their handling of
space was revolutionary, and congruent with the new con-

ceptions of physics. Planes were superimposed, lines were made to suggest rather than to define boundaries, and conventions of transparency and opaqueness were flouted. This art continued to take its cues from objects in the external world, but the difficulties that might arise in identifying these thereafter was conveyed by Picasso's declaration that, 'I paint forms as I think them, not as I see them.' As a result of this preference for the conceptual over the perceptual, the shattering of lines and planes had reached by 1910–11 a complexity that threw doubt on the cubists' ability to sustain for much longer any identifiable contact with ordinary visible phenomena. Then, relatively suddenly, Picasso and Braque turned to collage, and developed it in a manner that drew back from any imminent entry into a fundamentally non-representational art.

That breakthrough, though aided by cubist insight, was to be an achievement of expressionism. This label, then often applied to any manifestation whatsoever of the avant-garde, is one of the least precise. Even when associated particularly and properly with concentration upon inner feeling and a laying bare of the soul, it could not be limited to visual art alone. It had a musical relevance and, still more pervasively, it qualified many aspects of the anti-naturalistic movement in literature. The ambit of the expressionist movement in art includes for certain important purposes the work of Van Gogh and the *fauves*. There is also a special place for the Norwegian Edvard Munch, whose paintings and graphics sensitively explored unresolved tensions between instinct and convention. Five years before the completion of Wedekind's *Awakening of Spring* Munch was at work on the first, destroyed, version of his *Puberty* – part of a great series called *The Frieze of Life* into which he distilled the mental anguish both of himself and of contemporary society. Though Munch refined his talent in Berlin, it was elsewhere in Germany that the two leading groups of expressionist artists established themselves.

The first of them, called 'Die Brücke' ('The Bridge'), was formed by Ernst Ludwig Kirchner and others at Dresden in 1905. Their aim was to constitute an artistic community that would demonstrate its commitment to social reform through expressing, as Munch was doing, the psychological stresses imposed by many aspects of modernity. The second group, a secession from a secession, emerged at Munich in 1911. It was more loosely organized and less socially committed than Kirchner's circle. Yet the participants nurtured an intensity of vision and a cult of pictorial excitement that again rendered secondary all questions of imitation and optical realism.

The leaders in Munich were Vasily Kandinsky, a Russian, and Franz Marc, a native of the city who had a special interest in animal perception. There in 1912 they published *Der Blaue Reiter* ('The Blue Rider'), the collection which gave its name to the group. Its contents – essays, musical fragments, and pictures (some by children) – suggested the synaesthetic interests of those involved. In the same year Kandinsky issued *On the Spiritual [das Geistige] in Art.* The central term of the title had intentional religious connotations, but it denoted also the treatise's more general concern with the role of the mind and intellect in aesthetic creation. In residual naturalism Kandinsky saw a materialistic, and therefore immature, philosophy of art that was now on the point of exhaustion. He pleaded instead for a creativity that would shatter the limits imposed by the merely phenomenal. His declaration that 'the art of tomorrow will give form to our scientific convictions' intimated a concern to probe, like the new generation of physicists, the mysteries of hitherto invisible worlds. He had in mind an art that combined intuition and consciousness, an art 'expressive of a slowly formed inner feeling tested and worked over repeatedly'.

Such was the philosophy behind Kandinsky's *Compositions*, a series whose first seven paintings were completed between 1910 and 1913. In these he took to its logical conclusion the conviction that colours and forms possess expressive qualities which are inherent and therefore independent of material objects. Here any remaining trace of the phenomenal realm was merely incidental. A picture did not need to concern itself with anything external. The work of art, in itself, now constituted reality. Its creation was moulded not by exterior but by interior forces, by the mind operating at different and interacting levels of consciousness. This meant that, in turn, its appreciation by the observer depended on an exercise more subtle than one of spotting and judging correspondences between its components and the objects of ordinary perception. Such a challenge was already looming from the cubist quarter, but the development of an utterly non-representational art massively enhanced the urgency of the problems raised. In effect, Kandinsky and his associates were advocating not just a new manner of seeing but a major transformation in the way that men even talked of art – and of much else besides. The crucial steps were taken anything but blindly. In the fullest sense, there was being forged a revolution of the intellect as well as of the imagination.

The role of futurism in the artistic upheaval of this time was cruder and less central, but still far from insignificant. It enjoyed a brief but striking career of international success. Its influence rapidly had some effect on, for example, the Russian 'suprematist' movement led by Kasimir Malevich and the 'vorticist' school of Wyndham Lewis in Britain. Futurism, like expressionism, crossed cultural genres. It was the literary manifesto of the Italian poet Filippo Tommaso Marinetti and his associates that really launched the movement in 1909. They called for an aesthetic which, spurning tradition, would focus itself upon the dynamism of city and machine. It would encourage the love of danger and struggle (war being now the supreme expression of a mechanized culture), the habit of energy, the beauty of speed. The manifesto declared that,

A racing car having its bonnet adorned with great tubes like serpents with explosive breath . . . a roaring car which seems to run on
machine-gun fire is more beautiful than the *Victory of Samothrace* . . .
We will sing of great crowds agitated by work, pleasure and revolt;
the multi-coloured and polyphonic surf of revolutions in modern
capitals: the nocturnal vibration of the arsenals and the workshops
beneath their violent electric moons: the gluttonous railway stations
devouring smoking serpents; factories suspended from the clouds by
the thread of their smoke. . . .

In such a turgid and intellectually hollow manner did the bulk
of the futurists embrace the age of mass society.

Futurism, despite the fact that its literary manifestations
never got much above this level and that its musical ones
merely made a virtue of noise, did however achieve something more interesting in art. Its painters, who significantly
tended to group in industrial Milan, described themselves in
their 1910 manifesto as 'the primitives of a new and completely transformed sensibility'. This judgement was borne
out, partly at least, by their eclectic development of certain
features within the patterns of artistic innovation running
from impressionism to cubism. In particular, they had inherited the concern with materiality in flux. The best of them,
such as Umberto Boccioni and Carlo Carrà, valuably refined
the means available for its communication. The outstanding
example was a technique, already used by the cubists, analogous to multiple or continuous exposure in photography.
Indeed with Giacomo Balla, who showed himself especially
responsive to stimulation from revolutionary physics, this way
of handling the pictorial conversion of matter into dynamic
light and colour carried futurism into the borderlands of non-
representational painting. The more general significance of
these futurists sprang from their attempt to combine an acceptance of machine civilization with the development of a sensibility expressive of men's restlessness within it. In short, they

were elaborating one of the principal psychological components of most later art and thought.

An endorsement of modernity also marked the major shift in ideas about architecture and design that was developing just before the war. Nineteenth-century preferences, especially for variations on gothic or classical themes, had been backward-looking and imitative. The most influential critic to deplore this was William Morris. Because of this, and through his insistence on quality in popular design, Morris is rightly regarded as an inspiration to the so-called Modern Movement. But his positive contribution was lessened by failure to discern the potential benefits of machine technology. By the turn of the century there was already established a general European vogue for what, in order to stress its innovatory quality, Frenchmen termed '*art nouveau*' and Germans '*Jugendstil*'. This, though it rejected period imitation, was characterized by indulgent curves less related than ever to structural necessity. One possible reaction was suggested even through the mere title of a famous address published in 1907 by the Viennese architect Adolf Loos: *Ornament and Crime*. He was part of a new generation affected by the buildings and ideas of Frank Lloyd Wright and the Chicago school. From America came these first sustained responses to the challenge of finding elegance in functional form rather than in mere decoration – of forging more strongly those links between art and engineering present sometimes in the railway stations but absent usually from the other public buildings of the nineteenth century. From around 1900 a small but growing number of architects, especially in Germany, showed a readiness to use simply and directly such new materials as reinforced steel and concrete. In particular, the creation of authentically functional designs for both the structures and the mass products of the modern factory was one of the primary goals of such pioneers as Peter Behrens and Walter Gropius. The former's AEG turbine-

building in Berlin and the latter's Fagus factory at Alfeld
belonged, chronologically and stylistically, to the cubist epoch.
Initially, as Jacques Barzun notes, their creations 'incurred the
same scorn as other forms of cubist art, for they were similarly
bare, abstract, indifferent to the individual sensibility, and
hospitable to the anonymous mass'. Yet again, the critics
would have to accustom themselves to a novel way of seeing.
Meanwhile, in a very real sense, advanced ideas on architecture
and design were beginning thus to express some of the most
salient features of the contemporary social condition.

During these last pre-war years something comparable
occurred even in the creative sphere farthest removed from
the materiality of buildings and artefacts. For, similarly, the
forms of progressive musical idiom then being devised by
composers such as Arnold Schoenberg and Igor Stravinsky
not only were suggestive of distinctive features within modern
existence but also became the objects of much critical contempt. In the earlier part of our period Wagner, whose genius
as a composer sometimes obscured his banality as a thinker,
was the single most important influence on European music.
Signs of his ascendancy were particularly evident in much of
the nationally-inspired work, highly variable in quality, that
everywhere so characterized these years. He was also timely
in his pretensions to achieve supreme artistic synthesis – that
Gesamtkunstwerk best exemplified in the composition and
staging of his 'music-dramas'. His death in 1883 seemed for a
time merely to enhance Bayreuth's standing as a shrine to one
who, like many literary men of the day, had spurned moral
concerns in order to concentrate upon turning life itself into
an aesthetic phenomenon. As Thomas Mann later said, the
place was a musical Lourdes, 'a miraculous grotto for the
voracious credulity of a decadent world'. Even though their
impact began to diminish around 1900, Wagner's achievements retained some relevance to much that was best in early
twentieth-century music. One example – accompanied by

outstanding commercial success – was the final extension of
the German romantic tradition embodied in the symphonic
poems and operas of Richard Strauss. Another was the
deeper exploration into music's poetically expressive properties undertaken by Claude Debussy. Here the Frenchman
developed, even more intensely than Wagner, a chromaticism
rich with the promise of less restrictive rules of composition.
Debussy wanted more freedom in order properly to fulfil his
aim of intimating reality not through programmatic narration
but by capturing from the stream of sensations a particular
moment of imagination. He was providing, quite explicitly,
a musical complement to impressionist painting and symbolist
poetry. Indeed, his settings of Verlaine and Mallarmé suggested a new stage in the growing awareness of the insufficiency of words. Yet his musical impressionism, taken as a
whole, was no less significant for the manner in which it also
conveyed an appreciation of the insufficiency of music itself –
at least, so long as this was composed within the accepted conventions of tonality.

These were the bonds decisively broken by Schoenberg.
In Vienna around 1908 he, with his pupils Alban Berg and
Anton von Webern, began to write unequivocally atonal
music – pieces disregarding that relationship between keys
which was the central principle of Western classical composition. Schoenberg's *Theory of Harmony* (1911) showed that this
upheaval occurred in an atmosphere just as cerebral as the one
surrounding the expressionist breakthrough into non-representational art. The composer was indeed a painter too, a
friend of Kandinsky, and a contributor to the *Blaue Reiter*
collection. Schoenberg's essay there on the relationship
between music and text reflected his interest in the synaesthetic
quality of 'speech-song' that was giving rise to such pieces as
Pierrot Lunaire (1912). This, like other early atonal works,
showed that there was no clear line between the benefits of
compositional freedom and the drawbacks of sheer inverte-

bracy. Schoenberg was already seeking, but had not yet found, the kind of structuring that from the 1920s would characterize his twelve-tone method. But it was already clear that his new musical idiom resembled much of contemporary avant-garde art and architecture in seeming, on first acquaintance, uninvitingly austere, inelegant, incommunicative, and disorientating. The prevailing response was derisive incomprehension. In 1913 a Viennese performance of work by Schoenberg and his associates produced, according to one reporter, 'the greatest uproar that the oldest critics could remember'. Only a few weeks later, in Paris, it was the turn of the similarly unconsoling Stravinsky to occasion a still more extensive riot. Previous visits by the Russian Ballet, under Sergei Diaghilev, had introduced the composer's *Firebird* (1910) and *Petrushka* (1911). Some modest form of post-Wagnerian artistic synthesis seemed to be emerging from the combination of brilliant staging and dancing with inventive music. Stravinsky's contribution to the latter, though avoiding atonality, had shown his developing tastes for unconventional harmony and irregular rhythm. Now *The Rite of Spring*, in every sense percussive, brought these to a new intensity. There was a shocked reaction, partly to the ballet's theme of primeval pagan ritual but even more to the fierce savagery of the music illuminating it. The climax was human sacrifice. Very soon that would seem a mark of the immediacy, not the remoteness, of its relevance to the condition of contemporary European civilization.

The artistic and literary achievements of this period, considered as a whole, were extraordinary in the range and quality of their creative vitality. Despite their diversity, it has been possible to discern a pattern, however imperfect, of interconnections. Some of these links have become apparent only with the benefit of hindsight. But most had received already some degree of recognition from contemporaries. Basically, if to some lesser extent, that remains true even for the further connections suggested with the realms of scientific, philosophical, and social concern. No tight boundaries of subject or genre can contain the extensive interest shown by the intellectuals of this time not merely in the issue of their own social role but also in such topics as the nature of sanity or the workings of sexuality. Throughout the house of intellect there was debate about such tensions as those between normality and abnormality, consciousness and subconsciousness, reason and emotion, fact and value, description and evocation, objectivity and subjectivity, the perceptual and the conceptual. Perhaps most striking was the manner in which scientists and creative artists were, often quite independently, threatening hitherto received ideas about space and time – more generally still, about all such principles of order in the world. They shared increasing awareness that, everywhere, the tyranny of convention had reigned and that the previously accepted structures of reality were simply reflections of men's own frequently arbitrary assumptions. From this important standpoint, the scientific revolution was being complemented by the verbal experimentation of Mallarmé, the probing into memory of Proust, the rebellion against perspective in Picasso and against phenomenal representation in Kandinsky, or the revolution of tone, rhythm, and harmony in Schoenberg and Stravinsky. Moreover, like the discoveries of Planck and Einstein, each of these could be taken as intimating that many significant aspects of reality might correspond more closely to the dream world charted by Freud than to experience as more conventionally conceived. This underlined that the anomie discerned by Durkheim had more than merely social connotations. For not only science and philosophy but the creative arts as well were making contributions to the fundamental questioning of established norms.

The literature and arts of the early twentieth century fit therefore into the wider, and by now familiar, matrix of dissolving certainty. Their vitality did little positively to satisfy

the general yearnings for intellectual synthesis. Nor did it lead
in the direction of an adequate response to the equally widespread craving for clearer moral guidance. This latter problem
took a number of forms that have already been hinted. With
the various proponents of art for its own sake, who were
threatening to make large areas of aesthetic concern as remote
from ordinary experience as the new science itself, there was
a tendency proudly and explicitly to spurn the statement of
any values having public import. The kind of association
between creativity and impotence intimated by Thomas Mann
conveyed, in its turn, doubts about the sheer effectiveness of
any moral pronouncement that artists might indeed wish to
make. Again, the relativistic ethic discernible in Ibsen epitomized a brand of moralizing that certainly did not lack
powerful expression but which was nonetheless disturbingly
ambivalent and inconclusive. And in such writers as Barrès
there were suggestions of a mystique whose values, less
ambiguously but just as forcefully proclaimed, were perhaps
more discomforting still by virtue of their violently aggressive
nature. It could be argued, regarding any of these contexts,
that the creative artist – if magus at all – was becoming merely
a magus of dissolution.

   With hindsight, we know that much of the old European
order was, in social and political senses too, on the verge of
dissolution in war. It would be wrong to suggest that before
July 1914 most writers and artists were overwhelmingly more
conscious of the approaching conflict than the public at large.
Those of the minority actually concerned with the issue went
for the moment unheeded – though, once the fighting was
over, their earlier comments about the condition of pre-war
Europe certainly had considerable influence on social and cultural reconstruction. Many among them had warned against
war, not least as a threat to all that was most cosmopolitan
in art and letters. Yet a quite considerable number of others
had actually sympathized with ideas of violence. Moreover,

it is now easier to appreciate how this latter group had merely developed to extremes many of the fashions that intellectuals most widely accepted from around the turn of the century. No modes of thought were more readily resorted to than those, associated with debasements of Darwin and Nietzsche, that perfected the idiom of salubrious struggle and bracing domination.

The 'Neroism' that the French novelist Romain Rolland sensed in Germany during the later 1890s was the prerogative of no single country. Everywhere there had been some growth in sympathy for Dostoyevsky's view that man's true and authentic nature was revealed only in extreme experiences, of passion, horror, suffering. Central to the artistic drive of the time had been resentment against the constraints, hypocrisies, and mediocrities of bourgeois civilization. It was readily arguable that through violence these might be removed and boredom be dispelled. Thus too might the widespread demand for a greater liberation of the primitive forces of instinct and intuition be satisfied. Franz Marc, killed at Verdun, was not alone among the young and talented in sacrificing his life for the belief that the war represented a healthy purging of the European soul. But, here, there is no clear line between the purgatorial and the infernal. It is noteworthy that Auguste Rodin's sculpted brooding figure of *The Thinker*, today often regarded as supremely emblematic of an age so afflicted by doubt and disorientation, was first conceived within a larger work called *The Gates of Hell* (1880–1917). That fact simply intensifies its symbolic quality. Very particularly, the passage of European civilization beyond those portals was occasioned by the violent act of a Bosnian student; and of Gavrilo Princip, the Sarajevo assassin, it is recorded that he had an apposite fondness for Nietzsche's words. 'Insatiable as flame, I burn and consume myself.'

PART TWO

1914 – 1945

Chapter 6

THE
SOCIAL AND POLITICAL
ENVIRONMENT

THE outbreak of general hostilities in August 1914 rather surprised most Europeans. But the nature of the ensuing conflict utterly astonished them. Not even those who, fearfully or happily, had been anticipating war as the natural outcome of current international rivalries foresaw the extent of the horror. The basically patriotic, indeed enthusiastic, popular response to initial developments reflected images of swift and decisive warfare moulded in the Bismarckian era. This vision, which politicians and generals encouraged and partly shared, soon proved mistaken. In September, on the Marne, German hopes of a lightning victory over France faded. By the year's close, with stalemate on most fronts, the struggle was being transformed, against expectation and desire, into one of sheer attrition – a Great War proper. On balance, this change was more damaging to the prospects of Germany, Austria-Hungary, and Turkey than to those of Russia, France, and Britain (together soon with Italy) whose alliance created a potentially greater reserve of manpower and global material resources. During 1915 the daily slaughter reached the kind of horrific dimensions thereafter maintained. Warfare along the eastern front, though becoming more mobile, confirmed that the Russian commanders were prepared to accept huge losses in slowing the enemy advance. To the west there was also great bloodshed, but without any appreciable overall movement of forces. Amidst trenches and barbed-wire, craters and mud, defence was only marginally less self-destructive than attack.

The Germans' five-month assault upon Verdun, begun in February 1916, cost the two sides between them some 700,000 lives. Yet it shifted the battle lines scarcely at all. The Somme counter-offensive from July to November was similar in territorial inconclusiveness and even more wasteful of men.

At sea British and French power was employed in blockade. The Germans responded with extensive mining and, for the first time, with submarine warfare. They adopted unrestricted use of the latter early in 1917, when the need to transfer their own feeling of economic suffocation on to the British was pressing. This gamble on early victory failed only narrowly. Its main effect was to drive the United States into the anti-German alliance. Thus fortified, the Western forces were able to survive even the loss of Russia. Her internal chaos, indicated by the two revolutions of 1917, and her military dissolution, confirmed by the new Bolshevik regime's acceptance of the punitive Treaty of Brest–Litovsk in the following March, culminated too late to save the Central Powers. By July 1918 Germany's last great western offensive was exhausted. With Austrian and Turkish efforts along the South-Eastern Front faltering too, it became wise to seek armistice. In November, before the enemy advance could reach her own soil, Germany obtained it. What her Crown Prince had welcomed at the outset as 'a jolly little war' looked very different more than fifty months later.

The toll of lives was, literally, incalculable. Not for the last time in this period would precision in estimating slaughter reach no further than 'the odd million'. The battles themselves probably accounted for the killing of at least 8 million people, and for the disablement of some 25 million more. Another 3 million might be added from the Russian Civil War that lasted until 1920. Furthermore, taking Europe and other continents together, the early post-war period saw as many as 20 million deaths from the combined effects of epidemic and malnutrition upon societies directly or indirectly debilitated by four years of conflict. Alongside all such mortality figures should stand, ideally, some still more speculative estimate of the potential births denied. By 1939 the population of Europe, even though it had risen to some 530 million, was much lower than might reasonably have been expected without the Great War. Moreover the unprecedentedly concentrated bout of genetic destruction between 1914 and 1918 seems, on the battlefields at least, to have made exceptionally deep inroads into the most talented cadres of a whole generation. In short, the fighting annihilated many of the young men best equipped to tackle the very problems that it created or intensified.

The war was undoubtedly attuned to the mass age. Soldiers, increasingly recruited by general conscription, were subjected to a carnage that was appropriately indiscriminate and impersonal. In London or Paris homage to valour would be paid henceforth at the tomb of an Unknown Warrior – a novel conception reflecting how fitting it now was even for heroes to be nameless. Between combatant and civilian too lines were more than ever blurred. Massive artillery bombardment and sustained blockade ignored distinctions of age, sex, or class. Moreover, there was levelling in service as well as suffering. The reliance on female labour showed this most clearly. Once attrition of the enemy became the order of the day, all the human and material resources of each nation had to be mobilized. They were used according to the requirements of that machine technology which had already so profoundly conditioned everyday life in the pre-war world. Now there was gigantic conversion of productive into destructive capacity. At certain moments it seemed as if technical necessity had assumed autonomous significance, defiant of control by statesmen or generals. The machine, so long paradigmatic of the rationalization of the world, was here central to forms of wastage partaking of the irrational, even of the insane. Just as this paradox undermined some assumptions, so others were shaken by the nature of the mass propaganda which accompanied total mobilization. Psychological warfare attained new subtleties. The familiar atrocity story, for instance, was now developed into a minor art-form. This was only one area in which the extensive and calculated diffusion of inaccuracy was deemed acceptable for reasons of immediate expediency. In the longer run, there was no more insidious way of encouraging throughout whole societies a cynicism about, and disrespect for, every conception of morality and authority. Truth and language, like civilization itself, emerged more deeply wounded than ever before. The effects of their weakening would be seen clearly in later events.

Perhaps only war on this catastrophic scale could have shaken so severely that simple faith in rational progress – and especially in an alliance between material and wider civilizational advance – which had sustained the mass of men. Now some were so inured to violence that they readily accepted it as an instrument for propagating other creeds. But the blunting of conscience from which they suffered also afflicted many of those who, in their very nausea over carnage, henceforth erected the avoidance of war into a supreme principle that could disregard all others. Whatever his particular interpretation of it, the conflict provided each European with a new temporal landmark. The idiom of 'pre-war' and 'post-war' was soon an established expression of the modulation of consciousness engendered by the battles. To recognize this does not mean, however, that in the realm of ideas the war had its greatest significance as a point of origin. As previous chapters suggested, there had begun already a richly diverse revolution against established patterns of thought and expression. The war made its principal contribution through greatly accelerating their disintegration. It was the means of making some extensive confrontation with doubt and disorientation unavoidable for all. It accentuated the relevance, and much more widely generalized the acceptability, of new ways of regarding the world. Yet most of these, however affected by the great catastrophe, had taken some root before 1914. The intellectual history of the 1920s and 1930s therefore deals largely with ideas that were projected from the earlier period and refracted through the experience of war.

During 1919 the Paris Conference, whose participants represented three-quarters of world population, confronted the problems of international reconstruction. The fact that the three great dynasties of Central and Eastern Europe had fallen was a major indication of the magnitude of the task. Though unable directly to influence Russian developments, the victors certainly needed to deal with Germany and with the still more complicated matter of the Habsburgs' former dominions. With Turkey, where another imperial dynasty was soon overthrown, a form of settlement was completed only in 1924. The Conference was dominated by the United States, Britain, and France – powers committed to working broadly in accordance with the liberal-democratic ideals crystallized in Woodrow Wilson's 'Fourteen Points'. Amidst a multitude of conflicting claims, the principle of national self-determination was applied in an unavoidably arbitrary fashion. Poland, with a corridor to the sea at Danzig, and the Baltic states emerged with their independence. That of Hungary was made complete, though she lost much territory and population to an enlarged Rumania. The latter was soon allied, in the so-called Little Entente, with the two new but heterogeneous states of Yugoslavia (a much augmented Serbia) and Czechoslovakia. The Austrians, stripped of empire, were denied any right of uniting with a Germany whose own governmental structure was greatly transformed. The constitution of her Weimar Republic was symptomatic of a vogue for thoroughgoing democratic procedures that the victors aspired to consolidate throughout Central-Eastern Europe. But, except perhaps over Czechoslovakia, their hopes turned out to be excessively optimistic.

The prospects for some secure version of liberal democracy in Germany were weakened from the outset by the Republic's association with humiliating peace terms. Recognition of the Weimar regime by the winning allies had depended on prior acceptance of the Treaty of Versailles. This forced the German representatives explicitly to acknowledge their country's guilt in causing and conducting the war. By way of punishment, it imposed liability for the payment of a huge but indefinite amount in reparation and also demanded severe military limitations. Germany was also excluded initially from the League of Nations, whose covenant was an integral part of all the peace treaties. It was primarily because of the wide commitments which this new organization seemed to threaten that the American Senate refused to ratify the Versailles document. Thus the League was dealt an early blow. American non-ratification also caused Britain to cool about her own liability to act against any future German attempt at forcibly revising the settlement. An extra burden fell therefore upon the French who, though possessed once more of Alsace-Lorraine, were scarcely equal to the task. By the later 1920s, however, there seemed to be grounds for cautious optimism in international affairs. Though the United States and the Soviet Union remained outside the League, the conciliatory Locarno Conference of 1925 opened the way for German membership in the following year. In 1928 hopes were confirmed by the Pact of Paris, a renunciation of war that was soon supported by all major and most minor states.

Economically and socially too, the first decade of peace appeared to be ending on a favourable note. The war had caused vast material losses, as incalculable as the human ones. During the first post-war years the general situation remained grave, with currency problems particularly prominent. In 1923 the Germans made clear their inability to meet the reparations bill fixed two years before. Their own currency was collapsing and by early 1924 the nation had been devastated with an inflation so astronomical as to have effected something not far from social revolution. The tide was turned by the American investment programme contained in the Dawes Plan of that same year. The Young Plan of 1929, another symptom of general détente with Germany, furthered the realization that economic strategies based on expectations of substantial reparation payments were doomed to defeat. By then such growing realism and international cooperation seemed to be allowing the European economies to develop a real measure of prosperity. Though pre-war discrepancies between East and West continued, nearly everywhere the level of real wages and of consumption was ascending. The products of the electrical and chemical industries were now much more widely diffused. Sustained attention was being paid to issues of secondary education, health, and even leisure. The spread of motorized public and private transport, as well as the beginnings of passenger air-flight for a more limited number, was opening up new horizons. So too, in a different but crucial way, was the growth of wireless broadcasting. It was becoming possible to believe once more in the overall beneficence of science and technology. There was, in short, a renewal of rising expectations about material progress, and about the possibilities of its secure enjoyment within the structures of economy and politics sanctioned by the liberal-democratic victors of 1918. Yet, even as the 1920s drew to a close, such hopes were coming into peril both because of unparalleled economic collapse and because of accentuated strife between political ideologies.

The Wall Street crash of October 1929 was a turning point not merely for Americans but also for Europeans now enmeshed in a transatlantic financial system. Most of the world, indeed, suffered from the massive depression that ensued. Europe felt it worst over the two years following the collapse of the Austrian and German banking systems in the summer of 1931. Everywhere confidence in currency and in the established mechanisms of finance evaporated, as did the whole reparations issue. Goods were available, but primary producers and manufacturers alike could not overcome the problems of falling demand. As the volume of trade spiralled downwards, a rise in mass unemployment, with all its attendant human wastefulness, cut demand still further. So too did the reaction of most governments, who were at first reluctant to abandon the economic orthodoxy of meeting crisis with retrenchment. But the Great Depression was no mere cyclical complication of the nineteenth-century kind. For the second time within a generation, vast forces seemed to have escaped human control. The slump proved indeed just as influential as the war itself in hastening revision of old assumptions. It confronted Europeans with the paradox of an economic system immobilized by its very capacity to produce abundance, and with the tragedy of renewed poverty amidst plenty. Existing orthodoxies regarding the beneficially self-regulating nature of liberal capitalism were being exploded. The 1930s would see laissez-faire principles rapidly yielding further ground to the realization that, in one way or another, government must assume greater responsibility for economic regulation and strategy. This was not, however, the only sense in which the issue of state power now loomed still larger. For the Depression, by enhancing the popularity of alternatives to liberal democracy, was also aggravating conflicts of political ideology.

The Bolsheviks' dominance in Russia was by now firmly secured. Nonetheless, their original expectations about triggering off similar revolutions farther west had been disappointed. Early in 1919 the Berlin revolt of Rosa Luxemburg's 'Spartacists' failed, and the attempt at establishing a Bavarian soviet republic also came to naught. Soon similarly destroyed was the regime of Béla Kun, which had given Hungary four months of communist rule. Lenin, though sympathetic to such revolutionary efforts, was forced by civil war and famine to concentrate mainly upon consolidation within Russia itself. In pursuit of this he was prepared to make the kind of opportunistic compromises illustrated by the New Economic Policy of 1921 or the Rapallo friendship treaty with Germany of 1922. After Lenin's death in January 1924, policies based overwhelmingly on immediate Russian self-interest came even easier to the figure who was emerging as his successor. Over the next five years Joseph Stalin's 'socialism in one country' gradually triumphed against the doctrine of 'permanent revolution' purveyed by Trotsky. They disagreed, essentially, as to whether international revolution was the prerequisite for the completion of socialism in Russia, or vice versa. The difference between these assessments, though strictly one just of tactics, was never bridged. Trotsky's influence waned particularly after the outcome of the British general strike of 1926 had discredited his case for the ripeness of revolutionary opportunities in the West. By the time that the first five-year plan, concentrating on heavy industry and collectivized agriculture, was inaugurated in 1928 Stalin stood absolutely dominant. His policy of pragmatically extending the Soviet Union's circle of diplomatic and commercial relations alleviated only moderately the widespread European distrust of Bolshevism. Indeed most countries possessed elements obedient to Moscow's dictate that, while immediate revolutionary action might be premature, communist organization and discipline must be used constantly to exploit the weaknesses of the economic and political system. The Great Depression, against which Russia was somewhat cushioned by her own relative isolation, provided a fine opportunity to win support from those European masses hardest hit by this crisis of capitalism.

Yet there were other important forces, even newer than Bolshevism, hoping to derive political profit from these same ills. In October 1922 Benito Mussolini, a renegade socialist journalist, took over the government of Italy. He bullied his way into power as the *Duce* of a 'Fascist' movement that benefited from the nation's fifty years of accumulated disillusionment with uninspiring and inefficient parliamentary government. A similar emphasis on the need for strong authority against the perils of communist revolution already marked the Hungarian regime established by Admiral Horthy at the end of 1919. The fundamentally illiberal nature of Mussolini's movement was not yet generally appreciated at home or abroad. The conduct of the 1924 elections, followed by the murder of the socialist deputy Giacomo Matteotti, opened more eyes to its basic brutality. But this awareness dawned too late. Behind a parliamentary façade, Mussolini was establishing a personal dictatorship and destroying every organization or interest-group unsanctioned by current Fascist whim. His much-vaunted 'corporative state' subjected the forces of capital and labour alike to party control, so that during the later 1920s Italy was second only to the Soviet Union in her degree of governmental economic direction. Though the regime's propaganda machinery exaggerated the benefits, most Italians certainly experienced some rise in living standards. Even when they too became affected by the Depression, they were consoled by feelings of national self-importance that Mussolini had sedulously fostered. In Italy and beyond his standing had been, on balance, much enhanced through the conclusion of the 1929 Lateran Agreements with the Vatican. By the early 1930s he was preparing to exploit world chaos so that his popular oratorical intimations of future national glory might be given greater substance.

This was also the epoch at which Germany succumbed to Adolf Hitler's domination. His National Socialist Movement had been nurtured by the immediate post-war atmosphere of resentment against 'the stab in the back' that had caused sudden capitulation in November 1918. Hitler hammered home the conviction that, then and thereafter, Germany was being ruined by Judaeo-Bolshevik conspiracy. He exploited the kinds of humiliation involved in the Versailles Treaty, the reparations demands, and the French attempt at enforcing them through the Ruhr occupation of 1923-5. The Nazis, despite the failure of their Munich putsch of 1923 and their leader's subsequent spell of imprisonment, gained their first Reichstag representation during 1924. It was only, however, with the onset of Depression that they became a major force. Like Mussolini's movement, they had flexible appeal: to workers fearful of unemployment, to a bourgeoisie anxious about renewed inflation, to a rural population flattered by rhetoric about its future importance and security, and to nationalists of any class desirous of restoring their fatherland's honour. In September 1930 6·4 million votes secured the election of 107 Nazi deputies. The slump really hit hard during 1931, and by the spring of the next year a challenge to Paul von Hindenburg's presidential re-election, though unvictorious, brought Hitler a second-round vote of 13·4 million. At the Reichstag polls of July 1932 the Nazis were backed by 13·7 million and became, with 230 seats, the assembly's largest single party.

The loss of 2 million votes at further elections in November was merely a temporary setback. For Weimar moderation was being eroded also by the Communists, who now had increased their support almost to 6 million. To many it seemed therefore more necessary than ever that the Nazis, still the Reichstag's biggest group, should play a major role in averting Bolshevik triumph. This was the rationale which prompted leaders of the traditional Right to concede the Chancellorship to Hitler in January 1933. Soon exploded was their belief that his movement, once associated with governmental responsibilities, could be tamed. In March a new Reichstag, still lacking any absolute Nazi majority, passed the temporary Enabling Law which, in effect, gave Hitler irreversible dictatorial powers. He would use them to forge a national recovery whose economic and military aspects were inseparable. By July, when all rival political organizations were proscribed, the policy of *Gleichschaltung* (levelling) was gathering force. On Hindenburg's death in August 1934, the presidency itself was subsumed within the combined office of Chancellor and *Führer*.

Thus three major European states were now subject to totalitarian dictatorship. It was practised in Hitler's version of Fascism with a more efficient ruthlessness than Mussolini could maintain, but even in Italy the theory at least was unequivocal in commitment to total state domination of the individual's existence. Their movements on one hand and Stalinist Bolshevism on the other, despite great mutual hostility, refined regimes whose machinery of coercion revealed important similarities. As Mussolini's corporatism extended tentacles beyond economics into every sphere of life, as Hitler's henchmen intensified persecution of Jews and other 'non-Aryans', and as Stalin's trials and purges proliferated into a veritable reign of terror, Europe saw the apparatus of the fanatical political party becoming a vital organ of the repressive state. Denial of free speech and of effective democracy demonstrated the fundamental contempt for popular opinion. Mass acquiescence instead was engineered, not least by mobilizing every medium of communication in support of ideological orthodoxy. The disturbing findings of Tarde and Le Bon about the suggestibility of the masses were broadly confirmed. The new media of film and broadcasting were exploited to especially valuable effect. Similarly politicized was the rapidly developing sphere of mass sport and leisure. It was natural that formal education too should become, at every level, the victim of thorough ideological colonization. Totalitarian regimes aspired to make truly independent thought itself unthinkable.

Under these conditions the vitality of mind and art could not avoid atrophy. The sincerity of much work emanating from those enshackled by life under totalitarian rule is notoriously hard to gauge. There are blurred lines between those who, with differing measures of enthusiasm, positively served the dictators and those who, with varying degrees of honesty, took refuge in private dissent. Apart from the 'inner emigration' of the latter, there was sometimes – more commonly, during the 1930s, for Germans and Italians than for Russians – the potentially no less painful option of migrating in a directly physical sense. Flight from Nazi rule, mainly but not exclusively by Jews, reached especially massive dimensions. In it artists, scientists, and intellectuals at large were very prominently represented. As Peter Gay notes: 'The exiles Hitler made were the greatest collection of transplanted intellect, talent, and scholarship the world has ever seen.' Germany's loss (and that of other regions threatened by Nazism) was, in very many cases, a gain for the United States. Einstein, Schoenberg, Gropius, and the brothers Mann were among those who, permanently or otherwise, settled there and brought concentrated enrichment to the already remarkable complex of Euro-American culture. The multiplication of the persecuted, whether or not these reached exile, helped stimulate a dramatic return to social engagement on the part of those European intellectuals and artists who were still possessed of freer conditions for expression. Relatively few of these supported Fascism. Indeed its very threat led a larger number to adopt or develop allegiance to a Marxism more humanely inspired. These tended to treat whatever there might be of substance in tales of Stalinist repression as symptomatic of temporary aberration or passing necessity. Among others distaste for Fascism and Bolshevism alike prompted renewed awareness of the continuum between individual freedoms and the liberty of art and intellect. What the Depression had encouraged the divisions of ideology underlined: a very general feeling that any intellectual or artistic activity still spurning social relevance and judgement must be mere frivolity. Thus, although the nature of the process

differed significantly as between totalitarian and non-totalitarian contexts, the politicization of culture was everywhere
in full spate.

Urgency of commitment was reinforced also by the return-
ing threat of war. The Fascist powers especially were now
extending their aggressiveness from the domestic to the international scene. Hitler's accession to power brought Germany's
withdrawal from disarmament talks and from the League in
October 1933. Though a now increasingly apprehensive
Soviet Union was admitted to membership in 1934, the
organization proved incapable of acting effectively against the
German policy of major rearmament proclaimed during the
following year. In March 1936 no active resistance met Hitler's
remilitarization of the Rhineland. By May Mussolini's forces
had completed the subjugation of Ethiopia begun the previous
autumn. Formal condemnation of this pursuit of imperial
glory proved ineffectual, and at the end of 1937 the Italians
too left the League. Its impotence was apparent also during
the civil war that raged in Spain from the summer of 1936
until the final victory of General Franco's insurgent Nationalists early in 1939.

Amidst the widespread anxieties of the time this conflict,
though resulting from tensions essentially indigenous to
Spain, could hardly avoid occasioning some international
involvement. At the outset Frenchmen, like Spaniards,
possessed a recently installed Popular Front government
committed to opposing the Fascists. Its leader Léon Blum was
at first inclined actively to support the Republican cause. But
Britain's firmly neutral stance, added to deep divisions
within French opinion, provoked second thoughts. Franco–
British diplomacy then engineered a general non-intervention
agreement which was, in practice, largely ignored by the
totalitarian powers. The Soviet Union backed the Republicans
with arms and other material. The Fascist dictators, whose
'Axis' was established in October 1936, gave the Nationalists

similar aid. Further, they added regular troops in the guise of 'volunteers'. Rather more genuine ones from other countries arrived to fight for each side. In their battles the techniques of air and tank warfare, initiated during the Great War, reached new levels of sophistication. Retrospectively, we can see the extent to which the struggle was an important military prelude. Yet we also need hindsight to appreciate fully the over-simplifications in the common contemporary view of the Spanish Civil War as a complete emotional and intellectual watershed, beyond which the nature of future ideological alignment was clear. For this vision, imperfect rather than completely mistaken, underestimated the ambiguities that still remained within the triangular relationship between Fascism, Bolshevism, and more liberal democracy.

It was a continuing distrust of Soviet aims, as well as sheer desire to avoid general war, that helped condition the appeasement policy towards Hitler which the British and French governments for long maintained. There was some measure of foreign sympathy for his criticism that at the Paris Conference the application to Germans of the hallowed principle of national self-determination had been too rudely ignored. It was not surprising that Hitler, Austrian-born, should stress the arbitrariness and inadequacy even of the Second Reich's territory. Under his own Third Reich the natural extension of a racist ideology from domestic to external affairs produced claims for wider German *Lebensraum* (living-space), especially eastwards, that seemed superficially no more preposterous than many made by other national groups during 1919. The charitable could even interpret the annexation of Austria in March 1938 as the belated fulfilment of that desire for a Greater Germany so clearly expressed at Vienna by the Constituent Assembly nineteen years before. At Munich during September France and Britain capitulated to Hitler's demand for the Sudetenland. The Czechoslovak state, forced to comply both with this and with lesser Hungarian and

Polish claims, was so gravely weakened as to become little more than a German satellite. By March 1939, with the Little Entente still in disarray and devoid of effective support, Hitler had annihilated Czechoslovakia altogether. Steeled at last by this demonstration that Nazi objectives were really not limited to clearly German areas, France and Britain extended guarantees to Poland, Greece, Rumania, and Turkey. But meanwhile the Soviet Union was stalling during negotiations aimed at formally involving it in an alliance against Hitler. As the German threat to Danzig and the Polish Corridor approached a climax, the nature of Russian policy suddenly became clear. On 23 August 1939 Germany and the Soviet Union concluded publicly a ten-year non-aggression agreement. To it was added a secret protocol delimiting their respective spheres of potential domination in Eastern Europe and settling especially the partition of Poland between them. The Nazi–Soviet Pact possessed for both sides a certain tactical logic. Even so, their common hostility to free democracy lent it a certain ideological and intellectual coherence as well.

Hitler's invasion of Poland at the beginning of September caused Britain and France to declare war on Germany. However, the conflict did not become actively generalized until April 1940. Within two months Norway, Denmark, the Netherlands, and Belgium fell to the Germans. In June Hitler, with whom Mussolini was now actively allied, presided over the defeat of France. Even though failure to win decisive air superiority frustrated Nazi hopes of a similar British capitulation, the western *Blitzkrieg* had been successful enough to allow soon some more open indulgence of eastern ambitions. In these the quest for *Lebensraum* and the hatred of Bolshevism were complementary. During June 1941 Hitler took the momentous step of attacking the Soviet Union. In December, when Leningrad and Moscow were in peril, the war's scope widened still farther. The Pearl Harbor attack added Japan to the ranks of Germany's allies and brought the United States fully into the opposing cause. Over the next year Hitler's increasingly urgent need to register conclusive victory in the eastern campaign remained unsatisfied, and his enemies' now greatly superior resources of manpower and material became ever more significant. The turning of the tide stimulated more intense activity from valuably disruptive resistance movements inside occupied territory. By the summer of 1943 the Russians were taking the offensive, and the Western Allies were following their own North African victories with an attack on and beyond Sicily that soon brought Italy out of the war. After the Normandy invasion of June 1944 the Germans were in retreat on a revived Western Front too. This time the struggle continued even to Berlin itself. Upon it the forces of East and West converged, and there at the end of April 1945 Hitler killed himself. Early in May Germany surrendered unconditionally.

This second great war of the masses was, compared with the first, even more markedly global and more destructive of the resources, both human and material, so completely mobilized for its conduct. Fewer men were killed on the Western Front, but overall the casualties suffered – by the Americans as well as the defeated powers, but by the Russians above all – were greater than in the earlier conflict. A slaughter which there had possessed elements of miscalculation seemed here altogether more deliberately methodical. Once again every subtlety of science and technology was employed to promote devastation that made no discrimination between soldier and civilian, adult and child. This was shown clearest through the intensification of various forms of aerial attack. From 1943 Germany was subjected to the kind of massive air-raid that culminated in the saturation bombing of Dresden in February 1945. Meanwhile the Germans themselves had pioneered pilotless aircraft-bombs and supersonic rockets. In August 1945 war in the Pacific theatre was concluded by the American use of atomic bombs against the Japanese cities of

Hiroshima and Nagasaki. The new weapon, whose development involved the application of certain fundamental discoveries of twentieth-century physics, possessed a destructive
capacity which was unprecedented both in its immediate
effects and in its (then inadequately appreciated) longer-term
genetical repercussions. It was possible to have reasoned dispute as to whether the development and use, then or at any
time, of such bombs amounted to barbarism. But there was
no room for such doubt about the status of the Nazi extermination camps, whose nature and scale became fully apparent
at the end of the war. Within them millions of Jews and other
alleged racial degenerates had been murdered with an efficiency appropriate to the machine age and a deliberateness
indebted to ideological conviction. It was not self-evident,
however, that even the special horror of these camps could be
treated entirely apart from the numerous other examples of
massacre or terror which had so marked the years between
1914 and 1945.

Most European countries emerged from the war weakened.
Even those with global interests had soon to reckon with a
lessening of dominion or informal control. Over Europe herself the influence of the United States and the Soviet Union
was greatly increased. The military forces of the leading
capitalist state and of the pioneering communist one faced
each other throughout much of Central Europe. American
economic assistance, though at first available generally to a
continent that had suffered unparalleled physical destruction
and human displacement, soon became concentrated upon the
Western nations. The Russians – who had already shown their
cynicism in annihilating the independence of the Baltic states,
but who also had very genuine fears about the imbalance of
nuclear power – showed themselves prepared to use the Red
Army as the main instrument of an increasingly tight control
over much of Eastern Europe. Thus the liberation from open
warfare that followed the defeat of the Fascist powers was

destined to be insecure. Between the victors in East and West there existed little of the broad ideological consensus found among the leading figures at the Paris Conference of 1919. It was natural that the tensions within the anti-Fascist alliance should assume enhanced significance after the removal of the common menace. In this sense, the passing of Hitler certainly provoked ideological realignments. But it brought no immediate reversal of the tendency, clear from around 1930 at least, for some brand of confrontation between ideologies to constitute the most prominent feature of the European intellectual scene.

Chapter 7

IDEOLOGICAL
CONFRONTATIONS

No work accorded better with the mood of the years immediately following the Great War than Oswald Spengler's *Decline of the West*. This global history, planned before the conflict and completed during it, was published between 1918 and 1922. Though verbose and conceptually obscure, the book by the hitherto insignificant German schoolmaster quickly became an international best-seller. Of Europe's malaise it was both symptom and attempted diagnosis. Its thesis about the life-cycles of quasi-organic cultures and civilizations was presented in that mode of dogmatic determinism so characteristic of the uncritical positivistic spirit and so attractive to disorientated men. But there was no denying the vividness of Spengler's predictions about the continuation of violence and about the growing impracticality of liberal-democratic values. According to his analysis, everything for which the victorious powers claimed to stand was destined soon to go under. Over the next twenty-five years some parts of the Spenglerian prophecy seemed to be fulfilled, and the realization of others only narrowly averted.

The victory of 1918 certainly could not give the supporters of free government any charter of security. For liberal and moderate socialist democrats the war had intensified many difficulties earlier apparent. The supremacy of the popular will was now almost universally acknowledged, yet severe disagreements remained about the means appropriate for its expression and interpretation. Wartime jingoism provided one recent instance of mass passion being cultivated and exploited by calculating élites. The regimes of Mussolini and Hitler reinforced the point in due course. American congressional repudiation of Wilson's endeavours at the Paris Conference underlined the difficulty of implementing consistent policies in a context of effective restraint upon executive authority. More generally, the settlement itself confirmed the naïvety of the dominant liberal approach to the currently sacred principle of national self-determination. It had been invoked in the hope of promoting a sense of justice and a stable international system. But by the early 1930s, in an atmosphere of renewed aggressive nationalism, it was clearly contributing instead to grievance and uncertainty. The Bolshevik, or even the Nazi, vision of international order could readily seem superior, in consistency at the very least, to that realized at Paris.

The liberal attachment to largely self-regulating mechanisms for the harmonization of interests was weakened in domestic settings too. Politically, mass electorates seemed ever more acquiescent about authoritarianism; meanwhile, economically, capitalism was experiencing its traumatic Depression. The vast scale of the problems associated with the latter seemed to dictate that henceforth, as in wartime, a much greater stress be laid on public economic initiative. Along the road to material recovery, and soon to rearmament as well, liberal thinking on the role of the state came into much closer alignment with the democratic socialist view. The arguments mustered between them during the inter-war years in defence of non-totalitarian democracy were ideological only in an altogether looser way than those they confronted. Yet the former, despite their sheer diversity and inadequate coordination, had one crucial advantage over the officially tidied doctrines of a Stalinist or Hitlerian regime. They were produced within a tradition still broadly respectful of self-criticism. However wounding to pride or confidence over the short term, this was the quality most essential to the survival of rationality itself in political and other senses.

The challenge of evolving an effective free democracy was particularly pressing in Weimar Germany. Any contribution from intellectuals would have to be made initially in a situation where masses were succumbing either to political apathy or to various brands of extremism. Especially under such circumstances the relationship between fact and value, objectivity and commitment, maintained an urgent significance. Weber's last lectures, delivered in 1919-20 at Munich where the bitterness of confrontation between Left and Right was already very clear, dealt once more with this theme. He had featured among the drafters of the new republican constitution, but had failed in his pursuit of a parliamentary nomination. Now, perhaps seeking to exorcize the demons of frustrated ambition, he argued that a political career with all its passions and moral compromises was inimical to a career in scholarship. Thus he was suggesting once more the extent to which any usefulness in the latter – as a clarifier, though not a simple determinant, of value preferences – depended upon a primary commitment to maximizing objectivity. It was this that must not be imperilled. Such moderation was evident also in his own preference for the Weimar Republic as a means of reconciling loyalty both to democratic procedures and to certain special virtues within the German cultural inheritance. The historian Friedrich Meinecke was prominent among some still more conservative intellectuals whose nostalgia for the Second Reich did not prevent conversion to the view that, at many points, 'inherited ideals' must be properly subordinated to 'statesmanlike reason' and that the new republic was an appropriate instrument of such control. His major work of the Weimar years was *Die Idee der Staatsräson in der neueren Geschichte* (1924; translated as *Machiavellism*). There were echoes of Weberian concern in its analysis of centuries of discordance between the practice of political power and the needs of morality at large.

Karl Mannheim's writings on the sociology of knowledge

were influenced both by Weber's pluralism and by the vestiges of his own early Marxist allegiance. Soon after the war he had left his native Hungary – then another scene of oscillation between political extremes – and settled in Frankfurt. Now sympathizing with moderate socialism, he took a more straightforward attitude towards intellectual engagement than Weber. The fulfilment of Mannheim's aspiration towards subjecting all social problems to organized rational scrutiny involved the leadership of a creative intelligentsia. He regretted that the current state of intellectual fragmentation was inimical to such guidance and that meanwhile the habits of mass politics were developing in the direction of a 'democracy of impulse' rather than a 'democracy of reason'. He argued, most notably in *Ideology and Utopia* (1929), that intellectuals must strive to maximize their potential as *Freischwebender* – those whom he supposed to 'float' least trammelled by particularist social allegiance. Thus they might appreciate the partialness of every current ideology and persevere in such 'dynamic intellectual mediation' as would afford a 'total perspective' – broadly vindicating, of course, his own politics of moderation. Mannheim's claim that the resultant 'relationism' could transcend relativism was badly founded. Still, however flabby, it did constitute what Stuart Hughes calls 'a last supreme effort to bring about public understanding through entering into a sympathetic internal apprehension of each of the mutually destructive ideologies and Utopias that were tearing European society apart'. The Nazi triumph caused Mannheim to flee to the London School of Economics. There, until his death in 1947, he elaborated ideas about the ways in which rational social planning, now more than ever necessary, could succeed without totalitarian constraints.

Among others who wrote provocatively about the threat to rationality and freedom presented by unfettered mass political passions were the French cultural critic Julien Benda and the Spanish philosopher José Ortega y Gasset. In *The*

Treason of the Intellectuals (1927) the former argued, with acute perversity, that since the last years of the nineteenth century those best equipped to defend reason had been betraying its cause through their crude embroilment in the action and propaganda of mass politics. They had celebrated and fortified intuitive urges, realizing that 'the doctrines of arbitrary authority, discipline, tradition, contempt for the spirit of liberty, assertion of the morality of war and slavery were haughty and rigid poses infinitely more likely to strike the imagination of simple souls than the sentimentalities of liberalism and humanism'. Such diagnoses, though vastly oversimplified, had some value as salutary warnings. But there was little virtue in Benda's own cure. He offered only an ivory tower built upon the equation of rationality with complete practical detachment. As the 1930s progressed, evolving conditions under which it was increasingly unrealistic to separate political choice from intellectual integrity, his prescription became ever more patently inappropriate. Similarly Ortega, who left Spain in 1936 rather than commit himself to either side in the Civil War, was better at describing than solving this range of problems. His *Revolt of the Masses* (1930) depicted irrationality and violence rising in harness. Fascism and Bolshevism each represented not a welcome updating of liberalism but a capitulation to herd values. The spirit of the age was becoming one of mediocrity, wherein 'the commonplace mind, knowing itself to be commonplace, has the assurance to proclaim the rights of the commonplace and to impose them wherever it will'. This rebellion of the masses threatened to be triumphant in every sphere of life. In the moral context especially, it aspired not to exchange one code for another but rather to cast off all restraint. It was offering not a new civilization but the negation of civilization itself.

This was one of the issues that also engaged the now eminent Freud. After the Great War, which he viewed as a manifestation of 'the death instinct', he gave much attention to problems of civilization that seemed unprecedentedly urgent. He sought to elaborate, however speculatively, what had hitherto remained largely implicit: the vision of social life that must complement the image of man already suggested by psychoanalysis. Foremost among the resulting works were *The Future of an Illusion* (1927) and *Civilization and Its Discontents* (1930). In the first he showed awareness of the difficulties which men would experience while relinquishing religious belief, but also suggested that its retention would have consequences more baneful still. It constituted a point of crucial vulnerability. These words indicate what particularly Freud had in mind: 'Civilization runs a greater risk if we maintain our present attitude to religion than if we give it up ... Is there not a danger here that the hostility of ... the masses to civilization will throw itself against the weak spot that they have found in their task-mistress?' The second book developed this theme of tension between civilization and instinct. Again there was the suggestion, which came readily to one who leaned by temperament towards political conservatism, that the masses might be led all too easily into indulging the latter and harming the former. The work stressed how readily, once restraint upon their natural aggressiveness was removed, men might reappear as 'savage beasts to whom the thought of sparing their own kind is alien'.

Freud believed that civilization's function and fate was indeed to impose some such restraint upon any kind of instinctual pleasure which might destroy the less intense but more secure satisfactions of life within organized society. The visions of total social transformation offered by competing extremist ideologies were, to whatever extent they concealed or denied civilization's essentially repressive nature, themselves illusory. Yet their attractiveness would be enhanced so long as the proponents of moderation were reluctant to clarify those areas – well exemplified by religious and sexual taboo – where the toll levied against instinctual behaviour had been indeed excessive. Only through urgent and sustained rational scrutiny might some newly acceptable compromise between individual impulse and social need be established before the indiscriminate wreckers broke through. Once civilization was weakened beyond a critical point there might be no limit to the subsequent eruptions of aggression. Freud thought that enough violence was evident already, particularly within the totalitarian regimes. On the eve of disaster he was attempting, as George Steiner suggests, 'to devise a myth of reason with which to contain the terror of history'. The Nazi annexation of Austria, which caused him to spend his terminal months in London as an exile, was one painful testimony to his brave failure.

Of all contemporary endeavours rationally to modernize the broadly liberal tradition none was eventually more influential or successful than the revolution in economic theory dominated by John Maynard Keynes. His reputation was made first with *The Economic Consequences of the Peace* (1919), issued shortly after the author's resignation from the British delegation to the Paris Conference. This polemic against the practical unwisdom of imposing such massive reparation payments on Germany attracted extensive international attention. Over the next decade or so events seemed to justify the position taken by the Cambridge economist. In this sense at least, his work deepened that feeling of discomfort about the Versailles Treaty which during the 1930s so weakened any resolve by Germany's former enemies to oppose her belligerent revisionism. But the impact of economic ideas on policy was demonstrated more dramatically still in response to the Great Depression. Hitherto it had remained broadly plausible to regard infringements against classical liberal theory – for instance, the imperfect competition associated with monopoly – as anomalies capable of absorption within the overall structure. Yet even the feats of assimilation accomplished by economists such as Marshall became strained once the dysfunctions represented by massive inflation or unemployment became chronic in the manner experienced between the wars. Capitalism, its orthodoxies shattered by the impact of events, survived because of a reconstruction that was guided by theoretical innovation. Some governments did arrive independently at certain remedies soon elaborated by Keynes. The Scandinavian economies especially had been moving for some years into channels intermediate between capitalist orthodoxy and full state interventionism, and before his death in 1926 Knut Wicksell had led the Swedish economic school into perceptive speculation about liberal capitalism's potential for engendering an uncontrolled spiral away from general equilibrium. But only with Keynes himself came the kind of overarching revision that allowed each specific remedy to be evaluated as part of a systematic recovery programme.

Its author described *The General Theory of Employment, Interest, and Money* (1936) as 'a struggle of escape from habitual modes of thought and expression'. So rapidly was the import of this basically technical treatise conveyed to a wider audience that Keynes was largely justified in his hope of transforming within a decade much of the world's approach to economic questions. He saw the outstanding faults of the dominant version of capitalism as 'its failure to provide for full employment and its arbitrary and inequitable distribution of wealth and incomes'. The alternatives offered by Bolshevism or Fascism appeared to him wasteful of efficiency and freedom alike. The magnitude of the current crisis certainly necessitated greater economic intervention by governments. But this need not lead to authoritarianism, so long as the rules of beneficial involvement were carefully defined. Control of interest rates, for example, could provide governments with an important regulator of capital investment. Ability to adjust the volume both of taxation and of state expenditure provided another lever, powerful but hitherto much neglected, of economic management. Deficit budgeting, in particular, had been conventionally the object of criticisms that obscured its stimulative capacities and discouraged any helpful acceleration of public works and investment programmes during times of stagnation. Keynes' belief in the capacity of such instruments to enlarge, and not merely redistribute, economic activity derived from diagnosis of a major flaw in the prevalent obsession with self-adjusting mechanisms. Most particularly, he demonstrated the oversimplified psychological assumptions about economic behaviour behind 'Say's Law' and its later variants. There had been neglect of the drives towards liquidity preference. In Keynes' opinion this propensity, strongest under difficult conditions, for money to be hoarded rather than invested could launch an economy into a spiral of depressed income. It was precisely this kind of cumulative disequilibrium, made real in the Great Depression, that traditional theory had failed to accommodate.

Keynes presented his reassessment in a spirit loyal to liberalism: 'There will still remain a wide field for the exercise of private initiative and responsibility. Within this field the traditional advantages of individualism will still hold good.' Those who expected solutions via more authoritarian channels were confusing the task of transmuting human nature with the proper one of managing it. Successes in this latter and more realistic pursuit would act as an antidote to failure of nerve. They would amount to a substantial, and much needed, vindication of man's ability rationally to shape forces that had run seemingly beyond all human control. Robert Lekachman comments: 'If Keynes could be said to have possessed an ideology it was confidence born of the humane Locke-Hume-Mill tradition that intelligence in human affairs is both essential and possible.' It is evident, however, that from such a conviction no socialist needed to dissent. Nor necessarily had he to quarrel with many of Keynes' remedies. Certainly the latter himself remained distrustful of socialism, denying particularly that governmental supplementation of private effort at vulnerable points in the economy constituted any charter for public ownership. But Keynes, however unintentionally, had provided a theory which left room for compromise on that issue, as well as favouring and accelerating that high degree of reconciliation between democratic socialism and revamped liberalism so increasingly characteristic of Western Europe from the 1940s onward. In commitment to some degree of 'planning' – the obsession of the later Mannheim – there was important common ground between the two camps. It was particularly significant, moreover, that Keynes had encouraged such planning in order to achieve not merely greater productive efficiency but also some stimulating redistribution of wealth and income from the richer, who were in a better position for saving, towards the poorer with their greater propensity to spend. In the long run it was the similarities between his ideas and those of such socialists as Richard Tawney and Léon Blum that mattered more than the differences. Friedrich Hayek's *The Road to Serfdom* (1944) was one vigorous warning against the betrayal of older liberal orthodoxies but, especially in its hostility to economic planning, it seemed soon to be a cry from another age.

The manner in which many aspects of Keynesianism received cautious welcome from democratic socialists served to underline the divisions and confusions already existing on the Left. For twenty years moderates had been forced to identify for themselves a position somewhere between classical liberalism and the versions of Marxism promulgated from Moscow. From 1917 onwards the Bolshevik leadership had sought to define orthodoxy essentially according to whatever policies happened to be from time to time prevalent and convenient within the one state where Marx was officially canonized. The chief instrument for the exportation of current dogma was the Third International (or Comintern) founded in 1919. But everywhere beyond Russia its activities served to accentuate a split between those sympathetic to the Moscow line and

others, such as the socialist supporters of the Weimar Republic, more firmly committed to a democratic and parliamentary framework of action. Even in the Popular Front era
much of the energy of Communist and Socialist parties was
still being expended on the kind of mutual rivalry that meanwhile had facilitated the rise of Fascist influence. Whereas the
militancy of labour movements in Western and Central
Europe was predominantly democratic and reformist, the
Russian leaders found it natural still to advocate some version
or other of a revolutionary extremism not centrally concerned with electoral validation. In this they revealed, quite
understandably, both a general indebtedness to the deepest
historical and cultural traditions of their own nation and a
specific attachment to the methods by which their own rule
had been inaugurated and first consolidated.

During August and September 1917 Lenin worked on *The
State and Revolution*, which was published unfinished in the
following year. Composition was halted by the outbreak of
the very kind of revolution it aimed to justify. This selective
reading of texts from Marx and Engels rejected the Men-
shevik view that support for the Provisional Government,
which had been established through the 'bourgeois-democratic' February Revolution, constituted the best tactic
available to the socialist movement. Lenin advocated instead
another and immediate bout of revolutionary activity, aimed
this time against every element of middle-class rule. He had
criticized hitherto the view of Trotsky, who now became his
chief lieutenant, that the bourgeois and socialist stages of
revolution might be telescoped in this manner. However, by
referring to the changed conditions of wartime, Lenin was
able to render his own conversion more plausibly orthodox
than might otherwise have been the case. Now the goal was
prompt institution, by the Bolshevik party élite, of a workers'
dictatorship: 'The proletariat needs state power, the central-
ized organization of force, both to crush the existence of

exploiters and to guide the great mass of the population . . . in the work of establishing a socialist economy.' There was here little sign of that faith in the spontaneous revolutionary capacities of the masses which was soon to serve so ill the German revolutionary effort of Luxemburg. In Lenin's view, so long as traces of the class system survived then all issues of freedom or democracy must remain secondary. The forms of state authority involved in proletarian dictatorship would be redundant only when the final transition from socialism to full communism was accomplished.

The success of the October Revolution meant that Marxism could now develop, for the first time, as the ideology of an established ruling cadre. In this context it was natural that Lenin should continue the practice of his earlier preaching on organizational élitism. His party machine maintained a certain distance from the proletariat in whose name, but beyond whose control, it operated. Such autonomy eased its embarkation upon a task of which the theoretical status was disputable – that of using political power as the instrument of radical transformation in Russia's supposedly substructural economic conditions. Even the much vaunted federal constitution of the new USSR could not obscure the realities of dictatorial centralization. By the early 1920s it was clear that the Bolsheviks would countenance no rival political organization, socialist or otherwise, and that no significant separation was being made between party and government. Essential to the mutation thus imposed on Marxism was, as George Lichtheim claims, 'Lenin's (and subsequently Stalin's) systematic misuse of the term "proletarian revolution" to describe the totalitarian arrangement of society *after* the capture of power by a party which originally conceived itself to be in the "classical" tradition'. Under these conditions it was already far from safe openly to criticize the New Economic Policy for its compromise with profit motivation and its implicit recognition that transition to communism was anything but imminent.

The suppression of the Kronstadt rising in February 1921, shortly before the NEP's promulgation, suggested not only the intolerance already present within the regime but also the shape of worse to come.

In the light of the Russian past and of the perilous civil war and famine that soon preoccupied the new leaders such a bout of tough government was not surprising. There were, moreover, historical precedents for what followed: the conversion of temporary expedients into a more permanent way of life. The revolutionary leaders could argue that the continuing existence of a hostile capitalist world discouraged more relaxed policies. Indeed it validated the maintenance of proletarian dictatorship even beyond the point at which Russia's own bourgeois elements finally succumbed. The Bolsheviks had been simply wrong in their general assumption that the October Revolution would stimulate a wider European rising which itself would then assure the security and successful completion of their own. The best form of adaptation to a state of more prolonged isolation was the chief ideological issue of the opening years under Stalin. In such works as *The Foundations of Leninism* (1924) he sought to establish authentic continuities with the theory and practice of his predecessor. However, his orthodoxy did not go unquestioned. The severest doubts arose over his thesis, officially adopted in 1925, about the need to give greater immediate priority to consolidating 'socialism in one country' than to fomenting revolution on an international scale.

In this dispute, regarding alternative means towards the agreed goal of revolutionary fulfilment for Russia and the world alike, Stalin's chief rival was Trotsky. The latter had, like Lenin but unlike the new leader, a cosmopolitan political background. This showed in Trotsky's denial that a country as backward as theirs could establish, while isolated within a global capitalist system, a truly socialist order. Without proletarian revolution in at least some economically more advanced societies the Russian effort would be doomed either to self-betraying stagnation or to direct defeat by the forces of foreign capitalism. In Trotsky's view, any real progress from temporary success to 'permanent revolution' involved ceaseless activity on an international scale. For his opposition he was denounced, and in 1929 deported. Stalin had him assassinated eleven years later. In the meantime the exile had used his considerable literary and propagandist talents to the full. Even while the official chronicles were being revised so as to disparage his role, Trotsky was bringing out his own *History of the Russian Revolution* (1931–3). Such similarly vigorous later works as *The Revolution Betrayed* (1936) sought to illustrate the manner in which the USSR was succumbing to arid bureaucratization and to a perverted 'Bonapartist' cult of personality centred on the alleged mediocrity who had so unworthily followed Lenin into supreme power.

Stalin used this position of authority to legitimize the drastic change of course made at the end of the 1920s via the first five-year plan. Though its industrial programme soon registered notable triumphs, its agricultural collectivization brought no early tangible improvement in food production. But each part involved disruptions and sufferings on a vast scale. These were rendered acceptable to the party mainly through Stalin's skill in depicting them as the necessary price for revolutionary survival. At the same altar were soon sacrificed too every freedom of conscience and of intellectual or cultural expression. By the early 1930s Stalin had succeeded in establishing the first truly totalitarian state. In January 1934, at the Seventeenth Party Congress, he felt able to declare that within the USSR there was no one left against whom to fight. However, this finding did not prevent Stalin from applying his apparatus of terror with an intensity that grew to climax around 1936–8. Millions suffered arbitrary arrest, followed by condemnation to imprisonment in labour camps or to death or – in effect – to both. These purges, pre-dating the worst of the Nazi holocaust, swept not only across the nation but also throughout the ranks of the Party itself. The liquidation of stalwarts from the epoch of Lenin – figures such as Grigori Zinoviev, Lev Kamenev, and Nikolai Bukharin – underlined Stalin's craving to consolidate an undisputed personal primacy in power and ideological authority. This was the obsession that caused the murder of Trotsky too. By then many of his fears about the potential for perversion contained within the Stalinist dogma of 'socialism in one country' had been fully confirmed. Not least, this doctrine – whatever the strength of its original pragmatic justification – had become capable of underpinning something very similar to old-fashioned nationalism. Alterations in official historiography – no bad barometer of changing ideological climate – had been encouraging greater pride in certain aspects of that Russian past once so totally condemned by party orthodoxy. In practice much of Soviet policy appeared to be widening, at least for the foreseeable future, the potential discrepancy between the interests of Russia as a great power and those of the international proletariat beyond.

Doubts on this point, coupled with news of growing terror and censorship, rendered more difficult the acceptance of Soviet Marxism elsewhere in Europe. Matters were further complicated by the fact that, increasingly through the 1930s, Stalin's emphasis on the USSR's independent political development was being complemented by growth in self-imposed intellectual isolation. Russian Marxism, in theory as in practice, was reaching a level of dogmatism that could only be inimical to meaningful dialogue. Amidst the very crudest forms of dialectical materialism Soviet political ideology lapsed into stagnation. However, even despite such handicaps, the new regime had certainly managed to attract a considerable degree of sympathy from foreigners – and, not least, from foreign intellectuals. Some, like Bertolt Brecht, remained within the Communist Party; others, through the experience vividly recorded by the Hungarian-born Arthur Koestler in his novel *Darkness at Noon* (1940), were driven by its arid intolerance into defection. The fact that so many men of talent should, however temporarily, have lent support to Stalinism becomes explicable only within the wider context of malaise. The Bolshevik leaders bore no blame for the horrors of a Great War that had seared the European imagination. To a civilization desiring liberation from many aspects of a now ruinous past they offered a novel and total vision of ideals; for societies demanding restored hope they refurbished a theory of progress. Even as the capitalist world was slumping into economic depression the USSR was embarking upon a programme of state planning that brought striking industrial growth. Moreover, against this background of disillusionment with the politics and economics of democratic moderation, those who saw Fascism as the overriding menace were all the more ready to view Stalinist allegiance as the most effective bulwark against Hitler and Mussolini. Certainly it was from the parts of Central and Southern Europe most urgently vulnerable to the Fascist threat that there emanated the few really stimulating extensions of Marxism developed during these years. On the other hand, these were the very efforts which an ossified Stalinism was most likely to consider heretical.

The contributions of the philosopher and literary critic Georg Lukács made his career one long tale of tension between party orthodoxy and individual judgement. Though he wrote mainly in German, he was born in Hungary and during 1919 became a cultural commissar in its short-lived Soviet Republic. He then resided in Vienna and later Berlin until 1933. Thereafter he lived directly under communist regimes – first in Russia and then, from 1945, back in Hungary (with brief deportation to Rumania as punishment for involvement in the 1956 revolt). His talent for survival related, partially at least, to his reluctance to judge without equivocation

whether Stalinism was an authentic or an essentially perverted episode in Marxist development. It is clear, however,
that under Stalin he was compelled to repudiate his first,
and possibly most lasting, achievement'– the collection of
essays published in 1923 as *History and Class Consciousness*.
Here, even before the aridity of Soviet dialectical materialism was most fully apparent, Lukacs was striving to
establish a Marxist theory of consciousness that would
treat knowledge as something more than the merely passive
reflection of things material. By remaining within the Party
and bearing with its assaults upon his betrayal of 'science',
he gravely hindered all his own attempts at forging thus
some dialectically creative synthesis between current orthodoxy and the traditions of philosophical idealism. But it
proved crucial that, even in merely beginning this task,
Lukacs had been forced to draw upon his own youthful
Hegelian experience. For thereby he helped to fortify outside
Russia a realization that such idealism had been important in
the early career of Marx too and that it could release
insights which had been severely neglected in the thought of
Engels and Plekhanov, Kautsky and Lenin.

Fuller, less shackled, investigation of these matters was
achieved by 'the Frankfurt School'. This term covers the
men and ideas associated with the interdisciplinary Institute
for Social Research founded and affiliated to that city's
university in 1923 under the direction of Carl Grünberg.
Exiled to New York during the Nazi era, it returned in 1949
to Frankfurt and later attained a degree of fame not intimated
by its limited pre-war prestige. Among the leading figures of
the Institute's pioneering years were Max Horkheimer, who
was Director from 1931 to 1958, Walter Benjamin, Theodor
Adorno, and Herbert Marcuse. Despite other disagreements,
the school united around the necessity of providing a 'critical
theory' of Marxism. This sought to oppose all forms of
positivism, and especially those stressing the possibility of
value freedom in social science. Also countered was any

interpretation of Marxism itself afflicted, like Stalin's, with crude materialism and immutable dogma. Members of the school contended that only an open-ended and continuously self-critical approach could avoid paralysis in the theory, and therefore also in the practice, of social transformation. The accompanying conviction that some satisfactory alternative to present capitalist or Soviet society could become clear only during the actual process of revolution was seen by opponents as exemplifying opportunism and evasiveness; and these, in turn, were deemed reflective of certain irrational inconsistencies in the school's whole approach to the criteria of truth. Adherents believed, however, that they were in-augurating a timely programme of doctrinal reinvigoration. To this end, they helped promote the belated diffusion of Marx's early writings. Like Lukács but more consistently than he, the school thus encouraged particularly much deeper study of Marxism's debt to Hegel whose concern with conscious-ness as moulder of the world had been undervalued by the stark economic determinism of established orthodoxy. Some participants even blazed an initially unpromising trail between Marx and Freud. The study of personality was, in fact, only one of the topics that the Institute rescued from conventional dismissal as being merely superstructural. It strove, especially through its treatment of aesthetics in the mass age, to rescue from sterility the Marxist critique not only of society but also of culture. There was as yet, however, no widespread appre-ciation of Frankfurt's contribution towards rehabilitating Marx's more libertarian aspect.

The impact of Antonio Gramsci's theoretical efforts was also delayed, but for simpler reasons. In 1921 he had helped to launch the Italian Communist Party and three years later he became, at Moscow's behest, its leader. Between 1926 and the eve of his death in 1937 he languished in one of Mussolini's gaols. And it is for his necessarily fragmented and obliquely composed prison notebooks, published only in the late 1940s,

that Gramsci is now celebrated. In these he sought to subordinate *dittatura*, the temporary and merely political 'dictatorship' of the Party, to *egemonia*. Such 'hegemony' per-
tains to the ascendancy of that superior cultural order which
ought to be the natural and spontaneous accompaniment to
proletarian triumph. Gramsci treats this culture not as mere
superstructure but as a reality no less substantial and fulfilling
than the political revolution itself. His hegemonic concepts
revealed how important to him, as well as to Lukács and the
Frankfurt School, was a grounding in philosophical idealism
– developed this time amidst the Crocean atmosphere of pre-
1914 Turin. It informed Gramsci's conviction that *dittatura*
must be prevented from suffocating proletarian capacities of
a more truly creative kind than those offered in the dialectic
of mere materialism. The revolutionary intellectual should
aspire to mediate, not impose, an *egemonia* evolving from and
with popular consensus. Few would want to deny the nobility
and impressive ingenuity of Gramsci's endeavours at squaring
the circle connecting this cultural liberalism with élitist political dictatorship. Even so, the resulting ideas seem lacking both
in coherence and in grasp of practicalities. Any ultimate failure
to convince can be related, in part, both to the appalling conditions under which Gramsci had to work and to the fact that
he remained basically too faithful a Leninist. Moreover, from
inside a Fascist gaol the incompatibility between an allegiance
to Lenin's successor and an urge towards a more substantial
concept of Marxist freedom appeared, understandably, less
obvious than it might elsewhere. In the last resort, Gramsci's
pursuit of reconciliation manifested the weaknesses as much
as the strengths of Utopianism.

   To any Fascist version of dictatorship the Italian Marxist
leader was unequivocally hostile. But Gramsci's persecutors
did possess an ideology that was sufficiently novel to evoke
from parts of the European Left a certain ambivalence of
response. Just as liberals might fall into sympathy with Fascism

as a potential bulwark against red peril, so socialists of any kind might contemplate it as a less than utterly unwelcome symptom of capitalism's capacities for self-destruction. Particularly between 1928 and 1933 the Kremlin remained too sanguine about this very issue. Much contemporary Marxist analysis of the conditions giving rise to movements of the Fascist type was certainly helpful. Yet, generally, there was not even on the Left, let alone elsewhere, an early enough appreciation of the full scope and endurance of these new phenomena. Had communists and democratic socialists alike not thus miscalculated they would scarcely have done so much to ease, however unwittingly, the processes of Fascist consolidation. This was the simple product of a failure to mend, before the later 1930s, their own divided front. Many Marxists consoled themselves with the thought that Nazi annihilation of the Weimar Republic marked also the extinction of a form of democratic socialist rule which was potentially more inimical than anything else to the ultimate fulfilment of revolutionary processes. Such comfort was short-lived. There was, moreover, bitter irony in the fact that Hitler's movement had been learning from Soviet Russia itself, as well as from Mussolini's Italy, many valuable lessons in totalitarian control.

Between the political ideas of Stalin, on the one hand, and those of *Duce* and *Führer*, on the other, there were undoubtedly points of positive contact. Fundamental to their shared totalitarianism was contempt, intellectual as well as practical, for every form of effective representative democracy. All three dictators developed ideologies in which the leader himself was exalted as the supreme charismatic interpreter of the general interest, and all felt compelled to publish personal doctrinal testaments with pretensions towards sophistication. Formal justification of violence and of propagandist manipulation came easily to each. They aspired, in common, to impose through the power of the single-party state some standardized mode of life and thought that would embody fusion between practice and their own particular version of totalitarian theory. Together they sought to annihilate all meaningful distinction between public and private realms and to nullify the promptings of individual conscience. Any conception of politics as compromise was fundamentally alien to figures whose thinking about the resolution of conflict ran consistently into channels of relentless struggle and total domination. Their ideologies, however strong on internal logic, became closed intellectual systems equally defiant of real dialogue with critics beyond. Each system involved assumptions of absolute certainty – about, for instance, the destinies of class, or race, or nation-state – that might be, to its particular adherents, deeply reassuring. Each offered a reinvigorated sense of purpose, and promised redemption from a world of confused values or of no values at all. Even in the nineteenth century monolithic ideology had begun to flourish because of men's urge to be released from a sense of insecurity and disorientation. Now the intensification of this same malaise, and the dictators' undoubted skill in exploiting it, helped to make understandable the quite extensive sympathy soon being variously enjoyed by Stalin, Hitler, and Mussolini alike.

Fascism itself was fabricated by the last of these figures. Nonetheless many others proved capable of learning from the Italian model and of making whatever adaptations seemed appropriate to their own national context. Directly imitative movements of a minority nature characterized much of Western Europe; but in countries such as Spain, Hungary, and Rumania there was, rather, a tendency for Fascist techniques of political mobilization to be absorbed quite readily within stronger forces of traditional conservatism. Most significantly of all, Nazism came to be regarded as Germany's particular variety of a general Fascist species. The important distinctions between the Italian and German movements – provided these are actively recognized in the way shortly to be noted – need not lead us to revolt against such discourse about Hitler as

Fascist. Nor, with similar caution across a still wider comparative field, need we dissent from the view of most contemporaries that Fascism had become, in some senses, a broadly 'European' phenomenon. Everywhere it inclined to evoke strongest support from those whose anxieties about status were most acute. Its influence was perhaps clearest within the hitherto uncoordinated ranks of peasants and smaller bourgeoisie, whose interests seemed most immediately threatened by organized labour. Even so, industrial workers were certainly not immune to the Fascist spell. Loyalty to Fascism's national and other goals could vie with conventional loyalty to class as a means of appeal to proletarian support, especially in situations where the Left's own programmes against mass unemployment seemed unconvincing. Mussolini had been once the advocate of extreme socialism; and even the career of Hitler suggests that, at least until the dismissal of Otto Strasser in 1930, the Nazi movement's 'Socialist' title was not without some significance. Fascism's general aspiration was indeed to overcome much of the established dichotomy between Left and Right and to realize something transcending both socialism and capitalism as hitherto understood. It sought to make fundamentally irrelevant the habitual posture of confrontation between conservative and revolutionary by intimating their absorption within a higher form of community than either had previously envisaged. Youth especially heeded the Fascist claim to have discerned the wave of the future. But no limitation by age or class does justice to the wide variety of support gained through Fascism's brash confidence that upon this wave it could now launch an essential remaking of man.

This regeneration was conceived in a spirit of national or racial exclusiveness that was inimical to the humanely universalist ideals claimed by liberalism and by every type of socialist movement. Worship of force and of inequality was fundamental to the Fascist ethos. Élitist domination, exercised through the mode of cleansing violence, became virtually an end in itself. The cult of leadership in Fascism never embodied that note of apology – those allusions to mere temporary expediency – intermittently observable in the Stalinist setting. Doctrines of individualism were emptied of all real content. The Fascist rhetoric of freedom and fulfilment concerned the absorption of chosen individuals within some larger and morally more elevated entity. The pseudo-religious attributes of this assimilation are clear in Mussolini's exhortation that such a man be seen 'in his immediate relationship with a superior law and with an objective Will that transcends the particular individual and raises him to conscious membership of a spiritual society'. In pursuit of this kind of redemption Fascism perfected the practice of mass politics as ritual. The Nuremberg Rallies exemplify supremely how ordinary members of the Nazi Party, and through them Germans at large, were encouraged to share in the liturgical celebration of decisions and policies over which they were impotent to exercise substantial control. The Fascist leaders had grasped all too soon and too well certain leading principles of mass psychology. Certainly, at bottom, they were contemptuous of the claims of intellect. But, ironically, this did not prevent them from being during this period much readier than most of their opponents to appreciate the power of ideas – and, above all, the force of ideas and emotions in dynamic inter-action. Fascism gained no small measure of support from intellectual circles precisely because it drew so enthusiastically from the wells of intuitionism and irrationalism enlarged before the Great War. In this sense, not least, it embodied an aggressive modernity. Its élite-inspired myths were well-timed exercises in social poetry, and the two major Fascist regimes brought near to perfection this obsession with the epic state of mind.

Mussolini claimed that Fascism was, above all, 'a system of thought'. Yet this was not necessarily to deny that in Italy doctrine tended to develop posterior to action. Here Fascism elaborated the implications of Pareto's depiction of political ideology, as a potentially retrospective rationalization of material or emotional need and as an instrument of élitist control over mass behaviour. Ideas may have remained important, but intellectualism of the older and more coolly contemplative kind did not. Gentile, soon the regime's leading tame philosopher, castigated the men of letters for what he viewed as their traditional, and enervating, detachment from political action. He claimed that the new anti-intellectualism was 'not the enemy of culture but of bad culture, of that culture which does not educate and form a man but deforms him into a pedant'. Real cultural achievement would depend upon ideas arising from, and expressed within, action itself. Intellectual consistency remained, consequently, a consideration firmly subordinated to the requirements of pragmatic flexibility. Gentile declared that 'the meaning of Fascism cannot be measured in terms of the special theses which it adopts from time to time' and that he attached 'no value whatsoever to any thought which has not already been translated into action'. Switches of policy were conjured into insignificance through blanket expressions of the leader's infallibility. The Fascist Decalogue converted these into the simple formula, 'Mussolini is always right.'

Under these conditions the justification of action for action's sake seemed often the paramount ideological order of the day. There were, in short, intellectual parallels to the Bersaglieri trot. Inspired partially by Marinetti and the futurists, Fascism tried to cultivate a distinctive style of perpetual motion. This it developed to aid escape from the ethos of political stagnation which Pareto's generation had been drawn to analyse and which had so belied the great expectations aroused in the epoch of *Risorgimento*. During 1919–20 D'Annunzio – now cheered as soldier and aviator as much as author – demonstrated through his eccentric occupation of Fiume a new line in heroics. The *Duce* himself, as man of action and as ideologist, aspired to be the charismatic prophet of a future wherein Italy would recapture, indeed surpass, the glory that had once, or even twice, been Rome's. His was a myth of Italian destiny structured in Sorelian terms. Its truth and utility could be gauged only by reference to that future whose dramatic transformation the myth itself was designed to inspire. As a revolt against materialistic positivism and as a vision of dynamic fulfilment or 'becoming', it could draw also upon a debased Hegelianism. Nowhere was this more obvious than in the supreme ideological statement, an article on 'The Doctrine of Fascism' embedded in the *Enciclopedia Italiana* (1932).

Though Gentile collaborated, Mussolini was credited with sole authorship of the essay and its text does indeed reveal the ex-journalist's talent for exploiting all the worst rhetorical possibilities of crude philosophical idealism. These are employed in a discourse devoted, above all, to glorifying the State. Any thoughts about the desirability of its 'withering', so dear to Marxists, are absent. In Italian Fascism only the State itself – especially when operating under the 'corporativist' version of representation channelled through trade and professional associations – has potential to become a true spiritual reality. The *fasces* or lictors' rods now symbolize a discipline and an authority that relate not only to conventional laws and institutions but also to a higher realm of moral fulfilment. The State must embrace, synthesize, and transcend all other social phenomena. The individual commands respect merely

in so far as he coincides with the State, which is the conscience and universal will of man in his historical existence ... If liberty is to be the attribute of the real man, and not of the abstract puppet envisaged by individualistic liberalism, Fascism is for liberty. And the only liberty which can be a real thing, the liberty of the State and of the individual within the State. Therefore, for the Fascist, everything is in the State, and nothing human or spiritual exists, much less has value, outside the State. In this sense Fascism is totalitarian, and the Fascist State, the synthesis and unity of all values, interprets, develops and gives strength to the whole life of the people.

Not even the nation can effectively exist until it has been 'generated' by a State which, 'as the universal ethical will, is the creator of right'.

Contrast between the ideologies of Mussolini and Hitler is most important at two points. The *Führer* not only inverted the relationship between theory and practice but also treated the state as means rather than end. Whereas in the Italian case doctrine tended to be extracted from action, Nazi deeds were themselves directed towards the implementation of an ideological vision that was from an early stage broadly complete. Moreover, this passed beyond Mussolini's own idealist political philosophy of state-glorification and focused instead upon the supreme value of racial, or *völkisch*, fulfilment. The Nazi philosopher and educationalist Alfred Bäumler claimed that here was 'the Copernican idea of modern times'. It was certainly not an entirely new creation. In purveying it Hitler was short neither of predecessors nor of collaborating contemporaries. Nazi racist arguments were justified by reference (sometimes, of necessity, very selective and distorting) to many figures already mentioned: for instance, Gobineau, Darwin, Haeckel, Treitschke, Nietzsche, Wagner, Chamberlain, and Woltmann. Among other available sources were writers such as Paul de Lagarde (alias Bötticher), Julius Langbehn, and Arthur Moeller van den Bruck, all of whom Fritz Stern has illuminated within a context of pre-war 'cultural despair'. Moeller's *The Third Reich* (1923) was indeed one of the chief means through which the racial concerns of the 1890s were translated into terms appropriate to the requirements of a new generation. In 1934 Spengler, by then the world's most renowned commentator on doom, published *The Hour of Decision* – a work identifying Europe's very last hope as an altogether more urgent awareness of racial perils.

Outstanding among those even more directly involved in strengthening the ideological foundations of Nazism were Hans Günther, author of such books as *The Racial History of the German Volk* (1922), and Alfred Rosenberg whose major piece *The Myth of the Twentieth Century* (1930) brought racism to a peak of philosophical pretentiousness.

There is, however, no escape from the ideological centrality of Hitler himself. Though he had some acquaintance with the work of many of those just noted, his racist world-picture derived only very partially from such high-sounding sources. The received ideas of gutter life in pre-war Vienna tell, or at least symbolize, the rest. Hitler's talent was for synthesizing, and later for implementing in a terrifyingly literal manner, a variety of racist notions already widely current. Their characteristic mixture of commonplace vulgarity and misguided intellectual endeavour was eminently apparent in *Mein Kampf*, which the future dictator began to write while imprisoned at Landsberg and which appeared in two volumes during 1925–6. A best-seller from 1930 onwards, it stands among the most remarkable books of the twentieth century. Certainly it is rambling and often barely readable; and as personal or party history it is very misleading. Yet, unquestionably, it illuminates the essentials of Hitler's beliefs and character. It suggests that the author, whatever the arguments about his mental derangement, was devoid neither of intelligence nor of insight. Rather, *Mein Kampf* appears as the product of what Donald Watt has called 'a second-rate mind of immense power'. This is at work in, for instance, a candid alertness to the self-paralysing potential of any sustained concern for truth or moral scruple. The way that such a mind may operate is clearest in Hitler's observations on the mobilization of mass political sympathy, typified by the following:

All propaganda must be popular and its intellectual level must be adjusted to the most limited intelligence among those whom it addresses. Consequently the greater the mass it is intended to reach, the lower its purely intellectual level must be . . . The more modest its intellectual ballast, the more exclusively it takes into consideration the emotions of the masses, the more effective it will be.

This was cynical, but not unperceptive. Moreover, in the Nazi case at least, later events were to justify the complementary contention that such propaganda might be conducted best through the spoken rather than the written word.

These means subserved an ideology of Aryan supremacy. Hitler expressed it, typically, as follows:

All the human culture, all the results of art, science, and technology that we see before us today, are almost exclusively the creative product of the Aryan. This very fact admits of the not unfounded inference that he alone was the founder of all higher humanity, therefore representing the prototype of all that we understand by the word 'man'.

Hitler, in order to secure a political order rooted in acknowledgment of this supremacy, was willing to play upon German nationalist feeling. As a native Austrian, he was eager especially to exploit the discontent of those who regarded the so-called unification of 1871 as geographically too modest. As a legatee of pan-Germanism, he was also happy to endorse current convictions about superiority over degenerate Slavs or Latins. But he was also seeking to transcend the limitations of nationalism. Hitler tended eventually to deny both that all Germans were pure Aryans and that the noblest breed was found only in Germany-Austria. Concerning the first point, he did not view his own people as an exception to the general rule that there existed potentially within each nation some hierarchy of authority reflecting elements of varying ethnic value. It became clearly one of the primary tasks of the Nazi cadres, sifted and proved through the struggle for power, to exercise domination over those German masses whose imperfections seemed to the *Führer* ever more apparent. The second and complementary point involved the wider geographical application of the first, to the still more complicated racial gradations of areas beyond. Here the generality of Germans might be fit to wield authority over a whole hierarchy of inferior stocks, but only under the supreme direction of still purer Aryans. The latter were destined not only to stand at the head of a boundless new political order structured in complex racial terms but also, as the ideology emphasized increasingly, to do so as an élite of a truly international, indeed supra-national, kind.

By the time of the Second World War theory insisted that this élite had become organized into Heinrich Himmler's SS. It recruited, upon supposedly eugenic principles, both within and beyond the Reich. Though in practice remaining pre-dominantly German, it claimed to embody the most exalted images of supra-national Aryan manhood. Hitler declared that the SS, as a body of Knights seeking to protect the Holy Grail of Pure Blood, was making real the true meaning of Wagner's *Parsifal*. This racial élite was to form the vanguard for the triumph of Hitler's continental, and potentially global, New Order. Most urgently the SS would spearhead eastwards a programme of colonization and exploitation, according to those doctrines of *Lebensraum* pioneered by such 'geopoliti-cians' as Rudolf Kjellén and Karl Haushofer and clearly out-lined in *Mein Kampf* itself. Thus would blood and soil be brought into mystical union. Towards the end of the war Hitler promised Himmler that, following victory, the latter should have Burgundy as the heartland of a supra-national Aryan order maintained by the SS. This may have been the product of dementia, but not necessarily of any greater degree of dementia than that afflicting other aspects of Hitler's racism which were indeed implemented. His vision of the New Order was eventually pursued with minimal reference to practical economic and strategic considerations. Refusal to compromise about large-scale persecution of inferior stocks did incalculable harm to the German war effort. But to have expected from

Hitler a diversion of energy into more productive activities would have been to misunderstand the whole nature of his Nazi mania and the very essence of its drive to war.

The anti-semitic purges demonstrated most vividly these obsessive qualities in Hitlerian racism. The Jews, though far from being the only object of hatred, were undoubtedly Nazism's leading victims. Now viewed as an essentially biological entity, they were for Hitler the supreme manifestation of an Anti-Race pursuing on an international scale the total destruction of Aryan culture. In locating here the supreme responsibility for every social ill he was able to exploit that multi-faceted image of the Jew as enemy which has been noted already in the pre-1914 setting. Its further popularization in and beyond Germany was assured through the widespread circulation, especially from 1920 onward, of various versions of a forged compilation pretending to contain the master-plans for a Jewish conspiracy against the world. Within the genre of anti-semitic demonology these *Protocols of the Elders of Zion* were no less impressive even than *Mein Kampf*. From its earliest days the Nazi movement directed verbal and physical violence against the Jews –, as the agents of exploitative capitalism or of Bolshevism (according to choice and polemical need), as the rootless traitors of 1918, as the bacilli of biological and moral degeneration, and so on *ad nauseam*. After 1933 the attacks on non-Aryans, and on Jews especially, became official. Foremost among the many decrees imposing ever more stringent political, economic, and social disabilities were the so-called Nuremberg Laws of September 1935 dealing with Reich citizenship and with 'the Protection of German Blood and Honour'. Regarding the latter, the new regime prohibited Jews from contracting marriage, or having extra-marital sexual relations, with 'subjects of German or kindred blood'. In some senses, the removal of Jewish rights to citizenship revealed more precisely still racism's regression from the idea of justice that seemed to have won general acceptance in the civilized world. The relevant law did not penalize action at all, but merely a state of existence – and one that was indeed highly susceptible to capricious definition.

From 1941 the SS supervised the transformation of these policies into the pursuit of an exterminatory 'final solution' to the Jewish problem. For Hitler, a character whom Dostoyevsky himself might have hesitated to invent, this secret undertaking became an obsession to which even the efficient conduct of the war might be sacrificed. It was, quite simply, the practical enactment of Nazi ideology's ultimate logical conclusions. Every brand of racism, in establishing and generalizing rigid typologies to which its enemies must conform, tends to strip each victim of any claim upon personal individuality. But at Auschwitz and the other extermination camps the inmates were the objects of a process not merely of depersonalization but also of dehumanization. Types had become, at best, merely animal. Thus might the captives be all the more readily conveyed into the satanic mills of mechanized mass destruction. It was no great step from viewing the master race as the paragon of manhood to regarding others as semi-human or non-human, as closer to ape than Aryan. Not only did the SS treat its victims as animals, but in the process some of these did indeed seem to become animals. The fearful struggle for daily survival, as the central feature of life so close to death, helped make the prey more conformable to their image within Nazi ideology. Against this conscious and systematic policy of dehumanization it was immensely difficult to retain any grasp upon human dignity or any resistance to the moral nihilism so rampantly infecting the captors themselves. Within his family circle Rudolf Höss, commandant at Auschwitz, seems to have been an exemplary person. It was the racist ethos that helped such figures to reconcile home and work, just like men involved in a factory for the processing of cattle. That same ethos, and the traditions of anti-semitism especially, helped to numb the conscience of many other Germans who, while not directly cognizant of the extermination programme, were, as Albert Speer confessed, 'in a position to know and yet shunned knowledge'.

The Nazi regime was certainly unique in the pitch that its barbarities attained. They were seriously rivalled only by those of its Stalinist contemporary. In the latter case, however, it was possible to indicate some circumstances by way of extenuation, through observing that the Russian tyranny was in some degree a mere variation upon the political tradition nurtured by Tsardom and through recognizing that Soviet orthodoxy still professed ultimately humane aspirations. No such allowance remained relevant to Nazism. It was murderous in theory and practice alike. Not even amidst the Great War had barbarism been fostered with such calculated determination. When in 1945 the exterminatory horrors became fully revealed there was universal outcry against Germany. And yet, this should not be allowed to obscure either the bravery of those Germans who did resist Hitler or, still more crucially, those senses in which Nazism itself had merely intensified modes of thought and feeling common enough elsewhere. Not only was the Soviet regime guilty of a certain anti-semitism, but in some of the countries under German occupation there was no shortage of indigenous Jew-hunters who showed eagerness beyond any call of enforced duty. Regarding a still wider range of Nazi policies, foreign governments and peoples had earlier, in Speer's formula, 'shunned knowledge' on a disturbing scale. Alan Bullock's life of the *Führer* concludes with this valuable observation:

The conditions and state of mind which he exploited, the *malaise* of which he was the symptom, were not confined to one country, although they were more strongly marked in Germany than anywhere else. Hitler's idiom was German, but the thoughts and emotions to which he gave expression have a more universal currency.

Could the dictator convince himself, nor merely with sincerity but also perhaps with a grain of real justification, that in

exterminating supposed degenerates his Nazis were dealing
with a menace which many other Europeans also felt but had
not the courage themselves to destroy?

Such observations also illuminate a relationship between
barbarism and culture itself. There was a sense of shock that
Hitler's movement had originated within a Germanic world
which gave an impression of having matured beyond the
politics of primitivism. It seemed puzzling that the renewal of
savagery could be centred upon regions which, for at least
two centuries past, had contributed so richly and consistently to Europe's cultural development. But, whatever the
flaws particular to German culture, this was to view the
problem in terms that were too limited and, on the part of
outsiders, too self-flattering. For Nazism has to be seen also
as the supreme embodiment of those intimations of the infernal
already discernible before 1914 on a truly continental scale.
Like the recent war, it served to confirm that during the
epochs of Enlightenment and of ascendant liberalism fashionable visions of progress had dulled men's alertness to certain
brutalizing currents of unreason still potent everywhere within
civilization itself. As George Steiner has reiterated, only
following the Nazi experience came general recognition that

extremes of collective hysteria and savagery can co-exist with a
parallel conservation and, indeed, further development of the institutions, bureaucracies and professional codes of high culture ...
[and] that obvious qualities of literate response, of aesthetic feeling,
can co-exist with barbaric, politically sadistic behaviour in the same
individual.

Until then searing awareness of this more than merely Germanic weakness had been limited mainly to such exceptional
figures as Nietzsche and, less ambivalently, Freud. The latter
made this very malady the central object of his eleventh-hour
warning. He shared indeed with Hitler himself personal
experience of an imperial Vienna which had been simply the

supreme example of pre-war Europe's ability to nurture cultural achievement and barbarous intolerance side by side.

The Nazi leader intensified the latter without ever comprehending the former. By assailing genuinely gifted artists and intellectuals Hitler revenged himself on a world that had ignored his own claims to talent. The fundamental intellectual vulgarity of his movement is well illustrated by its special persecution of those Jewish communities which, out of all proportion to their number, had so enriched Europe's recent cultural development. Similarly illuminating is the fact that among the first tasks set for Joseph Goebbels as Minister of Enlightenment was the organization of public book-burnings. Having little cause actively to celebrate the arrival of Hitler's regime, most German academics settled for an attitude of ambivalent quietude which often evolved into an implicit denial of intellectual responsibility. In some ways their situation might have been more straightforward had Nazism itself condemned all scholarship in totally unequivocal terms. Yet the regime – whatever its intrinsic contempt for rationality, objectivity, and basic scholarly freedoms – did insist on maintaining some framework of erudition. Nazi ideology aspired, after all, to interpret the past, present, and future through a science of social processes that was pervaded by biological conceptions. In order to fortify the central racist tenets great effort was expended on, for instance, new subtleties of anatomical measurement and unprecedented horrors of medical experimentation. To the extent that the Nazis developed such scientific pretentiousness in a quest for dogmatic certainty they showed their indebtedness to forms of uncritical positivism. But an outstanding feature of the Third Reich was the readiness also to exploit, as an essentially complementary force in this drive to close the gap between knowledge attained and knowledge desired, the energies of myth and unreason. Everything that was best in the traditions of critical rationalism became imperilled, as the obvious common enemy of this striking alliance between scientism and mysticism. In combination they moulded an ideology that was pernicious because of its excesses of logicality and irrationality alike. Moreover, its debasement of mind had repercussions that spread beyond political thinking into every other area of intellectual and cultural endeavour.

Chapter 8

SCIENTIFIC, PHILOSOPHICAL, AND RELIGIOUS THOUGHT

UNDER totalitarianism the essential purpose of science and philosophy, like that of every other activity, became service of the regime. The procedures and conclusions of scholarship were subordinated to ideological need. However unnecessary it may be to catalogue at length the resulting crudities, there is value in stressing that this debasement was effected through extremism of Left and Right alike. The responsibility for its infliction was shared between the proponents of Soviet materialism and those who asserted the merits of Fascist vitalism. By 1921 Russia's revolutionary leadership had conferred upon Marxist approaches to knowledge an unhealthily monopolistic status. During the 1930s opportunities for debate narrowed further. Not only did intellectuals and others suffer progressively more restraint on their freedom of movement, but also Soviet Marxism itself was being reduced to a single and outstandingly arid version of dialectical materialism. Thus the method which Lenin had extended into every context now became also the only one applicable to each. Protected artificially from radical scrutiny dialectical materialism was, especially in its formulation of problems, increasingly marked by obsolescence. Its revolutionary intent could not conceal from critics the extent to which this approach was, in philosophical terms, reactionary. It also fortified a certain insularity in Soviet science, illustrated best by Trofim Lysenko's teachings on inheritance through acquired characteristics. The prolonged dismissal of the competing Mendelian theory as 'a bourgeois fraud', whether because it limited the operation of economic determinism or because it placed bounds upon a dictator's own capacities to transform men, was the outcome of political more than scientific judgement.

Enough has been said already of Nazism to indicate how, for similar purposes of social dogma, it perpetrated still grosser deformations on biological science and evolved, to boot, a philosophical method of incomparable arbitrariness. At Berlin Bäumler philosophized from a newly created Chair of Political Education, in whose title the adjective was redundant: under such a regime everything had to be a matter of politics. George Sabine sets out the resulting problem as follows:

A government that aims at a maximum of military power and also a maximum of intellectual control commits its educational system to a peculiar experiment. Essentially it has to find out whether it can debauch the social studies and the humanities and yet keep the natural sciences vigorous enough to support the technology. If it fails of the former the government loses its own self-assigned reason for existence; if it fails of the latter it loses the basis of its power.

On this tightrope Hitler managed less well than Stalin. Most particularly it was, in the long run, very fortunate for the Third Reich's enemies that the Nazis should have pursued Haeckel's aim of bringing even the superficially apolitical realm of physics within the organic unity of a total world-picture.

The intellectual degeneration of such early Nobel laureates as Philipp Lenard and Johannes Stark indicated the nature of the rot. Their condemnations of 'Jewish physics' would have been beside the point at any time; but in an era when Jews were prominent among the very best of physicists such attacks were also, in a most precise sense, self-defeating. Whatever the status of 'Aryan physics' may have been, a regime so disdainful of men such as Einstein did not, even for that reason alone, deserve to survive. Moreover, survival was indeed at stake. Under the Nazis Göttingen University ceased to sustain that claim to international eminence in work on the atom which had been established by Max Born and his colleagues during the 1920s. Enrico Fermi, who in 1938 did not return to Mussolini's Italy after accepting a Nobel Prize for researches into atomic chain reaction, followed quite literally in the steps of many exiled German scientists. They had found the ideology threatening to hinder scientific success; and, still more significantly, some were coming to realize that the placing of certain kinds of scientific discovery at the disposal of such an ideology would constitute the greatest horror of all. It was ironically fitting that a regime so contemptuous of mind should have debilitated those centres of scholarship most capable of providing, through the alliance of science and technology, an unparalleled instrument for the very domination which the Nazis craved.

The totalitarian disposition to force science and philosophy into a mould pre-determined by whatever vision of knowledge and order suited the ideology did have historical precedents. Over many centuries ecclesiastical authorities, in particular, had been just as eager to suppress any questioning of basic axioms that might threaten their own unverifiable claims to absolute knowledge: Galileo's fate was a case in point. But now, alongside the organs of science and more secular philosophy, the Churches themselves became victims. Their popular hold, even if probably waning somewhat, was still sufficient to produce complications that dictatorship could not afford to ignore. In the ensuing confrontation the ability of the Churches to represent the Christian tradition was imperilled especially by the competing but profane religiosity and messianism of the new ideologies themselves. This was most starkly apparent in the USSR where the Orthodox Church, already vulnerable through its sycophantic subordination to Tsardom, was ravaged openly by the militant atheism of a new order which

treated conventional religion as essentially an opiate or a cover
for class exploitation. Such limited toleration as the Soviet
authorities did allow – for example, as part of their drive to
consolidate patriotic feeling during the Second World War –
stemmed simply from considerations of expediency. The
Russian Orthodox establishment had the single advantage,
for what this was worth, of knowing pretty well the nature
and extent of its peril. Yet the less openly acrimonious relationship between Fascism and the Western Churches proved
almost as dangerous to the latter by drawing them into a
position that was, in the fullest sense of the word, compromising.

To many Catholic leaders the potential advantages of
appropriately directed forms of authoritarian and corporativist rule were just as evident as the drawbacks in popular
parliamentary sovereignty. The encyclical *Quadragesimo Anno*
(1931), issued by Pope Pius XI four decades after *Rerum
Novarum* as an updating of the Church's social teaching, condemned as 'twin rocks of shipwreck' the extremes of individualism and collectivism alike. It managed, however, also
to convey a certain tolerance of moderate corporativism.
Especially after the Lateran Agreements, the Italian regime's
token acceptance of some similarity between its own aims and
those of the Church had helped towards alleviating many
clerical qualms about Fascism. In Spain, where the universal
threat of Bolshevik atheism was soon deemed to be at its most
active, the Vatican greeted Franco's triumph as its own. The
German case was, however, more complicated. As early as
September 1933 Pius XI had concluded a Concordat with
Hitler. In this the Church's principal aim was to preserve
something of its influence over education. The strain imposed
by such compromises was especially apparent early in 1937,
when the Vatican circulated to Germany's bishops the message
titled *Mit brennender Sorge* ('With burning Sorrow'). This was
certainly a courageous denunciation of all secular ideologies

that might encourage their own idolatrous divinization at the expense of a truer moral law. But it was scarcely typical of the Church's general line over the Nazi period as a whole. Instead the German episcopate, and even more clearly the Vatican itself, sought normally to avoid any course that might tempt the regime to retaliate by inflicting further damage upon the organization of ecclesiastical institutions. Thus the bulk of Catholic resistance to Nazism stemmed more directly from individual rather than official initiative. Under Pius XII the dilemmas of leadership became more agonizing still. In 1941 Germany launched herself against the USSR, the supreme embodiment of atheistic government; and yet by the end of the following year the Vatican was also becoming aware of the Nazi extermination programme. It was a misguided, though perhaps understandable, form of prudence that prompted the Pope to refrain from public condemnation.

The German Protestant tradition had proved over generations just as important as the Catholic one in encouraging authoritarian rule and, not least, in maintaining an ethos hostile to Jewish religion and culture. As James Joll suggests, 'The Churches in general did not, and perhaps could not, rise above the prejudices of most of their members, who had welcomed or accepted the rise of National Socialism, just as other Germans had done and for the same reasons.' In such a context Protestantism's own most distinctive contribution stemmed from its well established association with extremist nationalism. This was evident in the widespread Protestant support for an organization founded by the Nazis in 1932 under the label 'German Christians'. It was soon led by 'Reichbishop' Ludwig Müller, whose bellicose reinterpretation of the Sermon on the Mount revealed a perversity bordering on genius. Still, having organizational structures less monolithic than those of the Catholic Church, Protestantism did manage more diversified forms of response to Hitler's dominance than mention of Müller alone might convey. Most notable here

was the *Bekennende Kirche*, or 'Confessing Church', founded
in 1933 by Martin Niemöller and others. This was scarcely
strong enough directly to challenge Nazi authority. Yet
adherents sought to keep a certain pietistic current of Christian
witness free from the processes of *Gleichschaltung* that the
regime was imposing in this as in every other field of thought.
In general terms, it seems reasonable to conclude that both
Hitler and the Churches at large found themselves playing for
time and that neither side was eager to enter prematurely into
a situation of openly total hostility.

The institutional compromises, whatever their rationale,
could hardly seem positively edifying. However, the dictators' challenge did help to inject into much religious philosophy something noted already within moderate brands of
contemporary political comment – an enhanced clarity of
purpose. In this same process a significant role had been played
even earlier by the Great War, which so dramatically illumined
the shoddiness of beliefs about inevitable secular progress.
Theological reinvigoration could be aided also by the development, being encouraged through social and natural sciences
alike, of a more modest estimation of man's rational capacity
and autonomy. Most strikingly, the early twentieth-century
revolution in physics, however impressive in itself, was now
tending firmly to suggest the limitations which necessarily
must surround any pursuit of knowledge conducted purely in
a scientific mode. Mystery was anything but banished from the
world. Many philosophers of religion were understandably
keen to explore the still patent opportunities for conferring a
complementary, or even higher, status upon knowledge
accumulated through forms of direct experiential perception
and intuition. This tendency was apparent in the work of
Jacques Maritain, the epoch's outstanding Catholic thinker;
of Karl Barth, his Protestant counterpart; of the exiled
Nicolas Berdyaev, Eastern Orthodoxy's most prominent
intellectual representative; and even of Martin Buber, seeking

a renovation of the Judaic religious tradition. All these shared, in varying degrees, a certain apocalyptic mood. This meant that the 'higher criticism', so favoured by many of their immediate predecessors, was not so much derided as rendered peripheral. Amidst a pastoral crisis of such dimensions that brand of scholarship seemed a luxury when compared with the urgent need to evoke an inspirational message more directly communicable to the mass of men.

In Catholic philosophy such developments had to be kept harmonious with the kind of anti-modernism promulgated as orthodox before 1914. Thus the mainstream continued to flow along channels first engineered by Aquinas. An outstanding feature of this neo-Thomism, exemplified best in the approach to questions of divine existence, was its elaboration of complementary modes for justifying belief: not only intellectually through rational and logical judgement, but also by non-inferential procedures associated with forms of direct intuition. Among current philosophies it stood unrivalled, except possibly by dialectical materialism, in the sheer number of its trained adherents and in the very bulk of its literary production. The University of Louvain in Belgium, even more than Rome itself, provided its academic focal point. But neo-Thomism's greatest impact on intellectual life at large occurred in France, perhaps the only country where religion made really positive overall gains during these years. Her 'Catholic Renaissance' had begun just before the Great War with Charles Péguy and others. Most prominent among those who sustained it thereafter were Maritain himself and, in a non-Thomist vein, Gabriel Marcel. Both were converts whose security within Catholicism had been earned not inherited. Maritain's switch of allegiance from liberal Protestantism dated back to 1906. He had then shared in the pre-war mania for Bergsonism, only to find eventually that its anti-intellectualism repelled him. He derived greater satisfaction from a vision of will not as irrational force but rather as something given by God for the mind to control, and thus he brought modernized Thomism to its fullest expression. In *The Degrees of Knowledge* (1932), his most widely read philosophical work, he explored the different, but not mutually exclusive, avenues to understanding granted by science, metaphysics, and mystical experience. By then, as the leading light in a wide circle of French intellectuals and artists, Maritain was well on the way to attaining international renown.

Protestant thinkers were, from the ecclesiastical standpoint at least, freer to undertake a really thorough renovation of their Christian message. Yet they too drew much inspiration from the past, being concerned progressively less with technical criticism than with recapturing central spiritual insights from the age of Luther and Calvin. The main version of the resulting 'neo-orthodoxy' incorporated a theology of 'crisis', but not in the ordinary sense alone. For, even sometimes at the expense of social concern, it also stressed men's abasement before, and utter dependence upon, the divine judgement (*krísis*). It contended that anguished recognition of this 'human predicament' was the necessary springboard for a 'leap' into faith; that the 'otherness' of God was so profound as to preclude any essentially rational demonstration of his existence; and that God was not to be comprehended but, in a spirit of bleak humility, to be felt, encountered, addressed. To all this Barth made an epochal contribution. His early thinking had followed the liberal theology of Ritschl. But Barth had found this increasingly irrelevant to that inspirational preaching which was so prominent within the pastoral tradition of his own Swiss Reformed Church. As he noted: 'Reason sees the small and the larger but not the truly large . . . It sees what is human but not what is divine.' Kierkegaard and Dostoyevsky were among the writers who inspired this deepening conviction that a humanized God was a God unreal.

Barth sought to put matters right through his *Commentary on the Epistle to the Romans*, issued first in 1918 and then again three years later in a still more radical version. It implied that theology would survive not by continuing a series of defensive responses to secular rationality but by taking the offensive so as to assert a world-transcending faith. Barth was denying that authentic awareness of God could be derived from rational argument, or indeed from the cultivation of religious experiences as hitherto conceived. Men needed to banish their current anthropocentric images of a deity whose actions are supposedly comprehensible according to criteria of everyday reason and morality. This was the mode of critical thinking with which Barth made his main impact. Nonetheless, subsequently he somewhat moderated his position by qualifying the stress upon divine otherness and upon the weakness of reason. The multi-volume *Church Dogmatics* exemplified his rehabilitation of some possibility of rational discourse about God. It began to appear in 1932, when Barth had been teaching influentially in a number of German universities for over a decade. Hitler's triumph not only led him to take refuge in Basel but also channelled his thinking towards worldly political concerns hitherto treated by him as very peripheral. In the end, from Switzerland, he was calling ever more insistently for practical resistance to a Nazism that embodied supremely men's capacities for harbouring delusive confusion between themselves and God.

Among those whom Barth encouraged in work for the Confessing Church was Dietrich Bonhoeffer. *Act and Being*, which he published in 1931 at the age of only twenty-five, suggested his potential for becoming the outstanding Lutheran theologian of his generation. During the war Bonhoeffer was gaoled for anti-Nazi conspiracy and yet, before his execution by the SS in 1945, he managed to produce a series of *Letters and Papers from Prison* which, posthumously published, became an inspiration to the religious sensibility of the postwar epoch. Other figures important in this phase of neo-orthodoxy were the German Rudolf Bultmann, whose rather

more revolutionary work on the 'demythologization' of
Christianity would come into its own only from the late
1940s onward, and the Swiss Emil Brunner. But between each
of them and Barth relations grew increasingly strained. He
criticized both, especially for undue anthropocentrism. The
alleged weakness took the form in Bultmann of stressing
inordinately just how human the human predicament was,
and in Brunner of over-extending the idea of religious truth
as a personal 'meeting' with God. *Wahrheit als Begegnung*
(1938; translated as *The Divine-Human Encounter*), in which
Brunner expounded this at length, itself owed much to Buber.
It was indeed suggestive of how the latter's *I and Thou* (1923)
had made greater impact on Christian than on Judaic thinking.
His small volume had pleaded that God should be considered
not as the impersonal 'It' of traditional speculative theology
but as an essentially personal 'Thou', and be treated not as
something about which one gathers information but as
somebody with whom one may enter into dialogue. In all
these developments Barth himself discerned excessive enthusiasm for a new philosophical fashion which was gaining
ground rapidly during these years and which had indeed
affected his own earlier work. Its application to thinking about
religion was pursued most vigorously within the Protestant
tradition by Bultmann and within the Catholic one by Marcel. This 'existentialism' had, however, far more than merely
religious implications. It needs therefore to be discussed in the
broader context of non-analytical philosophy at large.

Existentialist thinking developed more as a matter of mood
than as the expression of any firmly agreed philosophical
position. Among potential tutelaries the most universally
respected was Kierkegaard, for his probing into the anxieties
of the individual predicament; but Dostoyevsky, Nietzsche,
and Bergson were also commonly invoked. Much inspiration
was drawn both from earlier nineteenth-century romanticism,
particularly as found in Germany, and from the whole move-

ment around 1900 towards further enhancing the status of intuitive understanding. Indeed the most immediate source for existentialism was the 'phenomenology' then being pioneered by Edmund Husserl. His own most formative experience was study in Vienna with Franz Brentano on problems concerned with the introspective examination of consciousness. Between 1887 and 1928 Husserl, as a teacher at the universities of Halle, Göttingen, and Freiburg, gradually elaborated this into a general statement of phenomenological method which, he suggested, could solve difficulties familiar within the idealist tradition. *Logical Investigations* (1900–1901) and *Ideen zu einer reinen Phänomenologie* (1913; translated as *Ideas: General Introduction to Pure Phenomenology*) were the outstanding expressions of his desire to surpass the conventional neo-Kantian approach towards reconciling idealism with science, intuitionism with reason.

Husserl's proposed method involved, firstly, a minute scrutiny of phenomena from every domain of human experience. Next came an imaginative 'reduction', aimed at removing from each phenomenon every quality that was merely contingent – every feature that might be altered without the phenomenon itself changing into something fundamentally other. Only thus might the philosopher enter into the domain which properly concerns him, that of essences, of 'pure' experience, of necessary not conditional knowledge. In Husserl's view philosophy so defined has, like logic and mathematics, capacity to reveal fundamental presuppositions for natural scientific law and for all other attempts at systematizing experience. But the fulfilment of such promise must remain incomplete without a second feat of reduction. For, true to the idealist tradition, Husserl sees essences as logical structures embedded ultimately not in the phenomena to which men relate them but in consciousness itself. Therefore he advocates another exercise of imagination, intended to effect suspension of judgement about all acts of consciousness having an object independent of themselves. Rivalling Descartes in boldness, Husserl calculated that this would leave isolated and identifiable such other self-contained, irreducible, and 'immanent' acts as referred only to a truly pure state of consciousness. In the latter he discerned an Absolute producing novel insights. Acknowledgement of its importance seemed to him the essential foundation for any subsequent reconstruction of the world of phenomena. Experiences, whether emotional or rational in emphasis, could be assessed properly only according to their impact upon the naked consciousness. Phenomenology's aim was to analyse the structure of such particular experiences as they presented themselves to this brand of pure consciousness and, more ambitiously still, to clarify how men might employ that same Absolute to attain intuitive appreciation of the general laws controlling the structure of all possible experience. Husserl was confident that here he had evolved a new technique establishing 'an *a priori* psychological discipline, able to provide the only secure basis on which a strong empirical psychology can be built, and a new universal philosophy which can supply an organum for the methodological revision of all the sciences'.

Courageous panache marked this effort at restoring to philosophical activity its dignity and stature as 'the universal science'. Phenomenology, in so far as it was systematic, certainly possessed some capacity for limiting the current feelings of intellectual fragmentation. Nonetheless, being an essay in method rather than content, it could scarcely purvey the kind of comprehensive value system that was also craved in an epoch of anomie. This was the ethical vacuum that existentialism examined more closely. It developed first largely within German-speaking philosophical and literary circles; but from the 1940s onward, and increasingly under French leadership, it won much wider allegiance. Phenomenological techniques were borrowed, but in support of an altogether more personalized concern for men's anxieties and moral dilemmas. In illuminating the soon classic 'human predicament' the existentialists highlighted how man was fated, necessarily, to live amidst an alien world and to do so while contemplating the seeming absurdity of his own eventual annihilation through death. Yet they also suggested how the strains of such bleak existence within 'otherdom' were intensified, contingently, in situations of mass socialization. Each individual was now assailed by a worsening crisis of identity and of alienation which, if left unresolved, would preclude any effective conferment of value upon himself, or others, or the world at large. In Husserl's philosophy, however, the existentialists discerned some pointer towards reintegration. When all else was in flux that consciousness which he had so stressed did remain sure. The challenge was to render it truly active, so that even feelings of absurdity and despair might become instrumental in formulating values.

This search for authenticity of being was the leading concern of Martin Heidegger. In 1928 he moved from Marburg, where he had influenced Bultmann, to become Husserl's successor at Freiburg. A year earlier Heidegger had published *Being and Time*, soon recognized as the most seminal work of early existentialism. This identification of himself with existentialist philosophy proper was something that the author did in fact try to resist. Yet the incompleteness of his treatise helped it to be construed in a rather distorted manner, and one which was certainly no less influential on that account. In brief, Heidegger had not properly fulfilled a declared intention to make his study of 'Existence' the foundation for some adequate account of the fuller and distinctive meaning attached to 'Being' itself. Contemporaries, provided only with the former, tended to treat this *Existenzphilosophie* as something more substantive than the hermeneutical preliminary that its creator had in mind. They valued above all Heidegger's qualitative differentiation between levels of existence. This reserved the lowest plane for inanimate objects, ,

the mere tools of men. An intermediate position was allocated
to animals, as ordinarily defined; but here too were placed
human animals whenever these existed simply as the tool-like
objects of conditioning or command controlled by others.
Upon the highest level stood only those men who managed
to exchange such bare existence for a richer and less passive
conception of life. Heidegger indicated that the necessary precondition for its attainment was a fearless recognition of the
certainty of death. He believed that men who had thus confronted courageously the prospect of non-being might be
sustained thereafter in the resolve to follow a really authentic
mode of existence. In it they would have to defy every
attempt at anaesthetizing the spirit, whether through crude
tyranny or via the commoner and more insidious demands of
social conformity. A life of fulfilment must be lived as a continuous exercise in conscious and active commitment, according to choices that are freely made and distinctively one's
own.

The sheer intractability of Heidegger's style limited his
immediate impact. But Karl Jaspers, the other major moulder
of existentialist thinking between the wars, was much more
directly dedicated to what he termed 'communication'. The
Heidelberg professor showed, in comparison with Heidegger,
not only the deeper debt to Kantianism but also the greater
insistence upon applying existentialist insights to the contemporary crisis of civilization. Not least, the moral dilemmas
entailed by that crisis featured more prominently with Jaspers,
especially in such works as *Die geistige Situation der Zeit* (1931;
translated as *Man in the Modern Age*). Four years later he
commented: 'Quietly, something enormous has happened in
the reality of Western man: a destruction of old authority, a
radical disillusionment in an over-confident reason, and a
dissolution of bonds have made anything, absolutely anything, seem possible.' Jaspers certainly refined existentialism's
sensitivity to the yearnings endemic within ethically dis-

orientated societies. Yet, equally, his work typified this whole philosophy's inability lastingly to satisfy these needs by prescribing the content of some new and compensating value system. The existentialist reiterated the moral necessity for personal choice and commitment, even for action in advance of rationalization; but he refused to discern in, or confer on, existence any logic or structure capable of providing relevant bearings. It remained difficult to see how a philosophy recognizing no values save those generated through the play of subjective preference or 'inner disposition' could promote any real rescue from ethical nihilism.

Existentialism's instability of application was apparent at every turn. In religion, for instance, the philosophy could be made compatible with Christianity, and especially with the personal-affirmative urge of Protestant neo-orthodoxy. Nonetheless, as Barth's growing disquiet was meant to testify, an existentialist approach might lead just as readily towards the non-Christian theism basically favoured by Jaspers, or indeed towards agnosticism or even atheism. Might authenticity be deemed to depend upon men's active response not merely to the fact of their own mortality but also, in Nietzschean terms, to the necessity of facing death unsolaced by illusions about the survival even of God himself? The social implications of existentialism were equally volatile. At a quite fundamental level, its capacity to detach men from conventional structures of life and thought and to encourage self-contemplation led some adherents into believing that the imperatives on commitment could be satisfied through appropriately conscious justifications of 'disengagement' itself. But even among the greater number who avoided this paradox and who defined commitment less perversely there was little consensus about the causes worthy of attracting engagement. Such difficulties, relating to the particular context of Stalinism, encouraged acrimonious division within French existentialist circles soon after the Second World War. However, in many important respects, the kind of dispute into which Albert Camus and Jean-Paul Sartre then entered had its prototype in the disagreements over Nazism that earlier had polarized Jaspers and Heidegger.

In 1938 Hitler's regime conferred on Jaspers an unintended accolade – dismissal from his Heidelberg chair. Thereafter he moved to Basel. Heidegger, on the other hand, accepted the Rectorship of Freiburg University from the Third Reich. Reprintings of *Being and Time* carried no longer the original dedication to Husserl, a Jew. The book's obscurities of language now seemed to have a certain congruency with Hitler's own talent for bewitchment by the word. In short, Heidegger devoted to Nazism the choice arising from his conviction that 'thinking begins only at the point where we have discovered that thought has no more stubborn adversary than reason, this reason which has been glorified for centuries'. It is often suggested that such Nazi allegiance was somehow the logical outcome of his existentialist insights; but more helpful is the realization that his philosophy could 'justify' simply anything he pleased. Even so, Heidegger represented only an extreme instance of existentialism's more general weakness – its inability to offer release from a situation in which, to echo Jaspers, everything had been made possible.

Existentialists not only disagreed severely amongst themselves but also had still greater difficulty in sustaining debate with more analytically minded thinkers. To the latter existentialism seemed incapable of philosophical communication in any useful sense of the term. Indeed, between the wars something of Europe's more widespread cultural fragmentation was amply epitomized by the state of philosophy itself. Here two main currents were now flowing in ever greater isolation from each other. These promoted, in Anthony Quinton's words, 'on one hand a logical investigation of human knowledge and the language in which it is expressed, and on the other an inquiry, of a less disciplined and more imaginative sort, into the nature of human existence'. The political developments of the 1930s certainly accentuated a cleavage between the latter, more metaphysical, mode of discourse which became dominant on the European mainland and the former, more analytical, approach which was maintained principally in Britain, Scandinavia, and the United States both by natives and by many of the refugees from oppression. The divergence had begun, however, even before the totalitarian rape of freedom. Husserl, in seeking to combine introspective objectives with some real respect for the critical positivist image of philosophy as an impersonal cognitive study of the basic conditions of meaning, had offered a bridge. This was, however, swept aside by the insistence of Heidegger and others upon the complete primacy of the subjective. Interpreted thus, existentialism's concern with life had to work at the expense of logic. To the analytical scrutiny of methods and concepts it preferred exercises in intuitive sympathy. For what had to be expressed the formal treatise was increasingly a less appropriate vehicle than imaginative literature or the cinema; the café made a better base than the book-lined study. Existentialism could never deliver all that it offered, but such features helped to conceal its failings and to enhance its wider acceptability. The analytic approach, on the other hand, had very limited appeal to non-professionals. In general, it was the more technically daunting for laymen. Nor were these much comforted by its tendency to affirm that the provision of moral and spiritual anchorage was simply no part of the philosopher's task, and that metaphysical discourse was either an exercise in sheer nonsense or else something best left to poets and visionaries.

Until the early 1930s Central Europe was able to make real contributions to the analytical brand of philosophy. They were conveyed principally through the movement known first as 'logical positivism' and then, largely because 'positivism' had acquired so many unfortunate connotations due to the excesses of less critical practitioners, relabelled as 'logical empiricism'. The primary focal point was Vienna. It was therefore not surprising that Mach, who had taught there from 1895 to 1901, should have been regarded, alongside Frege and Russell, as a major source of inspiration. Indeed to Moritz Schlick, one of Mach's successors as Professor of the Philosophy of the Inductive Sciences, must go the main credit for forming in the early 1920s the group that would be known from 1928 onwards as the Vienna Circle. As will become clearer shortly, two very significant Viennese philosophers – Ludwig Wittgenstein and Karl Popper – stood at interesting tangents to it. Among the leading figures who, however, came properly within its ambit were Otto Neurath and Kurt Gödel. Perhaps the most articulate member was Rudolf Carnap, author of such books as *The Logical Structure of the World* (1928) and, still more influentially, *The Logical Syntax of Language* (1934). Hans Reichenbach, co-editor of the Circle's famous journal *Erkenntnis* ('Knowledge'), proclaimed the principles of logical positivism from Berlin; and Carnap's move to Prague in 1931 also aided their wider geographical diffusion. There was moreover some sympathetic reception in Poland where Kasimierz Twardowski and the logician Alfred Tarski were already engaged in broadly comparable activity.

The Vienna Circle's endeavour to effect, through the application of refined logical techniques, some systematic reconciliation between philosophy and science suggested a more restrictive assessment of the domains of each than had been current in the epoch of Comtean positivism. The effort also relied heavily on a particular principle of verification. As originally formulated, it insisted that all significant statements must fall into one of two categories: those that were not 'analytic' (logically necessary because their denial would involve a self-contradictory use of terms) must be 'synthetic' (susceptible to correlation with experiences capable of testing their accuracy). Conversely, assertions coming into neither of the preceding categories were judged to be devoid of meaning. This was the status of talk about God or morality or aesthetics, the position reserved for every form of metaphysical discourse and value judgement. Statements of this type might serve some psychological and emotional function but, because there was no possibility of verifying them, they could be of no concern to the philosopher as such. Carnap hoped that 'the logic of science' would now show how much of that 'inextricable tangle of problems which is known as philosophy' was really a matter of pseudo-questions and self-confusion.

Such aspirations involved a curious mixture of modesty and presumptuousness, and critics could attack the Vienna Circle for either or both. It was debatable whether members had indeed succeeded in distinguishing fact from value, not least in practical politics. The philosophical empiricism of the Circle certainly seemed to have spilled over into a broadly shared political commitment in favour of tolerant reformist socialism – something which meant, incidentally, that on at least two counts they could expect nothing but trouble from Nazi rule. From the extreme Left, moreover, they were assailed by figures such as Horkheimer who diagnosed in the Circle's quest for a bogus objectivity the cause of its failure to appreciate any great virtue in Marxism whether purveyed by the Frankfurt School or through any other channel. Much of the more technical criticism involved observations about the often confused relationship in logical positivism between meaning and verification. Above all, opponents queried where the principle of verification itself stood in relation to its own categories of significance. If it was indeed a statement, then there were difficulties in viewing it either as an analytical or as an empirical one; and, for its defenders at least, there were even worse perils in the third possibility that the principle was simply an expression of the dreaded metaphysics. Under pressure logical positivism evolved in due course certain more refined formulations of its basic argument. By the 1940s, writes R. F. Atkinson,

the verification principle had, in effect, been weakened in order to accommodate statements that logical positivists could not bring themselves to dismiss as meaningless. It began as an offensive weapon, potent enough to determine once and for all which statements were meaningful and which were not. It ends by being adapted to fit statements that are antecedently and independently held to be meaningful.

One major example of modification related to the difficulty (described by Carnap as 'inconvenient') that only statements of a singular nature seemed directly verifiable. The idea of 'indirect verification' was therefore elaborated so as to assert better the potential meaningfulness of the kind of generalizing statements that characterize, say, formulations of scientific law. Such adaptations were possible, however, only after relinquishing much of the dogmatic confidence in complete clarification that had made logical positivism initially so attractive.

This change of tone is epitomized within the history of the work most responsible for popularizing logical positivist philosophy among the English-speaking audience. In 1936 the opening sentence of Alfred Ayer's coruscating *Language, Truth and Logic* had proclaimed that, 'The traditional disputes of philosophers are, for the most part, as unwarranted as they are unfruitful.' Ten years later the original text reappeared intact, but with a new introductory essay suggesting that the matters which the young Oxford philosopher had quite dashingly surveyed no longer appeared in all respects so simple. Ayer, while making the methods of the Vienna Circle better known to his own countrymen, also revealed throughout his basic sympathy for the main tradition of British philosophy. This was marked not merely by general empiricist preferences but also, more distinctively still, by the tendency for these to be expressed through discussions of epistemology above all. The tradition's most classic problem, concerning what Ayer called 'our knowledge of the external world', stood indeed at the heart of his second book, *The Foundations of Empirical Knowledge* (1940). The sheer force of such anti-metaphysical currents meant that those who resisted them usually received less recognition than their due. For example, R. G. Collingwood's efforts to develop Croce's neo-Hegelian insights made little stir. Even the development by Whitehead of an organic metaphysics aimed at reconciling the scientific and religious spheres, expressed popularly in *Science and the Modern World* (1925) and more technically in *Process and Reality* (1929), had greater impact on Continental Europe and the United States (where from 1924 he taught) than on Britain. Indeed it was not he but the other author of *Principia Mathematica* who was regarded, with Moore, as doyen of British philosophy between the wars.

For the public at large Russell's stature was enhanced by his ability to produce a stream of writings commenting, often controversially and always entertainingly, upon issues of the day: books on *Marriage and Morals* (1929) and *The Conquest of Happiness* (1930) were particularly successful instances. In technical philosophy his most immediate concern following *Principia Mathematica* was to propound what he termed 'logical atomism'. This involved using that work's symbolic logic to construct a mechanical model of language. Only thus might the misunderstandings generated by aberrancies of conventional grammar be avoided. Russell's 'theory of descriptions' highlighted these. It also began to suggest how statements might be broken into their atomic parts and then reconstituted or translated according to some universal syntax of knowledge which, Russell believed, lay concealed beneath ordinary linguistic usage. He argued that this 'ideal logical language', even if wholly useless for daily life, would serve two invaluable purposes:

first, to prevent inferences from the nature of language to the nature of the world, which are fallacious because they depend upon the logical defects of language; secondly, to suggest, by inquiring what logic requires of a language which is to avoid contradiction, what sort of structure we may reasonably suppose the world to have.

The task was even more difficult than Russell initially envisaged. In time, his logical atomism appeared important less for what it directly achieved than for the problems that it raised and for the work from others that it stimulated.

Paramount here was the case of Wittgenstein. On Frege's advice he studied during 1912–13 at Cambridge under Russell, with whose work on logic he was already admiringly familiar. The pupil soon showed his own talent by confirming for Russell himself how this same logic indicated that mathematical propositions must be regarded as tautological rather than as providing information about some self-subsisting world of universals. Wittgenstein then embarked on a more general study of the nature of meaning. While in the Austrian army during the First World War, he assembled the collection of terse propositions known as the *Tractatus Logico-Philosophicus*. The original German text was published at Vienna in 1921 and, with Russell's encouragement, a parallel English version became available during the next year. In this treatise Wittgenstein suggested that philosophy was the application of logic for the purpose of clarifying thought. Moreover philosophical activity was, because of the essentially linguistic nature of thought itself, also inescapably a critique of language. In particular, it must be directed towards investigation of the conditions under which language has meaning. The *Tractatus* argued that the structure of language was the mirror-image of the structure of the real world, and that a meaningful statement must provide accurately some picture, or collection of pictures, of this world. The work claimed that the tautological propositions of logic could illuminate the structure of language and that therefore they were capable also of conveying, at one remove, the structure of factual reality. Here a major parallel between logical atomism and the *Tractatus* was patent.

For both were suggesting that behind the complexity of ordinary language the philosopher-logician might discern the form which propositions must take in order properly to mirror the facts they seek to represent.

Wittgenstein's conclusion that assertions which are neither factual nor tautological must be devoid of philosophical sense was one reached largely independently of the Viennese logical positivists. Even so, the *Tractatus* undoubtedly provided Schlick and his associates with clarification and encouragement. Any still closer involvement of Wittgenstein in their work was hindered by the harsher interpretation that the Vienna Circle placed on the agreed need to remove judgements of value and discussions of metaphysics from the realm of philosophical factuality. The distinction was, in brief, that he remained haunted by the reality of the ineffable. As Russell wrote somewhat distantly when introducing the *Tractatus*: 'The totalities concerning which Mr Wittgenstein holds that it is impossible to speak logically are nevertheless thought by him to exist, and are the subject matter of his mysticism.' Amid the smoke of common battle against conventional metaphysics the significance of such points was unduly obscured. But between Wittgenstein's position and that adopted by authentic logical positivists there was, in fact, much distance. Eventually the gap became wider still. The arguments of the *Tractatus* contained, admittedly, that same odd combination of modesty and presumptuousness already noted in the work of the Circle: the domains of philosophy had been reduced, but within them certainty was being consolidated with remarkable dogmatism. It must even be conceded that Wittgenstein believed his book to have solved, in all essential respects, the problems of philosophy so defined; and that he underlined this conviction by spending most of the 1920s in non-philosophical pursuits. However, by the time of his return to Cambridge in 1929, he was grappling with the realization that philosophy's ledger remained open. More precisely, he came to believe not merely that the logical positivism of the Vienna Circle and the logical atomism of Russell were alike misconceived but also that his own *Tractatus* stood fundamentally in error.

The painful elaboration of a new position, remote from Russell or the Vienna Circle, consumed the rest of Wittgenstein's life. He wrote much, but published nothing. Communications to the larger world of philosophy tended to be channelled through the small but distinguished band of intensely loyal pupils who gathered about him in Cambridge and who, after his death in 1951, organized publication of the writings from this second phase. Most notable among these was the *Philosophical Investigations* (1953), composed between 1936 and 1949. In such work Wittgenstein was still studying the structure and limits of language in order to grasp the structure and limits of thought itself. This was not the least of the positive links with the *Tractatus*. But the contrasts were even more striking. Wittgenstein now directly reversed his previous conviction that the structure of reality conditioned the structure of language. Nor did the premise of some common linguistic framework, from which the pre-existing model of reality had been deduced, any longer hold. Wittgenstein alleged that the *Tractatus* had erred in singling out one mode of language, dictated by logic, for the purpose of assimilating to it all other kinds. There was really a more elusive relationship between languages, such as might be suggested through the metaphor of 'family resemblance'. There was required a less restrictive theory of meaning that recognized the capacity of language in all its diversity to fulfil, like gesture, many communicative purposes besides those of mere assertion. Sheer variety of expression, previously treated as superficial, must now be accepted as fundamentally interesting – something to be explored empirically along lines already hinted in Moore's 'ordinary language philosophy'. The investigation of meaning must centre henceforth upon what men were actually doing whenever they believed themselves to be communicating significantly according to socially agreed conventions. It was for the philosopher to elucidate the various rules implicit in such customary discourse and thereby to clarify such confusions and paradoxes of thought and language as continually arose. This was the base for that 'linguistic philosophy' whose variants dominated the British academic tradition, especially in the Oxford of John Austin and Gilbert Ryle, for a generation after the Second World War.

More immediately, Wittgenstein's thinking exemplifies an intensification during the inter-war years of that sense of verbal crisis already discerned especially in the imaginative literature of the pre-1914 epoch. The *Tractatus* had suggested that words could deal meaningfully only with a very limited area of reality and that the rest must be silence. Relevant here is George Steiner's well-known view that this 'estrangement from language was, presumably, a part of a more general abandonment of confidence in the stabilities and expressive authority of Central European civilization'. Even the more flexible view of language found in Wittgenstein's later thought implied awareness of some such crisis. His growing insistence during the 1930s upon the linkages between meaning and customary usage contained indeed a warning – against bewitchment of the intellect through abuses of language that were now, more powerfully than ever before, produced by design as well as accident. For Wittgenstein the experience, and conquest, of one's own temptations to misconstrue language were necessary stages in the road towards philosophical understanding. Meanings had been bruised by the propaganda machines of the Great War, and then battered remorselessly by totalitarian regimes bent upon extending tyranny even to the very elements of discourse. The world and the word must be together remoulded: this was the dictatorial strategy that George Orwell's *Nineteen Eighty-Four* (1949), with its 'Newspeak', so vividly assailed. The perversities of 'Nazi-Deutsch', above all, added new dimensions to disorientation. In the hands of a Goebbels or a Reichbishop Müller, let alone of Hitler himself, the German language was daily devalued. No gloss is needed on the now infamous notice in the Sachsenhausen concentration camp which told of 'the one way to freedom' and named its milestones as 'obedience, diligence, uprightness, order, cleanliness, temperance, truthfulness, self-sacrifice, and love of the Fatherland'. When Heidegger's version of non-analytical philosophy was proving anything but a hindrance to obfuscation, and when (as Herbert Kohl notes) 'positivists were still talking of all non-verifiable statements being meaningless while Hitler pounded on table tops', it was Wittgenstein who embarked on a profound and necessary rescrutiny of language. Critics were free to find this unappealing; but, under all the circumstances, there was little defence for those among them who also found it totally pointless.

By describing philosophical activity as 'speech therapy' Wittgenstein suggested, however unwittingly, some resemblance between the way in which he and his fellow-Viennese Freud studied the workings of mind. Most particularly, what could not be expressed in words had to remain outside the domains of psychoanalysis and of Wittgensteinian philosophy alike. Both men concerned themselves with confusions in the different layers and modes of ordinary linguistic usage so as to illuminate the relationship between, on one hand, bewitchment or neurosis and, on the other, a general crisis of civilization and values. But, whereas Wittgenstein's almost eremitical posture delayed the diffusion of any pertinent message he might have, Freud had become by the 1930s a public figure prestigious both as therapist and as social commentator. Hostility from Catholic and Fascist circles – and, after a period of toleration, from Stalinist ones too – did not prevent the spread of his ideas through much of Europe and North America. Even the Vienna Circle's more measured warnings against the heavy reliance of Freudianism upon untestable propositions did little to contain the new fashion. Indeed, one of the main reasons for the speed with which psychoanalysis caught on was its own persistent claim not only to be scientific but also to constitute a science having a prompt therapeutic relevance to the strains of everyday life. In the case of Jung, the most influential of the schismatics, such therapy even involved open complementarity between science and mysticism. He postulated alongside the personal unconscious a collective one, embracing 'primordial images . . . older than historical man'. Religious experience, of almost any kind, was viewed as the chief means of accentuating an awareness of these. Jung believed that only through some more harmonious relationship with these 'archetypes' might modern man find spiritual and emotional security.

Despite internal schism the movement inaugurated by Freud had a general cultural impact sufficiently strong for many laymen to adopt the misconception – still common today – that psychoanalysis and psychology were virtually synonymous. In fact, the bulk of academic psychological study between the wars continued to rely, as before 1914, on more fundamentally experimentalist and physiological approaches. The most interesting development was growth in the Gestalt ('whole form') school, whose influence spread from its focal centre in Berlin under the leadership of Wolfgang Köhler, Kurt Koffka, and Max Wertheimer. It originated in engagement with philosophical rather than clinical problems, and became much concerned with controlled testing of processes in learning, memory and, above all, perception. Gestalt thinkers argued, contrary to associationist theories of sense impression, that the data of consciousness are grasped in organized and dynamic wholes. Each of these constitutes something more than the sum of its parts: just as, in the familiar musical analogy, melody is experienced as a unity beyond individual notes. Proponents aimed to establish systematic connections between such Gestalt qualities and underlying physiological processes. The pursuit was hindered not only by the formidable difficulties intrinsic to this task but also by the migration of the school's largely Jewish leaders from Nazi Germany towards an American culture distrustful of their necessarily anti-analytical stance in philosophy. Conversely, there was at much the same time some limited exportation from the United States to Europe of the 'behaviourism' initiated by John B. Watson, an approach to psychology more concordant with analytical method. The movement's influence, often merging with Pavlovian inspiration, was at the practical level particularly apparent in certain pioneering applications of psychology to industrial settings. Adherents, dismissive of any introspective probing of consciousness, concentrated on the externally observable and measurable aspects of behaviour. Especially when viewed in terms of stimulus and response, these facets seemed to constitute the field of study where physiological and psychological investigation came closest together. Behaviourists contended that only through this tight liaison could psychology become rigorously and objectively scientific.

In the natural sciences at large these were years of increasingly rapid advance and ever more dramatic technical innovation. Not surprisingly, they lacked any further intellectual revolution comparable to that which had erupted around 1900. Yet this had itself bequeathed to the next generation highly challenging tasks of assimilation and consolidation. Though many efforts were sadly hindered by ideological constraints, the overall response was vigorous. In biology the process of reconciling Darwinism and Mendelism was furthered by the employment of still more refined statistical techniques. These helped to produce a mathematical theory more satisfactorily relating the fluctuating frequency of particular genes within a population to the influence of natural selection. The practical benefits of applied genetics –

in the controlled breeding of plants and animals, rather than in the more sinister procedures of human eugenics envisaged by Hitler – became speedily obvious. No less clear was the relevance of more sophisticated biochemical study to improvements in clinical treatment as well as nutrition. The inter-war years have indeed been described by Stuart Hughes as 'a period of breathtaking innovation that brought more progress in medicine in a single generation than the profession had known in all previous human history'. Work on the identification of vitamins and on the development of insulin was, for example, already well established during the 1920s. In the early 1930s Gerhard Domagk discovered the anti-bacterial chemotherapeutic properties of the sulphonamides, and at the end of the same decade Howard Florey and Ernst Chain demonstrated the curative potential of the penicillin mould first cultivated by Alexander Fleming in 1928–9. This, the first of the antibiotics, was now exploited swiftly enough to be of huge value to servicemen engaged in the Second World War and to whole populations thereafter.

By 1945 the record of physics was intellectually perhaps more impressive still. Even so, after the Hiroshima explosion, it also looked socially the more problematic. The preceding three decades saw physicists preoccupied with exploring the implications of, and the relations between, those revolutionary theories of quanta, relativity, and atomic structure that had been pioneered at the opening of the century. Atomic physics, though still regarded in the 1920s as a somewhat bizarre choice of career for a bright young scientist, had undoubtedly come of age by the end of the period. In 1919 there occurred not only the observational confirmation of Einstein's general theory but also Rutherford's success with the first experimental transmutation of an element, achieved through an alpha-particle bombardment that converted a nitrogen nucleus into one of oxygen. Towards the mid-1920s certain drawbacks in Bohr's original model of electron movement, involving quantum leaps between orbits, were widely apparent, not least to the Dane himself. The revisions proposed almost simultaneously by Louis de Broglie in France, Erwin Schrödinger and Werner Heisenberg in Germany, and Paul Dirac in Britain all differed from each other rather more in form than in fundamentals. De Broglie and Schrödinger developed particularly the puzzling suggestion that electrons might have to be treated in some contexts as particles and in others as waves. Heisenberg and Dirac rejected even this degree of physical representation. The former, for instance, argued that the discussion of sub-atomic phenomena must be based upon the abstract language of differential equations rather than on any physical hypothesis such as orbits. However it was precisely, though solely, in such mathematical spheres that reconciliation between all these views became feasible.

The new quantum mechanics had generated, in essence, a system of equations capable of relating experimentally observable facts with their observable outcome. Yet the system, since it could not claim actually to delineate the mechanism underlying this relationship, had proved weaker on description than calculation. In consequence, it helped to encourage broadly conventionalist approaches towards the philosophy of science at large. These were further assisted both by Bohr's development of the 'complementarity' concept and, more famously still, by Heisenberg's exposition in 1927 of 'the principle of indeterminacy'. The latter was best exemplified by the suggestion that an observer might be able to specify either the position or the momentum of an electron, but never both together. Accurate measurement of one must lead necessarily to inaccurate measurement of the other, leaving an area of inherent uncertainty or tolerance calculable in terms of the quantum. This helped to explain the paradox of wave and particle: any reliable observation of the wave aspect of matter or radiation precluded reliable knowledge of the particle aspect, and vice versa. Heisenberg's principle also seemed to give elegant and connected expression to a number of features already noted in the pre-1914 development of physics. For instance, it confirmed that particle behaviour was predictable only in terms of aggregate probabilities. It suggested furthermore that there was a penumbra of uncertainty inevitably surrounding observation of cause and effect alike and that consequently the relationship between them must always remain blurred. Many physicists, though with Einstein dissenting, took this to mean that the very idea of causality had been finally overthrown. The indeterminacy principle was also commonly regarded as lending support to the view that science itself constituted an essentially operational interplay between observer and observed. As Heisenberg summarized this whole situation: 'Whenever we proceed from the known to the unknown we may hope to understand, but we may have to learn at the same time a new meaning of the word understand.'

The meaning now envisaged could do little to allay the serious problems of scientific disorientation already becoming apparent before 1914. Developments beween the wars did not restore faith in the capacity of science to provide some synthesis as satisfying as that so eagerly expected in the later nineteenth century. There was no precedent for the rapidity with which any view of the scientific landscape constantly shifted, as new areas of research were pioneered and relationships between older ones were replotted. None believed more firmly in the essential unity of nature than Einstein, and his was the most sustained and titanic effort to bring order out of intellectual revolution. 'In a lifetime', Jacob Bronowski says, 'Einstein joined light to time, and time to space; energy to matter, matter to space, and space to gravitation.' Even so, to the end, a unified field theory linking gravity and electricity, macrocosm and microcosm, eluded him. Moreover, there was not much he could do to alleviate the disquiet produced by a continuing retreat of scientific theory from the realm of everyday experience and ready intelligibility. It was not easy promptly to appreciate, for instance, that conflict between wave and particle could be resolved only in the realm of mathematics or, less adequately, of metaphor. Within such settings the Royal Society of London's motto, *nullius in verba*, assumed new poignancy. Bohr wrote to Heisenberg: 'When it comes to atoms, language can be used only as in poetry. The poet, too, is not nearly so concerned with describing facts as with creating images.' Strain upon words was clear also in ever larger and more esoteric technical vocabularies, which served sometimes to hinder communication between scientists and laymen and even to accentuate incomprehension across the sub-disciplines of science itself.

In these circumstances it was always likely that the natural tendency to popularize major concepts would operate very largely at the expense of accuracy. The manner in which Heisenberg's principle was often interpreted crudely as a straightforward vindication of free will against every form of determinism constituted one such case. It was however the idea of relativity, nurtured originally by Einstein's intellectual subtlety, which became most widely vulgarized. It cropped up as a catchword in every conceivable cultural context, with scant regard for the appropriateness or otherwise of the transfer. A civilization characterized by intellectual, social, and moral disorientation did not spurn to make 'relativity' pivotal in the explanation, or justification, of its condition. Sometimes the debased concept proved useful to those who, merely for the purposes of greater obfuscation, wished to exploit tidings that science was confirming human awareness of mystery in the universe. Even more commonly, relativity became devalued into synonymity with relativism; became remoulded to deny all objective truth; became distorted to assert that every value was expressive only of whim and convenience. Early on in this process Einstein protested wryly to *The Times*:

By an application of the theory of relativity to the taste of the reader, today in Germany I am called a German man of science and in England I am represented as a Swiss Jew. If I come to be regarded as a *bête noire* the description will be reversed, and I shall become a Swiss Jew for the German and a German for the English.

Such comment conveyed clearly enough Einstein's distaste for the distortion of his work; but it was also, in one area, tragically prophetic of his own personal fate. Shortly before Hitler's takeover he left Germany, never to return. By the end of 1933 he was established in Princeton.

Such instances of prudent withdrawal from the Nazi threat suggest one of the ways in which scientific and social considerations were becoming more than ever before entwined. On superficial acquaintance, the career of Popper might seem to do no more than illustrate this theme in just the same manner. Certainly he too was a refugee – one who left Austria shortly before the German annexation and who then taught in New Zealand and later, from 1946, in London. Yet Popper did manage also to illuminate the interaction of matters social and scientific in a more profound sense still. His chief task as a philosopher became that of forging links between certain views on the nature of scientific procedure and others about the intellectual foundations for social reform, with the overall aim of dispelling myths common to both spheres. The outcome was a series of seminal, though also particularly controversial, works within the tradition of critical positivism. Popper's *Logic of Scientific Discovery* (1934) contended that a theory should never be accorded more than provisional acceptance, and added that even this could not properly depend upon processes of inductive verification. It argued that any enlargement of provisional knowledge must begin with the conversion of hunches or other imaginative insights into hypotheses. Then, once the conditions for their falsification had been deductively established, these hypotheses must be tested through sustained search for negative instances. According to Popper it is, strictly, this falsification – rather than the verification favoured by his acquaintances from the Vienna Circle – which stands as the appropriate object of experimental and observational effort and which separates science itself from metaphysics. A distrust of ultimate explanations and an insistence upon the essentially self-critical nature of all properly rational endeavour were similarly central to such more explicitly social writings as *The Open Society and its Enemies* (two volumes, 1945) and *The Poverty of Historicism* (1957). In them Popper discussed the essentially authoritarian nature of social theories that were rooted in mistaken notions of certainty. The books also expressed, no less importantly, his own competing preference for projects of piecemeal social reformation. Only these would be fully concordant with the spirit of critical self-scrutiny embodied already in the principle of falsification.

The social bearings of scientific activity were, however, most straightforwardly apparent in the growing scale and complexity of research work itself. European laboratories – often in imitation of those now developing so quickly in the United States – were ceasing to be centres of small-scale, and often largely individual, endeavour. There was demand for more extensive buildings, for more sophisticated equipment, and for more highly trained and specialized staff to be employed in the increasingly typical setting of collaborative teamwork. In making adequate organizational response the more authoritarian regimes, whatever wounds they might otherwise inflict upon science, enjoyed certain advantages. For example, accommodation to the new requirements occurred remarkably successfully in the USSR, at least during the 1920s when scientific fields were still relatively free from ideological colonization. The overall European situation is described thus by Raymond Sontag:

Governments and industries began to subsidize research, sometimes in the universities, sometimes in their own laboratories. This seemed an inevitable trend, not only because of the demonstrated practical advantage of group research, but because the instruments provided to the scientists by technology, as they increased in power and delicacy, increased astronomically in cost.

Under conditions of close correlation between scientific or technological expertise and commercial well-being, such developments worked naturally in parallel with the wider tendency for the state to assume more control over the direction of economic policy. Additionally, and with increasing urgency during the 1930s, governments needed to concern themselves more deeply with the military implications of scientific discovery. Here, at least, any otherwise defensible generalization about the cosmopolitanism of science runs into complications. Above all, the latest advances in nuclear physics – whose history had been marked until now by a truly international exchange of ideas – were beginning to be cloaked in secrecy as the 1930s drew to a close.

As late as 1937 Rutherford, so much the grand old man in this sphere, was still declaring that the work of his Cambridge team on the artificial transmutation of atoms was devoid of practical significance. But very soon it became clear that, on the contrary, this line of research could give access to energies capable of annihilating a whole civilization. The major achievement of the years immediately preceding was to render the image of the atomic nucleus more complex. In particular, the existence of a whole series of fundamental particles – including those that would be known as neutrons, protons, and mesons – became apparent. The most critical breakthrough had come from Rutherford's own Cavendish Laboratory in 1932, when James Chadwick demonstrated the existence of a particle without electrical charge. This, the neutron, was soon recognized as the leading feature of nuclear structure. Its own non-electrical nature also made it the particle best fitted to penetrate into the positively charged nuclei of atoms. Chadwick's discovery therefore stimulated increasingly intensive work on neutron bombardment. Among leading students of the resulting atomic transformations were Frédéric Joliot and his wife Irène Curie in Paris and Leo Szilard, a Hungarian whose German academic career had been ended by the Nazi triumph, exiled in London. During 1934 Szilard filed a patent specification containing the term 'chain reaction', and two years later the Italian Fermi announced that his own neutron assault on certain heavy elements had produced a number of new ones more ponderous than any known hitherto.

The full significance of these developments was clarified only during 1938. Here the interpretative talents of Lise Meitner played a key role. She was an Austrian physicist who had been working on neutron bombardment with Otto Hahn and Fritz Strassmann in Berlin but who, being Jewish, had just taken the precaution of moving to Sweden. Meitner was the first properly to appreciate, from correspondence with Hahn, that during recent experiments their team had succeeded in splitting, and not merely probing or chipping, the nucleus of the uranium atom. Her insight suggested, furthermore, that even earlier experiments by Fermi and the Joliot-Curies must now be re-interpreted as having also achieved nuclear fission. Henceforth a race was on to obtain proper technical mastery over nuclear chain reactions – processes productive of sufficient neutrons to be self-sustaining. With the rate of reaction strictly controlled, any such process seemed likely to offer a major new source of practically available energy; left uncontrolled, the reaction could become an explosion on a scale never before contemplated. In such contexts a Nazi regime which, for instance, still scorned much of relativity theory as mere 'Jewish physics' put a severe handicap on its own ability successfully to utilize science.

Under all the circumstances – and considering, not least, just how much talent had fled elsewhere – it was perhaps surprising that the physicists left in Germany achieved as much as they did. Even so, in the competition of the early 1940s to develop nuclear power, they proved no match for those working against Nazism. The latter included not only American, Canadian, and British physicists but also colleagues exiled from many parts of the European mainland. Through their joint endeavour the great tradition of scientific cosmopolitanism was asserted anew.

On 2 August 1939, at the behest of Szilard and others, Einstein had signed the final draft of a letter to the President of the United States. Eventually submitted in October, this drew attention to recent work particularly by Joliot in France and by Fermi and Szilard himself in America. Einstein reported the imminent possibility of creating 'a nuclear chain reaction in a large mass of uranium, by which vast amounts of power and large quantities of new radium-like elements would be generated'. He outlined briefly the conceivable military implications, and alerted President Roosevelt to the significance of similar research in Berlin. The letter requested official enquiry into the desirability of protecting uranium sources, of establishing closer liaison between government and the scientists engaged in study of chain reaction, and of lending support to an accelerated experimental programme. It was evidence of the prestige now possessed both by Einstein and by the scientific community at large that President Roosevelt had no real choice other than to listen, and to act. Thus began the Manhattan Project. By December 1942, in a squash-court at the University of Chicago, an international team guided by Fermi and Szilard was operating a graphite-uranium 'pile'. Inside it occurred the first self-sustaining chain reaction giving controlled release of nuclear energy. By 1945 an atomic bomb, employing Fermi's man-made plutonium, was ready for testing and soon for use. Szilard was prominent among those who made unavailing pleas that it be 'demonstrated' to Japanese leaders in some way other than by being dropped on centres of population. But such efforts were unavailing. In the shadow cast by the Hiroshima and Nagasaki explosions whole societies had thereafter to live. Another great anxiety was thus added to the burdens of an already harassed world. The creation of the bomb undoubtedly constituted, in terms intellectual as well as technical, an outstanding landmark even among the many triumphs of twentieth-century physics. No less significantly, however, it had thrown further doubt upon any automatic concordance between the advance of mind and the betterment of civilization. Moreover, it had intensified moral problems about the uses of knowledge that scientists seemed even worse equipped than philosophers and theologians to solve.

Chapter 9

LITERATURE
AND THE ARTS

THE war which began in 1914 had been greeted by some as a cleansing purgatory. That which ended in 1918 was regarded more readily as a demoralizing hell. By the time of the armistice even those writers and artists who earlier had been prominent in advocating conflict as a healthy release from stifling convention needed to question the price finally paid. Hostilities had stimulated, at least initially, little writing of the first order. Such as did emerge – for instance, from Wilfred Owen in English poetry – was inspired far less by romantic heroics than by the horrific wastefulness of war. At a less exacting level of craftsmanship literary celebrations of struggle naturally survived, but even there on a diminishing scale. The German war-hero Ernst Jünger, author of *The Storm of Steel* (1920), was one novelist of wide appeal who persisted in treating battle as essentially the occasion for that heightened experience and deepened comradeship which made any sacrifice worthwhile. Yet, certainly for another decade or so, such sentiments were less typical in Europe at large than the numerous expressions of anti-war feeling. These were exemplified early on in such French works as Romain Rolland's *Above the Battlefield* (1915), a Nobel prize-winning essay advocating international pacifist solidarity amongst intellectuals, and Henri Barbusse's *Under Fire* (1916), a fast-selling novel about life in the trenches. The latter's naturalistic exposition of the manner in which war constituted a betrayal of ordinary men did not exhaust the market. Indeed, still more phenomenal sales were achieved by a novel from Germany that appeared only in 1929, perhaps the last year in which Europeans could cherish any easy hopes of secure peace. Within eighteen months Erich Maria Remarque's *All Quiet on the Western Front* had sold 2·5 million copies in twenty-five languages, and it was soon adapted for the cinema. Literary critics have dealt harshly with Barbusse and Remarque alike. Nonetheless authors like these, who gave dramatic form to revulsions so widely felt, retain real historical significance as representative and popular chroniclers of disillusionment.

For creative figures in every genre the holocaust was a searing experience. War had disrupted much work in progress, had driven many artists into hurried migration and painful exile, had severed numerous international liaisons, and had given renewed authority to xenophobic cultural judgements. Given peace and time, such matters could be remedied. But the battles had also eaten deep into the very ranks of the young and talented, and those losses were not reversible. The names of the French sculptor Henri Gaudier-Brzeska killed in 1915, of Franc Marc slain during the Verdun assault of 1916, and of Owen who fell in the very last days of fighting stand emblematic of many. These men of talent died while a new barbarism seemed to be triumphing over conventional patterns of culture as well as of politics. The conventions had certainly failed to stifle some vast collective atavistic urge; and there were even those who argued that the urge itself had thrived precisely because of need for a bracing conflict against suffocating orthodoxies. On these and other counts it is tempting simply to suppose that the war had inflicted upon European art and letters a trauma so profound as to have severed almost every nerve of connection with pre-war sensibility. Yet this would be to ignore the distinction between modulation, however sudden and dramatic, and sheer discontinuity. The dominant post-war mood was undeniably far more sombre than the preceding one. But that did not hinder its tendency to find imaginative expression largely along lines pioneered already between 1890 and 1914.

Such continuity is less surprising in the light of the abundant evidence for a major questioning of former certainties even before the war itself. By 1914 there was little unfamiliar either about feelings of disorientation or about iconoclastic experimentation as an appropriate means of cultural response. The real contribution of war was to accelerate a process by which the former became more profound and the latter more widely acceptable. It appeared ever more normal that confusion or alienation should be expressed through those modes of abstraction and introspection which typified much of the modernist movement in culture. The growing influence of expressive forms so resistant to the demands of easy public communication suggests how, in one sense, the war encouraged cultural fragmentation. The possibility of maintaining authoritative criteria of aesthetic judgement tended to be not so much doubted as denied – a stance speciously supported by the vulgar applications of relativity theory to artistic contexts. There thrived indeed throughout the 1920s a spirit of coterie that seemed to put general intelligibility at a greater discount than ever. Even so, there was a related sense in which the war actually helped to bring artist and audience closer together. For the conflict did more than works of imaginative and intellectual talent by themselves ever could to promote disillusionment with a civilization which had failed; and, just as significantly, it intensified awareness of the need to transcend that civilization's discredited modes of seeing and thinking. In this shocked atmosphere it was understandable that there should be an improved public reception for those cultural innovators whose critiques of exhausted values had been too simply underestimated before 1914. The origins and first achievements of modernism clearly belong to the pre-war years, but only in the 1920s did its full impact become everywhere apparent.

There was one particularly striking effort to repudiate the whole of pre-war culture, whether in traditional or avant-garde form. But this came from a circle which showed, at many turns, its own unavoidable debt to futurism and expressionism especially. It originated in 1916 among a cosmopolitan group of writers and artists meeting at the Cabaret Voltaire in neutral Zürich under the leadership of two poets, the Rumanian Tristan Tzara and the German Hugo Ball. After the armistice Paris became their focal point, and Berlin, Cologne, and Hanover their major outposts. Participants adopted the label 'Dada'. This echoed the babble which could convey, on principles hinted already by expressionism, child-like authenticity. Here was a nonsense word for a nonsense world. This awareness of absurdity – suggesting links with simultaneously developing existentialist insights – was clearest in the Dada attitude to four years of war: the slaughter had been senseless, and yet it was also in part the product of rationally planned and mechanized procedures. Culture, no less than political affairs, needed liberation from such discredited conventions of logic and order. As Tzara declared, 'The beginnings of Dada were not the beginnings of an art, but of a disgust.' For him the movement was essentially 'a state of mind', one alienated from the complacencies of received bourgeois culture. Dada was alert to the therapeutic benefits of the instinctual, the illogical, the uncompromisingly outrageous. It organized events which were, like those of the futurists, works of art – or, more specifically, 'anti-art' – in themselves: exhibitions staged in lavatories, festivals devised to end as brawls. The Dada revolt against the total European cultural inheritance was epitomized by Marcel Duchamp's reproduction of the Mona Lisa – with beard, moustache, and obscene caption. So too was the cult's overwhelmingly negative and often trivial quality.

By 1922 Dada was largely exhausted. Yet something of its capacity to startle survived, transmuted through the more resilient movement that the French poet André Breton launched in its wake. This 'surrealism' – a term that Apollinaire had coined recently for other purposes – was greatly inspired by Freudian ideas. Breton, who had received some psychiatric training, defined it as 'pure psychic automatism, through which one seeks to express verbally, in writing or in any other way, the true process of thought'. He hoped that the movement, by exploring such conditions as those of semi-consciousness, hypnosis, hallucination, and dementia, might convert 'those two seemingly contradictory states, dream and reality, into a sort of absolute reality, of surreality so to speak'. Writers and artists must be given more freedom to transmit the promptings of subconscious mind and vision. This would involve putting at discount every conventional conception of morality, rationality, and order. Thus the surrealist desire to expose and transcend the limitations inherent in hitherto accepted notions about the creative-psychic mechanism carried implications that were revolutionary in senses both aesthetic and social. The positive aspiration to raise reality close to the level of men's dreams led often to a broadly socialist, and sometimes even to a specifically Communist Party, allegiance. In distinctively literary terms one of surrealism's most provocative habits was the production of sentences, by automatic writing or other means, that were deemed to possess meaning even while violating logic or syntax. Critics might be confounded with the observation that a random flow of words was properly concordant with the elements of chance now recognized as fundamental to the physical structure of the universe itself. Even more notorious than such commentary on verbal crisis was the work of surrealist painters. They exhibited nightmarish pictures replete with unexpected juxtapositions, with incongruities perceptual and conceptual alike. Most notable were the Belgian René Magritte, for his fastidious fudging of the boundaries between reality and illusion, and the Catalan Salvador Dali, for an almost photographic naturalism dedicated to paranoiac images defiant of nature itself.

For European painting at large these were years of consolidation rather than of technical or intellectual innovation on the scale encountered earlier in the century. In particular, neither the cubist nor the more essentially non-representational idiom had yet achieved its full potential by 1914. The French capital remained pre-eminent as a centre of progressive art by attracting the galaxy of international talent known loosely as 'the School of Paris'. This kept largely within the bounds of representational technique, though not without such major distortions and exaggerations of vision as were indebted particularly to cubism. Picasso, already the most renowned artist in Paris, exhibited a stylistic restlessness which seemed timely in itself. Certainly he did not long maintain the tranquil form of neo-classicism adopted in the early post-war period, most apparent in his monumental studies of woman and child. During the 1920s this gave way to essays in savage deformation, many of which suggested surrealist inspiration. These culminated in the great *Guernica* of 1937, painted during the Spanish Civil War to commemorate the horror and violence perpetrated through the bombing of the Basque town. Meanwhile such public commentary seemed alien to the aspirations of his formerly close associate Braque. The latter remained more straightforwardly faithful to the cubism that they had together pioneered, and aimed, particularly in still-life and figure painting, to create pictorial harmonies valuable for their own sake alone.

Outstanding among others who sustained the cubist vision was Fernand Léger. He too was keener than Braque to accept some social function for art. The war had convinced him that his painting should convey images of contemporary mechanized existence. Léger generated a distinctively curvilinear cubism, with forms derived from the geometry of cylinder and wheel. It was employed, just as the futurists had used their own techniques, chiefly to represent the objects of modern mass production. This developed even to the point of repeatedly treating the human figure itself as a mere metallic automaton. His interpretation of man as machine helped Léger to become one of the most eloquent commentators on the twentieth-century city. Similarly, as George H. Hamilton says,

it was he, not Braque or Picasso . . . who saw the artistic significance of the artefacts of urban life, the bold designs and blatant colours of posters on hoardings and billboards, the movement of advertisements on passing vehicles, the spare tensile strength of electrical transmission towers, the ceaseless, changing lights in streets illuminated by flashing signs.

The resulting pictures revealed his training as an architectural draughtsman and his concern for design in every aspect of man's environment. To state in addition that Léger's work sometimes verges on the purely abstract is to indicate his great significance as a point of contact with developments in non-representational painting. For there too much closer links were being forged with architecture and design, principally by supporters of De Stijl in Holland and of the Bauhaus in Germany.

The Dutch movement, which flourished for over a decade, took its name from a monthly review launched by the painter and poet Theo van Doesburg in 1917. The opening issue claimed 'to state the logical principles of a style now ripening, based on the pure equivalence of the spirit of the age and of the means of expression'. These principles were deemed to derive from a universal geometrical and mechanical order expressing simplicity of line and form. De Stijl sought to introduce them not merely into art as narrowly conceived but also into every sphere of design bearing upon the man-made environment, whether concerned with buildings, furniture, utensils, typography, posters, packaging, or whatever. Henceforth the 'plastic reality' of man's surroundings must be treated as being within, not beyond, art. The movement had special relevance to the city, both as the paradigm of humanity's previous attempts at constructing artificial order and as the setting for the most acute strain and anxiety. It proposed to bring especially into the urban environment conceptions of harmony that would enhance the quality of art and life alike. De Stijl's intellectual claims were expressed best by Van Doesburg's fellow-Dutchman Piet Mondrian, working largely from Paris. It was he also who most successfully conveyed the movement's association with non-representational art, even to the extent of becoming Kandinsky's equal as an influence on the later evolution of such painting. Mondrian criticized cubism for not accepting the logical consequences of its own discoveries, for refusing 'to develop abstraction towards its ultimate goal, the expression of pure form'. His aim was not to derive pictorial facts from nature but to create pictorial structures that were real simply in themselves and without reference to nature. The 'neo-plasticism' of Mondrian came to rely predominantly on a carefully restricted vocabulary of vertical and horizontal lines, segmented often by primary colours and held in tension by their actual or potential points of rectangular intersection. This was the form of tonal and geometrical discipline which became most characteristic of De Stijl's lastingly influential approach to design in general.

The Bauhaus, though partly inspired by De Stijl, was essentially the creation of Gropius. He founded it at Weimar in 1919 to promote the principles of architecture and design which, both as practitioner and theorist, he had enunciated before the war. It moved in 1926 to Dessau, and in 1932 to Berlin where it was forced to close soon after the Nazis assumed power. It managed to combine, in Peter Gay's words, the qualities of 'a family, a school, a cooperative business, a missionary society'. Gropius declared his desire to establish a modernized conception of craftsmanship reconciling art and technology, 'to eliminate every drawback of the machine without sacrificing any of its real advantages'. In practice, the relationship within the Bauhaus between fine and applied arts was often uneasy. Yet Gropius did succeed in attracting as teachers such impressive figures as the Hungarian Laszlo Moholy-Nagy, outstanding for his experiments on the aesthetic properties of new materials like plexiglass, and the Swiss painter Paul Klee, who had been a member of the Blue Rider group. More striking still was the decision of Kandinsky himself, who had spent the years from 1914 to 1921 in his native Russia, to teach at the Bauhaus from 1922 onwards. There the theoretical foundations for non-representational composition as 'the sum of inwardly organized tensions' were further developed, particularly in the treatise entitled *Point and Line to Plane* (1926). Meanwhile processes of intellectualization were equally apparent in Kandinsky's own paintings, where the expression of abstraction tended now to be more strictly controlled in terms of geometrical ordering.

All these Bauhaus associates shared with Van Doesburg and Mondrian some belief in the socially redemptive qualities of an enhanced visual environment. Here again careful attention was paid to simplicity of design in everyday objects. But especially influential was Gropius's conception of architecture as, essentially, a rational interpretation of fundamental human needs. This was the idea behind both his pre-war scheme for Fagus and such later designs as that for the Dessau Bauhaus itself. It was also the view of his great Swiss contemporary Le Corbusier, who called the house 'a machine for living in' and whose *Towards an Architecture* (1923) constituted the outstanding manifesto of functionalist building. Similar sentiments were indeed prominent among the others, such as Ludwig Mies van der Rohe (Bauhaus Director from 1930 to 1933) and the Finn Alvar Aalto, who in the inter-war years consolidated and extended the tradition of Behrens and Lloyd Wright. Perhaps only in Holland and Germany did this have before

1945 much significance for the housing of ordinary Europeans. Even so, especially in regard to prestigious public buildings, it was already well on the way to justifying the label 'International Style'.

The post-war search for principles of order within abstract modes of expression – promoted by Mondrian, Kandinsky, and Gropius alike – was characteristic also of progressive music, another sphere in which many features of an earlier twentieth-century revolution required further refinement. Thus it was no mere coincidence that Stravinsky should have been a distinguished visiting lecturer at the Bauhaus. He and Schoenberg, the other leading figure in avant-garde composition, presented rather different interpretations of modernism. Yet they agreed about the desirability of imposing more formal controls upon the richly anarchical musical tendencies that they had inspired before 1914. Stravinsky, now resident in Paris, increasingly adopted a neo-classical style. This was simpler in form, more economical in use of instrumental resources, and less overtly emotional than the idiom of *The Rite of Spring*. He stayed aloof from atonality, engaged instead with what Eric Salzman terms 'the thorough renovation of classical form achieved through a new and creative rebuilding of tonal practice independent of the traditional functions which had first established those forms'. Stravinsky's influence – along with that of the eccentric Erik Satie – was most immediately apparent in a basically French group of composers known, over-simply, as 'The Six'. Its most notable figures were Darius Milhaud, Francis Poulenc, and the Swiss Arthur Honegger, and among its leading traits were borrowings from popular music and experiments in polytonality.

The largest step towards a regulated consolidation of atonal idiom was Schoenberg's introduction during the early 1920s of twelve-tone method. This laid down that a composition should be based on an initially random succession of all twelve notes in the chromatic scale, with each used only once. Thereafter the serial ordering of notes within this 'row' had to be strictly observed. Yet, as the composition developed, the row as a whole might be inverted, or used backwards, or subjected even to retrograde inversion, while also remaining constantly available for transposition across the scale. The row's movements thus became analogous to the rotations of a physical object in space. Among the first masterpieces of this dodecaphonic technique was the uncompleted opera *Moses and Aaron*, composed between 1930 and 1932 but not performed until the 1950s, in which Schoenberg revealed the continuation of his synaesthetic concerns by preparing text as well as music and by freely employing speech-song. Some considerable flexibility even within the basic twelve-tone regime was maintained both by him and, to still larger degree, by Berg. On the other hand, a greater strictness characterized the manner in which their associate Webern explored the possibilities of compositional control offered by the technique. These were demonstrated through pieces whose every sound was meticulously fashioned and whose every silence was an integrally positive element in performance. For some time the impact of this whole Viennese school upon the European avant-garde remained secondary to that of neo-classicism. But by the time of Schoenberg's death in 1951 things were changing, and even Stravinsky himself was beginning to compose on dodecaphonic principles. It would soon be widely claimed that, having laid the intellectual as well as the artistic foundations first for atonality and then for twelve-tone method, Schoenberg represented posthumously the most important influence in contemporary European composition.

None of this should obscure the fact that the music which most Europeans enjoyed in these inter-war years – usually under conditions revolutionized by wireless and by improved gramophone technique – was something rather different from what Stravinsky or Schoenberg might produce. Even still within the highbrow sphere, new works remained pre-

dominantly traditional in form: for instance, the persistence
of national inspiration behind composition was expressed
more typically by the basically romantic idiom of the Finn
Jean Sibelius than by Béla Bartók's atonal and dissonant
experiments with themes from his native Magyar folk song.
The outstanding feature of really popular musical culture was
the conquest of Europe during the 1920s by the jazz style that
had originated with the blacks of New Orleans and by the
lively dance forms derived from it. Paul Whiteman and Louis
Armstrong were prominent among those who became internationally renowned as a whole demotic culture flourished
around the bandleaders and virtuosi. Nor was the phenomenon without relevance to 'serious' music, as primly defined.
Just as Debussy had shown interest even before 1914, so now
Stravinsky and Milhaud were among the numerous composers attracted by the habits of rhythm, syncopation, and
extemporization displayed in jazz. Its idiom even provided
important stimulus to non-musical creativity. This tendency
was exemplified outstandingly in some of Mondrian's most
vibrant abstracts, associating the rhythms of jazz with those of
city life.

The second important sphere of American cultural influence
was the cinema. In these years the products of glamorous
Hollywood, or cheaper imitations, came to dominate film
programmes through much of Europe. They were shown in
what the British called, significantly, 'picture palaces' – one
kind of public building where functionalism made little progress against pretentiously ornamented décor. By the time
that soundtrack arrived in the late 1920s the cinema was
already a substantial factor in popular culture. It drew people
from their homes – almost as often as the wireless or the
gramophone held them in – by serving a predominantly
trivial diet of gangster movies, westerns, slapstick comedies,
and romantic spectaculars. Even so, particularly in Europe,
there were those determined to show that the film could

become a serious art form and a major medium for communicating ideas and values to a mass audience.

One of the first great screen classics, *The Cabinet of Dr Caligari* (1919) directed by Robert Wiene, aided expressionism's extension into Weimar Germany. In this film of distorted and vertiginous vistas the audience was challenged, as Paul Rotha observes, 'to take part and believe in the wild imaginings of a madman'. Moving pictures also augmented the resources available for use in surrealistic explorations of dream and fantasy, as shown by Dali's collaboration with Luis Buñuel on *Un Chien Andalou* (1929). Among pioneers of abstract film were Hans Richter, a German member of the Zürich Dada group and creator of *Rhythm 21* (1921), and Léger whose *Mechanical Ballet* dates from 1924. The cinema's potential for humour – especially at the expense of bullies human or mechanical – was realized through the work in France of René Clair, no less than through the American productions of the Englishman Charlie Chaplin. Under the leadership of John Grierson, with such studies as *Drifters* (1929), Britain made its best general contribution to the documentary form. The political relevance of cinema was most urgently clear to those who supervised cinematic activity in totalitarian settings. During the 1920s at any rate, Soviet notions of revolutionary art perhaps nurtured rather than stifled an exceptional pioneering spirit in this least traditional of genres. Pre-eminent among Russian film-makers were Vsevolod Pudovkin and Sergei Eisenstein, whose masterpiece *Battleship Potemkin* (1925) testified particularly to his opportune talent for handling crowd scenes. The treatment of mass emotion was also prominent in the work of Leni Riefenstahl, whose stature as the leading German director under Nazism derives from such documentary epics as those recording the 1934 Nuremberg Rally and the 1936 Berlin Olympics.

No other art form bore more signs of modernity than film.

Concordant with Einstein's physics or Proust's novels, it developed a special ability to express fluidity of temporal and spatial perspective. Flashback, montage, and many other editing techniques could give an unprecedentedly forceful impression of time itself as discontinuous and even reversible. The cinema was equally effective in capturing the sheer pace and bustle of modern life. Seasonable too was the fact that production for the commercial screen involved an apparatus of collective collaboration even more complex than in opera or stage drama. The application to filming of the term 'industry' seemed natural. Here, to an extent unmatched in any other creative genre, science and machinery were crucial – for shooting, chemically processing, editing, printing, and at last projecting the work of art. As Benjamin noted, 'In this case, mechanical reproduction is not, as with literature and painting, an external condition for mass distribution. Mechanical reproduction is inherent in the very technique of film production.' It also helped to make the commodity readily available to an immense public. In the darkened auditorium mass man was cheaply, contentedly, and anonymously accommodated.

The commercial cinema, with its largely casual and informal mode of attendance, appealed across boundaries of age, sex, and class to a degree unparalleled by any other form of public art. Even so, it constituted simply the most marked example of more general tendencies towards a lowering of social barriers in the arts and a blurring of traditional distinctions between élite and mass culture. These were phenomena that attracted attention particularly from literary critics, though without producing much agreement about their desirability. Marxist commentators were perhaps keenest to stress potential advantages in the changing situation. But, as indicated by the example of Benjamin and the Frankfurt School at large, even they might harbour anxiety about the destructive elements in mass taste. Perhaps the survival of these elements was not, after all, limited purely to conditions of capitalist domination. This was a problem to which Lukács also was sensitive, though his own efforts at commentary were frequently compromised by dependence on the Kremlin's cultural whims. Proponents of more classless culture were indeed little assisted after 1930 by the Soviet example, for Russia gave increasingly ample evidence of a withering of artistic freedoms and a capitulation to the most banal brand of social realism. For non-Marxist critics it was a rather more straightforward matter to highlight how the rise of the masses could endanger culture as valuably conceived. Benda's observations on treason by the intellectuals and those of Ortega on the triumph of 'the commonplace mind' are again relevant. In 1930 Frank Leavis, an exacting Cambridge critic committed to the sheer moral and social power of a great literature scrupulously read, crystallized similar sentiments by observing that, 'Civilization and culture are coming to be antithetical terms.'

Another who preached this kind of message from Britain was the American-born T. S. Eliot. For some the social conservatism of his cultural commentaries seemed at odds with the modernity of technique evident in his more widely known poetical writings. Yet there was no real inconsistency. Even as a stylistic innovator Eliot showed deep respect for classic verse forms. Moreover, the poetry which established his reputation shortly after the Great War concerned itself in large part with rarified spheres of private meaning scarcely communicable to the philistine mass. Thus it suggested, like the *Charmes* (1922) of Paul Valéry or the final *Sonnets to Orpheus* and *Duino Elegies* (1923) of Rilke, a continuation of symbolist hermeticism. There was nothing easily accessible about the polyglot allusions or the complex code of anthropological reference fundamental to a full reading of *The Waste Land*, which Eliot published in 1922 after revision by Ezra Pound. Nonetheless the poem was soon famous, being interpreted – sometimes too simply for the author's own taste – as an essentially public commentary on the moral and cultural aridity of the epoch. Its vignettes of contemporary London, a city where the anxious and disillusioned hordes were drifting from one empty pleasure to another, suggested a larger image of European civilization in disarray. Even the poem's own fragmented form seemed reflective of a world whose structure of traditional values had broken asunder. In Eliot's later work, especially after his conversion to Anglo-Catholicism in 1927, redemptive hopes came through more strongly. The intensified religious sensibility pervaded *Murder in the Cathedral* (1935), his first and most convincing piece of verse drama. It also helped him to reach the peak of his poetic achievement with *Four Quartets* (1935–44). But not even these perennially challenging meditations on time and eternity could match in broad impact the earlier and bleaker vision of *The Waste Land*.

Easy solutions were just as alien to the two authors who in this period most inventively used theatre as a medium for expressing ideas. Fame greeted the Sicilian playwright and novelist Luigi Pirandello only in his fifties, upon the appearance of *Six Characters in Search of an Author* (1921) and *Henry IV* (1922). Yet he had already epitomized their leading theme – the relativity of truth – in the very title of a piece first performed in 1917, *It Is So* (*If You Think So*). In such works Pirandello allowed full scope to ambiguities of relationship, including those between the actor and the character portrayed. More generally still, and quite independently of Freud, he probed into the unconscious and cast doubt on every accepted criterion of identity and sanity. The real-life ordeal of his own wife's withdrawal into madness acted upon him as a creative stimulus much more openly than it did upon Eliot in parallel circumstances. In the world of Pirandello no single reading of reality was authoritative. Like Chekhov, he explored both the comic and the tragic potential of men's failure even to communicate adequately their competing versions of factuality. Pirandello's plays were inhabited by characters, drawn particularly from the middle class, whose very desire to survive seemed dependent on the maintenance of their illusions. All were striving to preserve intact their own private systems of ordered experience, each at any given moment as consistent in its own internal logic as it was irreconcilable with the notions of reality cherished by others.

It was also in the early 1920s that Bertolt Brecht, a German poet and dramatist of a younger generation, began to make an impact on audiences. His first play *Baal* (1922), with its memorable dismissal of the world as 'God's excrement', was typical of his expressionistic and anarchical opening phase. But by the end of the decade his distaste for the bourgeois values on which he had been reared was assuming the more positively Marxist form maintained thereafter. This shift was apparent in two pieces presented with musical collaboration from Kurt Weill, *The Threepenny Opera* (1928) and *Mahagonny* (1929). The former enjoyed particularly remarkable success, though this stemmed more from its sheer entertainment value than from its social message about the parallels between capitalism and criminality. Such didactic concern was, however, central to the idea of epic theatre now elaborated by Brecht. He advocated the use of 'distancing effects', such as slogans draped across the stage or interpolated announcements about the artificiality of the action in progress. His aim was to block the audience's conditioned expectations about a need to empathize with the characters presented. This emotional involvement on the part of spectators could only weaken their capacity to judge the dramatist's essential message in an appropriately dispassionate manner. In Brecht's view, any suspension of disbelief about the reality of the stage action was misguided. A drama was not real to the extent that it managed some illusory imitation of the world outside but according to its measure of success in creating within the theatre an occasion for collective educational effort. This whole approach was capable of generating its own brand of tedious banality, especially when adopted by imitators. Indeed, without Brecht's implicit willingness eventually to accept some greater complementarity between his new distancing and the older empathy the impressive stature of his final works, written during exile from Nazi Germany, would have been diminished. Among these plays were *The Life of Galileo* and *Mother Courage and her Children*, both composed in the late 1930s, and *The Caucasian Chalk Circle* which was completed in 1945.

An even more vital force in the literary dissemination of ideas was the novel. Its potential as a vehicle for social criticism was still much exploited in the traditional realist mode. Typical was the English novelist John Galsworthy whose *Forsyte Saga* (1908-28), a tediously extended cycle about possessiveness in the moneyed class of his time, met with wide acclaim. A realism more engaged by psychological complexities characterized the novels of his less garrulous compatriot E. M. Forster, one of the Bloomsbury Group centring on Virginia Woolf. Among Forster's works was *A Passage to India* (1924), which documented the uneasy relations between Europeans and Asians as the certainties even of overseas empire began to fade. Others wrote in the context of more immediate imperial dissolution within Europe itself. Most notably, the Habsburg decay helped to inspire not only brilliant essays from the Viennese ironist Karl Kraus but also such minor masterpieces of the novel as *The Good Soldier Schweik*, by the Czech Jaroslav Hasek who died in 1923 before finishing it, and *The Confessions of Zeno* (1923) by Italo Svevo of Trieste.

Under the new German regime Heinrich Mann continued his indictment of the old, completing by 1925 the *Kaiserreich* trilogy which had begun with *Man of Straw*. The first great literary sensation of the Weimar Republic was provided however by Hermann Hesse, in self-imposed Swiss exile. Through *Demian* (1919) he too sought to champion a humane individualism alien to the militaristic ethos of the departed Reich. Like his later *Steppenwolf* (1927), it was an almost poetical creation which over-indulged a mysticism drawn from oriental and Jungian sources. But Hesse's works did reflect, in their concentration upon the hidden depths of inward experience, the kind of concerns now dominant in the most outstanding novels of all. From this point of view, a great landmark was the award to Proust of the 1919 Prix Goncourt. For there were some marked parallels between him and those who were now making the finest attempts at further enlarging the virtuosity of prose fiction, especially as a medium of ideas: Franz Kafka, James Joyce, D. H. Lawrence, André Gide, and Thomas Mann. Not least, like Proust, each had begun to write even before 1914 along lines which suggested that only through some transcendence of conventional realism could the rich diversity of mental states be adequately communicated. Another Frenchman, younger than any of these, might have sustained a claim to be added to their number – but Alain-Fournier did not survive the war to fulfil the extraordinary promise of his first, dreamlike, novel *Le Grand Meaulnes* (1913; translated as *The Lost Domain*).

Kafka was brought up in Prague, doubly distanced from its dominant Czech population both by his German language and his Jewish origins. Physical and psychological vulnerability soon became the hallmark of his whole existence. His early death in 1924, two years after Proust's, came when most of his writings were still unpublished. Only slowly did it become clear how accurately he had depicted the world of nightmare necessity, in such stories as *Metamorphosis* (written 1912; published 1915), *The Trial* (1914–15; published 1925), and *The Castle* (1921–22; published 1926). Each compelled the reader to share some painfully puzzling experience. In the first, the protagonist awakes convinced of his transformation into a huge insect; in the second, he comes to believe in 'his guilt upon charges equally obscure both to himself and to the remote judges; in the third, he confronts a secretive bureaucracy bent upon administering through paradox. In many of Kafka's tales one viewpoint only is vouchsafed. Thus there is often no way of knowing whether the experiences narrated in such limpid prose are to be taken as strictly accurate, or as calculated falsifications, or as genuine but distorted products of dementia or hallucination. As in *Dr Caligari* or the plays of Pirandello, reality and illusion merge. There are myriad questions, but none is ultimately answerable. Such stories reflected, in part, Kafka's own experience of the declining Habsburg Empire. But much more noteworthy is the manner – frequently very precise – in which his tales would prove prophetic of later developments. Soon millions of men were indeed being treated as vermin, distinctions between guilt and innocence wilfully confused, and new bureaucratic labyrinths constructed – under totalitarian regimes existing in a realm of quite indubitable reality. More broadly still, Kafka succeeded supremely in translating his own anxiety into terms that could be recognized anywhere as convincing images of mass man's collective loneliness and loss of bearings.

With Joyce a similar universalization of personal disquiet had its point of departure in the social alienation of the young artist. More specifically, it originated from a sense of suffocation amidst the bigotry and parochialism of the Dublin in which he was reared. Indeed his contribution to an Irish literary renaissance – whose other luminaries included the poet W. B. Yeats and the playwright Sean O'Casey – was to be made from Continental Europe, and from Paris especially. Yet, even in exile, Joyce's writings constituted a sustained evocation of his native city, its sights and smells and noises, its streets and bars and brothels, its people above all. His collection of short stories *Dubliners* came out in 1914. Over the next year there appeared in serial form *A Portrait of the Artist as a Young Man.* This semi-autobiographical work traced from childhood into student years the mental development of a hero increasingly at odds with an unsympathetic environment. Thereby it introduced the figure of Stephen Dedalus, who was to stand also at the heart of *Ulysses* published from Paris in 1922.

The action of this huge masterpiece spanned a mere twenty-four hours of Dublin life in the summer of 1904. It was narrated in forms of prose-poetry which displayed Joyce's accomplished blending of naturalistic detail and symbolist inspiration. To interior monologue particularly this gave new depth. Thus the book captured quite consummately those 'streams of consciousness' which would loom so large in twentieth-century literature thereafter. It managed, as John Gross says, 'to demonstrate as no previous novel had done the sheer density of the individual's mental life, the incredibly rapid succession and complexity of thoughts as they swarm past'. *Portrait of the Artist* had concentrated, like Proust's great cycle, on the flux within a single mind; but *Ulysses* penetrated deep into the mental universe of others in addition to Dedalus, expressing this variety through shifts of style and of narrative technique. Consequently it reinforced communication of a relativity in the perception of ideas and events, which Joyce himself deemed analogous with the condition of physics in the Einsteinian age. As if to emphasize the fluidity of time too, he worked on various sections of the book quite simultaneously; and the reader himself, like the casual explorer of a great city, loses little by moving randomly to and fro across it. The dreamlike quality present in the novel was something which Joyce sought thereafter to intensify. The reverie of an unidentified dreamer provided indeed the very substance of his final work *Finnegans Wake* (1939), in which literary conventions strained by *Ulysses* were now shattered altogether. It attempted to express through creative literature the very language of dreams which Freud had elucidated already in his own mode.

Here Joyce indulged the verbal ambiguities and confusions which psychoanalysis cherished also, not for being meaningless but for being so luxuriant in symbolic significance. Words as well as syntax were distorted, fractured, and spliced, in an orgy of punning, neologism, and onomatopoeia. The untranslatable text that resulted was simultaneously opulent and resistant to ready comprehension. It remained debatable whether 'Wake-language' amounted to a courageous reassertion of the vitality of words or was merely itself one of the most flagrant symptoms of contemporary verbal crisis.

The public tended to link Joyce merely with filth. For many years neither in Britain nor in the United States could an unexpurgated *Ulysses* be published. At the heart of the difficulty stood the author's insistence on writing with complete sexual and scatological candour, on articulating that which was readily thought but which politeness ordered to remain unspoken. The episode of Leopold Bloom's masturbation, and much else besides, constituted an attack upon conventional respectability in its most sensitive and vulnerable regions. Joyce was thus associated with the still early stages of, arguably, the profoundest shift in social attitude experienced by twentieth-century Europe: towards greater licence in the discussion, the practice, and even the exploitation of sexual activity. In the long run, creative literature's contribution to publicizing the case for a less restrictive approach was probably even more influential than that of Freudianism or of social science at large. The years before 1914 had witnessed pioneering efforts from writers such as Ibsen and Wedekind, and over the ensuing period Joyce was far from striving alone. Indeed, from the standpoint of straightforward social relevance at least, the works of Lawrence and Gide also seemed significant most of all for their further exploration of this topic.

Lawrence was less revolutionary than Joyce in technique. Yet he was just as keen to depict the complexities of consciousness and of what lay below. Among his abiding themes were the vitality of hitherto stifled subconscious forces and the multi-faceted creativity inherent within a sexuality purged of conventional hypocrisy. This miner's son found the advance of industrialization hideous and soul-destroying enough; but a more long-standing and still graver charge against European civilization was its perversion even of the sexual urge into something shameful and ugly. Lawrence's own defiant counter-proclamation of instinctual vitalism found expression in works such as *Sons and Lovers* (1913), *The Rainbow* (1915), and its sequel *Women in Love* (1920). The concern with a more authentic sexuality became most explicit in the notorious *Lady Chatterley's Lover*, a final though lesser novel first privately printed at Florence in 1928 and not openly available in Britain until the 1960s. Nothing so shrill came from Gide. Born into a wealthy bourgeois family, he was reared upon French Protestantism. Whereas Joyce resisted utterly any asphyxiation by Catholic orthodoxy, Gide lived with subtler tensions between his essentially puritanical upbringing and the 'immoralism' of his own homosexual desires. When the Great War ended he was nearly fifty, and already an established author in various genres. But only after 1918 did he become an indisputably central figure in the modern literature of introspection, exploiting fully the artistic analogues of Calvinist self-examination. In the Socratic dialogue on homo-sexuality entitled *Corydon* (1924) and especially in his auto-biography and journals Gide's self-revelation attained an impressive dignity. He wished to purge from sexual conven-tion all that was unnecessarily restrictive. Yet, like Lawrence, he desired this not essentially for its own sake but rather as a contribution to the renewal of civilization at large. This was apparent in *The Counterfeiters* (1926) – the only one of his stories that Gide himself termed a novel (*roman*) – which had as leading motif the contemporary hindrances to evolving humane and consistent criteria for authentic moral behaviour of any kind.

Not until the 1920s did the significance also of Thomas Mann begin to be fully appreciated. His major achievement of the inter-war period was *The Magic Mountain* (1924), a novel surpassed in subsequent literary influence only by *Ulysses* and the Proustian cycle. Here too the fluctuating perception of time's passage was a prominent topic, treated through Hans Castorp's seven-year sojourn in an alpine sanatorium. But, no less significantly, the hospital itself represented in microcosm the contemporary European condition. Behind the superficial tubercular bloom there ravaged inner decay. The soul of Castorp stood for that of a whole continent. And on these mountain slopes Mann staged a sustained confrontation between forces competing for dominion over both. His Settembrini embodied the Enlightenment's tradition of liberal rationalism; his Naphta, a remarkable amalgam of Jew and Jesuit, personified what Stuart Hughes calls 'the forces of terroristic authority unleashed by the war and its aftermath'; and his Peeperkorn symbolized the rising energies of naked charisma fortified by verbal necromancy. Settembrini's victory – if indeed it amounted to so much – was far from unequivocal. Yet it was evident enough that Mann's sympathies were moving closer to the kind of humane involvement which his brother Heinrich had been hitherto forced to champion against him.

This was confirmed by the appearance in 1930 of Thomas's *Mario and the Magician*, which could be interpreted only as a hostile reference to the hypnotic demagoguery currently rampant in Mussolini's Italy. The work met with Nazi denunciation, and after 1933 Mann had no future in Germany. Soon he became a major symbol of resistance to the new regime. His *Joseph* trilogy (1933–43) emerged eventually not only as the product of his own exile but also as a protest against the expulsions and persecutions inflicted on Jews, and others, in any age. With *Doctor Faustus* (1947) an earlier theme of artistic self-destruction re-emerged, but now it was incorpor-

ated into a vast allegorical treatment of disease in the language
and spirit of twentieth-century Germany. Only painfully, and
with residual ambivalence about the merits of liberal democracy, had Mann been converted to the view that some
reconciliation of creativity and political commitment was
inescapable. However, by thus gradually accepting that the
season of unpolitical man had passed, he was epitomizing the
most significant modulation in the cultural history of these
decades.

The advance of totalitarianism, added to the general
economic crisis, made inevitable a closer intermeshing of
politics and culture throughout Europe. According to Benjamin, the Fascist effort to render politics aesthetic must be
countered by a communist striving to politicize art. Those
who were not very sympathetic towards either camp tended
to see less crucial difference between these two aims than
he; but even they were having to treat as redundant luxury
any form of cultural activity that was not somehow engaged in
promoting political values, albeit of a more moderate kind.
Every country witnessed, among circles both literary and
artistic, a slackening of concern with further stylistic experimentation in modernist modes. Instead, emphasis was put
increasingly upon the transmission of readily comprehensible
messages. The most important outcome of this trend was an
intensified cult of social realism. Now, as in the preceding
century, it remained all too often artistically hollow. Yet, in
matters of propaganda, banality does not work necessarily
against efficacy. Their very combination was soon clearest in
Russia and Germany alike. Already from 1917–18 onwards
there had been in each of these countries a more than usually
close link between politics and the sphere of art and literature.
For some years – even if for rather different reasons across the
two cases – this association had proved capable of stimulating
genuine cultural achievements. But in the 1930s – and now for
quite similar reasons of totalitarian censorship – the Russian

and German politicization of culture became almost entirely philistine and destructive.

In the case of the USSR this transition was not the product of some sudden realization that the creative imagination must be made to serve political purposes. Of this the Soviet regime was, from the very first, convinced. The truly remarkable thing is that, for a time, the Communist Party allowed the revolutionary role of culture to be interpreted with some real measure of zestful flexibility. Thus the arts reflected much of that excitement with experimentation which originally characterized Soviet political life. There was nothing coincidental about the fact that the USSR enjoyed some of its first cultural triumphs in film, a genre as little compromised by the past as the regime itself. Lenin's Commissar for Education was Anatoly Lunacharsky, whose years of exile in the West had alerted him to the potentially revolutionary antagonism between modernist culture and bourgeois civilization. To the Russian avant-garde he gave unprecedented respectability. The regime's capacity for some good judgement in cultural matters is instanced by its appointment of Kandinsky to supervise picture-purchasing for the state museums. In the whole sphere of visual art there were, very early on at least, some particularly outstanding achievements. The Soviet authorities countenanced extensive experiment with abstract forms. These were essential, for example, to the efforts of Malevich's school towards expressing 'the supremacy 'of feeling in creative art'. Paintings inspired by such suprematism, as well as by futurism more generally still, bedecked Moscow on May Day 1918.

A drive greatly to intensify the sheer social usefulness of the abstract typified the no less remarkable 'constructivist' movement. Like De Stijl and the Bauhaus, this was concerned to exploit – in harmony – the functional, the symbolical, and the aesthetical properties of the machine. Its epitome was Vladimir Tatlin's plan, implemented only in model form, for a tower-monument to the Third International. This was due to stand over 400 metres high, and to contain within its tilted spiral structure various counter-revolving meeting-halls. By the early 1920s, however, the Russian proponents of abstraction were becoming sorely divided by differences over the proper balance to be kept in art between public and private purpose. Friction was growing, as cultural innovation and bureaucratic convenience continually collided. Soon neither Malevich, with his bias towards art as a personal statement, nor even Tatlin, with his stress on the practical application of creative activity, was finding it easy to work as he pleased. There was wisdom in Kandinsky's early return to Germany. At the Bauhaus the relations between pure and applied art remained problematic; but there they could be at least explored with a frankness now growing rarer in every sector of Russian imaginative endeavour.

By the early 1930s the bleak cultural future was clear. Lunacharsky had been replaced and the hunt against 'formalism' begun. Paramount henceforth would be orthodoxy of content – which meant a revived naturalism concerned with easily assimilable description of proletarian muscles, hard hammers, sharp sickles. The novelist Maksim Gorky returned home in 1931 to lend his prestige to the regime's new cultural policies. He assisted Stalin with the formulation of a programme for socialist realism in literature, and become first chairman of the Union of Soviet Writers which was dedicated to its implementation. Issues of literary judgement and of party discipline were thereafter totally entwined. Authors were encouraged to laud the USSR's technological achievements, but prohibited from recording the human tragedies that accompanied the drive for industrialization and collectivization. The great tradition of the Russian novel was swiftly imperilled. There was some ponderous merit in *The Quiet Don* (1928–40) whose attribution to the pen of Mikhail Sholokhov alone has been questioned. But even its volumes were readable only to the extent that the author or authors had managed some transcendence of socialist realism. More typically, what Trotsky called 'assembly-line romances' became the order of the day.

Accomplished poets fell silent: Boris Pasternak for nearly a decade after 1934, Vladimir Mayakovsky for ever. The motives behind the latter's suicide in 1930 remain obscure. Stalin gave posthumous praise, but it was already clear that his Russia retained no genuine place for the mixture of passionate lyricism and stylistic innovation which Mayakovsky had used to convey so powerfully the world-transforming enthusiasm of Lenin's epoch. The pioneering theatre of Vsevolod Meyerhold was forced to close, and the creative freedoms of Eisenstein and other film-makers were ever more tightly circumscribed. Musicians too felt the pressure of state-censorship. Assessment of the ideological purity of compositions was difficult but, from the official standpoint, indispensable. Here some scope for originality did remain, if only because the authorities had few consistent ideas about how to apply social realism to this sphere. Dmitri Shostakovich was the Soviet composer best able to produce work of quality even while navigating, far from smoothly, through the unpredictably shifting shoals of formalist error. His opera *Lady Macbeth of Mtsensk* (1934) was one notorious instance of shipwreck. Perhaps the visual arts, which during the early 1920s had promised so much, suffered the greatest loss of vitality. The progressive painting and design once welcomed as concordant with Soviet revolutionary aspirations were now exhibited, if at all, only for their cautionary value – as embodying what the official labels called 'the fundamental contradictions of bourgeois society'. Under Stalinism, as Lunacharsky soon conceded, 'the workers too have a right to colonnades'. No remark captures better the sense in which socialist realism degenerated into mere imitation of all that was most moribund about the bourgeois culture it aspired to discredit.

Into a curiously similar bathos Nazi culture also eventually descended. Yet the earliest post-war years had seen in Germany, as in Russia, immense creative enthusiasm. During the 1920s Berlin was second only to Paris as an intellectual and aesthetic focal point, and among provincial cities Munich especially nurtured talent. It seemed as if German writers and artists, for long much more remote from political influence than their French counterparts, might exert at last some real leverage upon the course of national development. In this sense, writes Peter Gay, 'Weimar culture was the creation of outsiders, propelled by history into the inside, for a short, dizzying, fragile moment.' Much of their excitement related to an atmosphere of sheer political experimentation, partially similar to that being experienced by the Russians. But in Germany the embroilment of culture with politics resulted from the regime's weakness rather than its strength. The Weimar authorities elicited much implacable hostility from extremes of Left and Right, and yet little heartfelt affection from supporters. The new regime was neither as freely able nor as fully keen as the Bolshevik one firmly to supervise cultural activities. Their substantial politicization remained likely, however, so long as the Republic itself was quite patently vulnerable to every shift of mood and argument. This was appreciated, from very diverse standpoints, by Spengler, Jünger, Hesse, Remarque, the Mann brothers, Gropius, Benjamin, Brecht, and a host of others. Their country's proximity to political, even moral, disintegration was perhaps most vividly suggested through the masterly satirical drawings and paintings of George Grosz, one of the founders of Berlin Dada. His close, though increasingly difficult, association with the Communist Party is emblematic of the fact that nowhere outside the USSR were there more links between the forces of political and cultural innovation than in Germany.

Artists and writers in the expressionist mode were especially keen to underline the relevance of their work to the task of socialist revolutionary transformation. But something of expressionism's pursuit of intense inner vision was germane also to the mystical irrationalist ethos of the Nazis and other right-wing extremists. This connection is exemplified in much of Gottfried Benn's poetry or, at a vastly less talented level, in Goebbels's otherwise unremarkable novel *Michael* (1929). Still, Hitler's accession to power meant prompt dismissal of expressionism along with every other manifestation of modernist culture. No time was lost in dignifying mere banality. Exiles sought to salvage something of worth in the German spirit, but within the Reich itself there flourished nothing besides the hollow-heroic and the sickly-sentimental. These were the weapons with which hated *Kulturbolschewismus* was opposed. Literature and art, music and film, were all made to evoke 'the spirit of the German homeland', to suggest the sacredness of Aryan blood and soil, to announce the imminent triumphs of the master-race. Benn was one of the few writers of any real worth to give creative support to the Nazi regime. Yet by 1938 even his work was banned. Meanwhile through every medium the authorities intensified their onslaught against language itself, until words became instrumental not in the clarification but only in the obfuscation of thought.

The process of ideological cleansing was applied during the late 1930s to Germany's museums as well, so that art might make its own purified contribution towards the new political order. Works by such painters as Van Gogh, Munch, Picasso, and Braque suffered in the purge. As in Russia, the official labels proliferated. They bedecked particularly the House of German Art at Munich, and the Exhibition of Degenerate Art which in 1937 was staged instructively nearby. Within the ambit of the latter might fall anything that deviated from the pedantic naturalism through which the regime expected its images of strength and joy to be projected. Nothing appealed more to Hitler's own taste than the sexually-obsessed realism with which Adolf Ziegler, president of the Reich Chamber of Art, portrayed one naked Germanic form after another. Ultimately, paintings of Nazi-Aryan muscle and paintings of Soviet-proletarian muscle tended to look, in many respects, very similar. And in both the German and the Russian case they stood a good chance of being consigned to some new public building notable only for the tasteless monumentality with which it aped classical form.

Heroic pomposity was also a prominent theme in the official culture of Fascist Italy. But that regime never matched in thoroughness the contemporary Nazi or Soviet standardization of literary and artistic activity. For example, though neo-classical monuments certainly proliferated in the capital, there was also soon in Rome a central railway station impressively executed according to advanced modernist principles of architecture. Similarly, after his brief phase of compromise with Fascism, Croce was allowed to survive inside Italy as spokesman of a kind of criticism which would have been promptly silenced under Hitler or Stalin. In much the same way the subtly hostile Alberto Moravia too was partially tolerated. His novels *The Time of Indifference* (1929), *The Wheel of Fortune* (1935), and *The Fancy Dress Party* (1941; censored personally by Mussolini) caused official discomfiture. Yet the authorities might refrain from totally silencing such a writer if he was able like Moravia to illuminate the tawdriness of traditional bourgeois values. As Raymond Sontag notes, 'Italy was ruled by the middle class under Mussolini no less than earlier; but Mussolini never lost his youthful contempt for the middle class, and he was indulgent towards artists who shared his view.' This was not the least of the reasons behind the support given to the *Duce* by Pirandello, one of the most enthusiastic champions of the Ethiopian War. An even more remarkable believer in Mussolini's ability to restore something of ancient Roman glory was the American-

born Pound, who did much of his best poetical work on the
epic *Cantos* (published over some forty years from 1925 onwards) while living in Fascist Italy. Any attraction that the
regime exerted upon intellectuals was likely to be linked
somehow with the elements of sheer flexibility characterizing
its proposed alternatives to the exploded values of the recent
past. Marinetti and the other futurist supporters of Fascism
were more concerned with dramatic means than defined ends;
the movement's very lack of precise objectives had helped
Croce to underestimate at first its harmful potential; and the
same vagueness encouraged Pound's attempts to make it a
vehicle for his own idiosyncratic vision of economic reform.
Mussolini's rhetoric involved, positively, little commitment
to anything constant or definite. On the other hand, negatively, its denunciations were quite fully and precisely concordant
with a widespread mood of intellectual discontent.

Even in countries still free from dictatorial control there
was now increasing pressure for clearer social commitment by
writers and artists. Most of the resulting engagement did turn
out to be anti-Fascist in tone. But this is not to say that the
minority which offered sympathy, or even fuller support, to
Fascism was derisory either in number or in quality. No other
leading writer in English quite matched Pound's half-deranged
enthusiasm; but Yeats, Eliot, and Lawrence were prominent
among those who at times assessed quite favourably Fascism's
potential contribution to cultural and social regeneration. In
the French ranks much the same was true of the novelist and
dramatist Henry de Montherlant, and deeper still went the
involvement of Maurras and the Action Française circle
especially during the Vichy years. Such figures genuinely felt
that traditional liberalism had been largely discredited; and
they found even less palatable what they took to be the universal leftist dismissal of creative activity as merely epiphe-
nomenal. Drawn towards the Right, they tended to feel the
allure of Mussolini's movement more strongly than that of

Hitler's. Nazism came relatively late to power, and its cultural vulgarity was more difficult to conceal. Moreover, the greater rigidity of Hitlerian ideology rendered it a harder product to export and adapt than an Italian Fascism which made a fundamental virtue out of doctrine's dynamic flexibility. Until the mid-1930s or so, Mussolini offered a suggestive starting-point – or even something more – for literary and artistic figures who were variously at odds with society as currently democratized. What these usually had in common was the desire to protect culture from mass debasement, to reconcile creative spontaneity with the properly hierarchical requirements of authority and order in art and politics alike. Some of them even believed that in a broadly Fascist future the artist or intellectual might come into his own as a guardian of ultimate values. Of this most were sooner or later disabused, as Fascist organizations revealed ever more starkly their fundamental affinity with political and cultural mediocrity.

The counter-mobilization of cultural resources against Fascism was evident soon in Britain and, above all, in France. Many of the relevant writers showed that outside Stalinist Russia an allegiance to communism – or, perhaps more often, some relatively transient sympathy with it – could stimulate work valuable in terms both aesthetic and political. Much of the best verse from a new generation of English poets, including Wystan Auden and Stephen Spender, was prompted by a phase of infatuation with Marxist ideas. These came to exert a more durable influence on the French poetry of Louis Aragon and Paul Éluard, both of whom allowed a greater social realism to supplant their earlier surrealistic style. The virtues of Marxism were propounded also in Aragon's prose fiction. Thus he typified also those who were injecting into the novel altogether stronger elements of social and ideological commitment. François Mauriac was pre-eminent among authors who linked such engagement to the more general intellectual revival of French Catholicism, aided by the Papal condemnation of the Action Française in 1926. A number of other Frenchmen contributed in the genre of the *roman-fleuve*. Here such sustained essays as Roger Martin du Gard's *The Thibaults* (seven volumes, 1922-40) and Jules Romains's *Men of Good Will* (twenty-seven volumes, 1932-47) expressed, broadly within the social-realist idiom, views which came to characterize the more moderate aspects of the Popular Front mentality.

The roles of novelist and man of action seemed most completely harmonized in the career of André Malraux. Indeed, to him at least, the search for an heroic style in politics was ultimately more important than any precise ideological allegiance. Through most of the 1930s he was intimately associated with the communist movement. Even while eschewing actual membership of the Party or indeed any deep philosophical allegiance to Marxism as such, Malraux was bent on living out as well as describing the contemporary condition of alienation. For *The Conquerors* (1928) and *The Human Condition* (1933), which both dealt with the rising tide of revolution in China, he could draw upon first-hand experience. Similarly, his involvement with the Republican forces during the Spanish Civil War provided material for *Days of Hope* (1937). But by 1939, when the Nazi-Soviet Pact was signed, he felt that gnawing doubts about the wisdom of accepting Stalin as the most crucial bulwark against total Fascist triumph had been confirmed. Three years before, Gide – the most eminent of all French literary fellow-travellers in the early 1930s – had returned from a Russian visit more disheartened than uplifted. An Italian counterpart was Ignazio Silone, organizer of the communist underground resistance to Mussolini, who as early as 1930 had been driven by disgust with the Stalinist contempt for freedom into leaving the Party and adopting an independent socialist stance. Henceforth he wrote from exile novels, such as *Bread and Wine* (1937), which were enthusiastically greeted abroad less strictly for their literary merit than for their vivid condemnation of bureaucratic tyranny whether communist or Fascist. These figures were representative of many in their generation – idealists who had looked readily to Soviet Russia for a re-invigorated sense of moral purpose and whose hopes had been sooner or later dashed. Of all novels, it was Koestler's *Darkness at Noon* which most vividly conveyed an author's personal experience of this disillusionment.

Once the conflict in Spain had begun the evasion of some kind of political commitment became rare indeed. Upon that country's own cultural life, so enriched since the turn of the century, the Civil War inflicted deep wounds. The slaughter would evoke the *Guernica* masterpiece, but after Franco's victory the inclination of Picasso and others to reside abroad was massively reinforced; Ortega would withdraw from his homeland, once it was evident that the Republicans' atrocities rivalled those of the enemy; Unamuno, as Rector of Sala-manca University, would spend the last months of his life striving bravely to halt the erosion of intellectual freedoms within Nationalist-held territory; and the Republican poet and dramatist Federico García Lorca would be merely the most renowned of many talented figures summarily executed or killed in action. Foreign writers and artists also felt greatly involved, and many came to the battle-zones as participants or observers. No novel inspired by the struggle was more widely read than the American Ernest Hemingway's *For Whom the Bell Tolls* (1940). Of lasting documentary value were such accounts as the Austrian Franz Borkenau's *The Spanish Cockpit* (1937) and Orwell's belatedly appreciated *Homage to Catalonia* (1938). Another notable report, especially on Nation-alist barbarity in Majorca, was *Great Cemeteries Beneath the Moon* (1937) by the French essayist and novelist Georges Bernanos. The war caused him to abandon his hitherto broadly Maurrassian and pro-Fascist position. Now he became one of the Catholic writers who, defying most of their co-religionists in a deeply divided France, joined Mauriac and Maritain in condemning the Nationalist cause.

As Spender has recalled, the Civil War seemed to offer every European an experience comparable to the revolutions of 1848–9 – a significant opportunity to stand and be counted. In countries where freedom to choose and to express choice still survived, the great bulk of support from intellectuals went to the Republic. But it was a notable feature of the Spanish hostilities, as of the European revolutions ninety years before, that they complicated some issues even while clarifying others. This was particularly true on the Left, where experience of a real and bloody struggle tended to strip away the more naïve idealism which had dominated the earlier 1930s. Here many were alerted, above all, to the manner in which a popular indigenous revolution had been cynically exploited for Stalinist ends. With Koestler – observing, for instance, the fabrications introduced into his newspaper dispatches by Comintern officials on the spot – the Spanish visit became the occasion for thorough rethinking. Amidst the praise for Republican heroism which suffuses *Days of Hope* there began to emerge a similar disillusionment on the part of Malraux. To the English author of *Homage to Catalonia* the necessity for rescrutiny was already clearer still.

Orwell, though accused of succumbing to reactionary attitudes, remained in essence a socialist. The Spanish experience merely led him to contend more strongly than before that, in the last resort, individual conscience must take precedence over the dictates of any party organization. Around the end of the Second World War it was quite reasonable for someone so repelled by every brand of authoritarianism to direct his most urgent warnings not against the defeated dictatorships but against the comparable potential for tyranny within communism. Orwell's hostility towards the latter was particularly apparent in two novels, which were successful principally because of the timeliness of their political message.

Animal Farm (1945) had as leading theme the perversion of the Russian Revolution's initial idealism. In this allegorical fantasy pigs could suffer no worse fate than that of becoming indistinguishable from greedy humans. Ideas for *Nineteen Eighty-Four* – published in 1949, a year before the author's death – had been shaped while Orwell was working on war propaganda at the BBC. In so far as it suggested how scientific and technological advances might be made to assist in enslaving rather than in liberating men, the novel contained a vision of future society not unlike that already presented by Aldous Huxley's *Brave New World* (1932). Yet Orwell's image of dystopia was remarkable even more for its representation of the manner in which the totalitarian aim of annihilating individual conscience might be helped, subtly yet powerfully, by distortion of language. Under the dominion of Big Brother and of 'Newspeak' the double-talk of Sachsenhausen has become universalized: everywhere war is peace and ignorance equals strength, propaganda is truth and freedom equals slavery. This was scarcely the 'ideal logical language' which Russell had envisaged: but it was not, on that account, any less ideally concordant with the logic of totalitarianism at least. 'In the end,' declares one of Orwell's characters, 'we shall make thoughtcrime literally impossible, because there will be no words in which to express it.' Contemporaries saw promptly enough that *Nineteen Eighty-Four* constituted a further indictment of Stalinist Russia. What many – even on the Left – failed to grasp was the extent to which the book also condemned mass capitalist societies, for their own drift towards unthinking conformism.

Similarly sombre was the whole mood in which this period of European cultural history drew to a close. The increasingly horrific circumstances which had driven so many intellectuals and artists into some potentially fulfilling engagement with social issues left no room for comfort or complacency. Spengler did not seem to have been in all respects a false prophet. In an unfinished novel, *The Man Without Qualities* (1930–43), the Austrian Robert Musil communicated feelings about cultural collapse that were broadly typical of an entire literature of social decadence. From the early 1930s onward images of disease, decay, and putrefaction exerted an ever stronger hold. No one gave them more startling expression than Louis-Ferdinand Céline, through novels and anti-semitic diatribes whose language violated every received idea concerning French literary idiom and yet brought even to visceral obscenity a touch of genius. It was under the title *Nausea* that in 1938 his more cerebral fellow-countryman Sartre published a first novel, dwelling on the negative and morbid aspects of existentialist insight. But perhaps the most illuminating statement of such widespread pessimism came from a writer who would not, like Sartre, live to promote some intellectual reconstruction in the era after the Second World War. In 1945 the dying H. G. Wells published a small book with the altogether significant title *Mind at the End of Its Tether*. These ruminations upon 'a jaded world devoid of recuperative power' possessed a special poignancy. Over many years their author had impressed millions with his passionate hopes for the perfectibility of mankind through the advance of science and reason. Now Wells confessed that he had been 'clever, but not clever enough'. He was not the only figure nurtured in the great age of buoyant positivism for whom that made a perfect epitaph.

PART THREE

Since 1945

Chapter 10

IDEAS AND SOCIETY
IN POST-WAR EUROPE

EUROPE emerged from the Second World War deeply divided. It was unavoidable, following the defeat of Hitler, that the relations between the USSR and its Western allies should have become more strained. Less predictable, however, was the sheer intensity of misunderstanding and acrimony which characterized the first years of the Cold War. By the end of the 1940s 'People's Democracy' had been established nearly everywhere in Eastern Europe. Its rapid advance had much less to do with spontaneous revolutionary feeling than with the Red Army's presence or proximity. Stalin was certainly eager to exploit every opportunity of spreading Soviet authority; but, to a degree inadequately appreciated elsewhere, his colonizing efforts were conditioned also by real anxieties about Russia's own security, particularly while the United States maintained large forces in Europe and had sole possession of the atomic bomb. Whatever the balance here between aggressive and defensive intent, the enlarged sphere of Soviet dominance was soon a basic political fact. As early as March 1946 Winston Churchill declared: 'From Stettin in the Baltic to Trieste in the Adriatic, an iron curtain has descended across the Continent. Behind that line lie all the capitals of the ancient states of Central and Eastern Europe.' This sense of confrontation was not a matter of geopolitical or narrowly ideological division alone. It expressed also an accentuated divergence between Eastern and Western Europe in every sphere of intellectual and cultural concern. The mere names of Auschwitz, Dresden, or Hiroshima now encapsulated horrors from the recent past that none could evade. Western ideas about how to avoid their repetition were bedevilled by a continuing dearth of firm reference-points. Farther east, on the other hand, the first post-war years saw Stalin intensifying his drive to impose a monolithic system of values that could generate standardized responses to every crisis of individual or collective existence.

In the Soviet bloc the development of ideas over the whole period since 1945 has been greatly affected by the Kremlin's fluctuating assessment of how much freedom of expression it is prudent to tolerate. The nature of the alliance against Hitler had raised some expectations that henceforth the USSR might sustain a more relaxed and less isolationist policy regarding communication with the West. Yet the fact that great numbers of Russian soldiers had been in contact, however temporary and imperfect, with alien influence actually made Stalin all the more determined to minimize such exposure during peacetime. This further tightening of state control over all aspects of intellectual and cultural life was supervised by Andrei Zhdanov, until his death in 1948. Under his direction the scholar or creative artist in search of audience and livelihood was ever more strictly compelled to operate within an appropriate craft organization policed by the party bureaucracy. Officialdom dictated to painters not merely the style but often also the subject of their work; the products of the Russian cinema declined in quantity and quality alike; even a composer of Shostakovich's eminence could be reprimanded for writing music insufficiently concordant with mass taste. Genetics and linguistics were prominent among the academic subjects about which Stalin himself professed to have something authoritative to say. He claimed to be a better economist than Yevgeny Varga, whom he denounced publicly for daring to suggest that the West was capable of rapid and sustained material recovery. The continuing condemnation of Einstein and Freud exemplified the sense in which the regime was, despite its theoretical internationalism, fundamentally xenophobic – and often quite specifically anti-semitic. Stalin certainly proved himself the enemy of cultural diversity both amongst the non-Russian populations within the USSR itself and amongst the various nationalities of the new 'satellite' states beyond.

Recovery from the nadir of 'the Zhdanov years' was slow and halting. Stalin's death in 1953, together with Nikita Khrushchev's subsequent exposure of the former leadership, inspired renewed hopes about liberalization that were only very partially fulfilled. There developed a pattern of bewildering alternation between freeze and thaw. For example, the widespread dissent which surfaced in Hungary and Poland during 1956 and in Czechoslovakia during 1967–8 was sternly suppressed; yet, at other times, the Kremlin behaved as if it believed that such crises might be better averted through some carefully calculated relaxation of intellectual censorship. The shadowy zones between the officially approved and the officially condemned were constantly shifting. Their exploration offered the best chance of self-fulfilment to those who wished to assert some real intellectual autonomy while also preserving a reasonable measure of personal security. Success here was often dependent upon skill at camouflaging independent comment beneath a web of respectably orthodox phrases and allusions. Among the Russian authors who proved too outspoken were Andrei Sinyavsky and Yuli Daniel, arrested in 1965 and condemned to a labour-camp. Their talents were not of the highest order, yet there was no doubt either about their courage or about the West's keenness to exploit it. Another prominent protester had been the poet Yevgeny Yevtushenko, but by the 1970s his differences with the regime seemed to have narrowed to the point where he was content to serve it as a peripatetic cultural ambassador. The rise of any Russian artist or intellectual towards international eminence frequently caused the authorities more embarrassment than joy. Such fame lent to figures of this kind some qualified immunity. Thus the relative freedom of Andrei Sakharov to protest against the USSR's continuing violation of basic human rights derived from his global reputation as a physicist. The Soviet government viewed his 1975 Nobel Peace Prize as part of some sustained Western effort to exaggerate the worth of Russian dissidents.

There were, from the Kremlin's viewpoint, outstandingly painful precedents in the cases of Pasternak and Alexander Solzhenitsyn. It was as novelist rather than as poet that the former won renown abroad and disgrace at home shortly before his death in 1960. *Doctor Zhivago*, denied Russian publication, appeared first in Italy during 1957. Only with the English-language edition of 1958, however, did the novel make really sensational impact. By the end of the year Pasternak had been awarded the Nobel Prize for Literature. His government forced him to decline the honour, and it expelled him from the Writers' Union. *Dr Zhivago* did not condemn utterly either Marxism or the Russian Revolution. The book was all the more subtly dangerous for suggesting, rather, their simple inadequacy. Pasternak hinted at attitudes towards life which were more diverse and more spiritual than Marxism alone could inspire; and he criticized the particular transformation that had occurred in Russia over the past four decades by contrasting this with a more individualistic vision of what, ideally, revolution should mean. Solzhenitsyn too was concerned with highlighting perversions of the revolutionary process. His own imprisonment at the end of the war, on a Kafkaesque false charge, provided material for his first important work, *One Day in the Life of Ivan Denisovich* (1962). The authorities allowed Russian publication because they saw the story as a condemnation simply of the Stalinist epoch. Nonetheless it became increasingly evident, through such novels as *The First Circle* (1968) and *Cancer Ward* (1968), that Solzhenitsyn was mounting a much wider indictment of the Soviet system. *August 1914* (1971), the opening volume of the work which he himself rated most highly, and *The Gulag Archipelago* (three volumes, 1974–6), a documentary study of repression in and beyond the time of Stalin, went unpublished in the USSR. Only when Solzhenitsyn came to the West as an exile in 1974 was he free to accept the Nobel Literature Prize offered four years earlier. It remained to be seen whether, in a new environment less threatening than the old, he could maintain the creative impetus which had brought him world-wide fame.

No critic of comparable eminence emerged elsewhere in the eastern bloc. There was, all the same, considerable dissentient feeling within the satellite countries at large. Here even those most sympathetic to communism itself might have severe reservations about the Kremlin's constant tendency to interpret the creed mainly according to Russian convenience. Intellectuals were prominent whenever there surfaced nationalist, or other, resentment. To the extent that they did accept dictation from Moscow they risked being isolated from ideas and debates upon the wider European stage. This was nowhere more tragically apparent than within the new German Democratic Republic, whose inhabitants had been tossed almost directly from Nazi to Soviet dictatorship. They lived henceforth in perhaps the most tightly organized police-state of the Russian bloc. Under these conditions the many radicals from the Weimar years who did indeed settle in East Germany stood no chance of recapturing the cultural excitement of the pre-Nazi epoch. The only figure of outstanding stature was Brecht, who was now concerned mainly with directing the Berliner Ensemble. Such was his significance in developing this theatrical company as a cultural showpiece that the regime tolerated some degree of Brechtian irony even against itself. By the 1970s strategies of straightforward repression were proving, throughout most of Eastern Europe, ever more difficult to sustain. Even in Russia itself, the authorities were

troubled by the tide of *samizdat* – the illegally produced pam-
phlets, magazines, and other documents of dissent. Westerners
were increasingly insistent that the sincerity of Kremlin rhetoric about détente might be gauged according to the Soviet
Union's willingness to allow, in practice, a much greater
measure of cultural, intellectual, and – perhaps above all –
personal exchange. Under contemporary conditions of communication, Russia's leaders could scarcely resist this pressure
completely. But, equally, they were understandably anxious
about how such wider contact might erode their own
authority both at home and throughout the Soviet bloc.

Although important ideological differences between Eastern
and Western Europe persisted, it seemed from the mid-1960s
onward that the most acute phase of the Cold War was over.
The peril of sudden mass destruction remained, and indeed
grew as more states acquired nuclear weapons; yet men
appeared to have made such mental adaptation to the threat
as to suffer rather less of the urgent anguish which had been
so evident a generation before. China's emergence as a world
power, proclaiming a brand of communism increasingly
remote from the Kremlin's, helped to make the USSR less
aggressive in dealing with the countries of Western Europe.
Meanwhile most of these had been developing variants on the
theme of 'the welfare state'. Thereby they had come to accept
a much greater role for government in economic planning and
in the universally avowed pursuit of social justice as a whole.
The Russian leaders seemed to have acknowledged that under
these circumstances the Western socialist parties had lapsed
still further into pragmatic reformism. Even more crucially,
the Kremlin had also to concede implicitly that such major
communist movements as the French and the Italian had lost
much of their distinctively revolutionary impetus. Memory
of events in Budapest during 1956 and in Prague twelve years
later did nothing to help the morale of would-be sympathizers with Russia. Thus it was realistic to recognize

throughout Western Europe the waning of any prospects for imminent revolution, on the Soviet model at any rate. None of these factors was deemed to render redundant the ultimate communist objective attainable through class struggle. Yet all of them contributed towards an increasing Russian willingness to talk, at this epoch of historical development, principally in terms of 'co-existence'.

One of the most delicate areas of dialogue concerned the meaning of Marxism itself. After the war intellectuals in non-communist Europe showed a sustained, even growing, desire to benefit from its insights. But this necessitated some identification of the perversions suffered by Marxism, especially after its founder's death. There was criticism, above all, of the particular way in which it had been adapted to Russian circumstance. Conversely, more attention was also given to the doctrine's first emergence within a predominantly Western social and philosophical context. Significant here was the increasing availability of Marx's early writings. These made clearer his deeply moralistic and humanitarian qualities, and his connection with Hegelianism. Their emphasis was not upon deterministic economic analysis as such, but rather upon capitalism's capacity to alienate men and to render individual freedom at best illusory. Lukács, Gramsci, and the founders of the Frankfurt School were now widely recognized as having helped to pioneer the recovery of a more libertarian Marx. The teaching of academic philosophy and social science, even on the part of non-Marxists, was deeply affected by their ideas. These provided during the later 1960s much inspiration for the widespread movement of student protest identified with 'the New Left'. It tended to generate such nihilistic currents that some early mentors – like Jürgen Habermas, now pre-eminent in the Frankfurt School – dissociated themselves. The revolt was directed primarily against the repression deemed inherent in neo-capitalism. However, it soon became an indictment of the oppressive complexity of

all 'advanced' societies, including those in traditional communist hands. The movement was a further example of how
little direct comfort Moscow (as opposed, possibly, to Peking)
could derive from the West's rescrutiny of Marx. There had
been special poignancy in the flight from East to West Germany of the philosopher Ernst Bloch. None welcomed more
shrewdly than he Marxism's embodiment of 'the Hope
Principle', his title for a treatise of 1959. Yet, by migrating,
Bloch indicated that the West understood better than the
Kremlin much of Marx's meaning; and that the capitalist
world might be, in Walter Laqueur's words, 'a more con-
genial place in which to live and work not only for Western
liberals but also for their severest critics'.

Assessments of Marxism were also highly relevant to the
major post-war development in Continental European philosophy. This is identifiable as a rapid diffusion, chiefly through
non-communist countries, of those broadly existentialist attitudes cultivated on a more limited scale during the preceding
generation. The allure of such attitudes in an epoch of mass
disaster was now amply shown. Existentialism's insistence
upon the significance of constant confrontation with death
assumed new force under wartime conditions. Moreover this
concern seemed no less relevant immediately thereafter, when
men were not yet used to living beneath the shadow of
imminent atomic destruction. In an age of such epic tragedy,
actual and potential, there was something specially appealing
about a movement so deeply concerned with the human condition and about a philosophy so often communicable through
works of the creative imagination. By the later 1940s the main
source of existentialist inspiration had shifted. Heidegger certainly continued to be the leading philosophical force in
Germany, but it was prudent for one who had embraced
Nazism to be now altogether more hesitant about the social
bearings of his thought. The new existentialist oracles were
found, rather, in France – particularly among those whose

personal choice, at the hour of loneliest anguish, had committed them to resisting Hitler.

None rivalled Sartre in influence. His talent for formal philosophy was apparent in *Being and Nothingness* (1943), a huge treatise on 'phenomenological ontology'. Yet his great impact in France and beyond was due even more to activity as novelist, playwright, critic, and political protester. Only after the war did his earlier emphasis upon the mutual isolation and enmity of individuals yield to a growing concern with their capacity for self-fulfilment through social cooperation, or 'being-for-others'. There were a great many ways in which post-war existentialists, like pre-war ones, might interpret any consequential commitment. Unfortunately the activists with whom Sartre himself chose to cooperate were Stalinists. Prominent among fellow-countrymen who shared this political naïvety were Camus and – rather more clearly within the main existentialist tradition – Maurice Merleau-Ponty. These two, however, saw the light somewhat sooner than Sartre. Only after the Budapest slaughter of 1956 did he have substantial second thoughts. His hopes for the attainment of revolutionary sociability continued to develop in a form that was even more fundamentally Marxist than existentialist. Nonetheless the focus of these aspirations had moved from Russia to the so-called Third World. As for existentialism itself, by the 1960s much of its vocabulary and insight had been absorbed into the wider fabric of European culture. Its strangeness had clearly diminished, but so too had a large measure of its once seemingly urgent relevance.

The broad geographical division which had emerged during the 1930s between more metaphysical and more analytical philosophers persisted into the post-war period. The latter continued to have their firmest European base in Britain, where the most significant centre of activity was now Oxford rather than Cambridge. Variants on the issues raised by logical positivism maintained importance in the United States, where

the use of symbolic logic reached new planes of sophistication
through the work of W. V. Quine at Harvard, but the British
tended to give greater attention to the 'linguistic philosophy'
derived more directly from Moore and the later Wittgenstein
than from Carnap or Russell. Two of the most influential
exemplars of its approach to the rigorous analysis of ordinary
discourse were Gilbert Ryle, author of *The Concept of Mind*
(1949), and John Austin, whose posthumously-edited notes on
Sense and Sensibilia appeared in 1962. Even those critics who
did concede that such work might generate some shafts of real
philosophical illumination usually felt obliged to condemn a
certain narrowness of beam. Accusations about desiccating
triviality came thick and fast, most frequently from Continental commentators puzzled by what they took to be an insular
and donnish indifference to philosophy's human relevance.
One very vigorous assault was made from the London School
of Economics by Ernest Gellner, who had been born in Paris
of Czech-Jewish parents. His *Words and Things* (1959) was
endorsed by Russell, who approved especially the observation
that such linguistic philosophy 'has an inverted vision which
treats genuine thought as a disease and dead thought as a
paradigm of health'. Gellner identified in his opponents a
'preference for and vindication of the simple unspoilt popular
view against the reasoned subtleties of the ratiocinator' which
led him to dub them 'the Narodniks of North Oxford'.

It was, however, easy to underrate both the sheer variety
of Oxford philosophers and their underlying concern with
wider problems. This became much clearer with the publication, also in 1959, of Peter Strawson's *Individuals* and of Stuart
Hampshire's *Thought and Action*, studies which reached out
towards questions significant within the idealist tradition.
These figures managed – perhaps more emphatically than
Austin and Ryle – to transcend the triviality undoubtedly
afflicting some Oxford debates of lesser stature. The later
Wittgenstein himself had intimated that the exposure of verbal

bewitchment was an essential prerequisite for proper involvement in broader issues of civilization and values: he had no wish to sunder language from life. As Raymond Plant writes: 'Actions in a sense embody ideas, concepts, beliefs, and to look at language is to look at the possibility of acting in a determinate manner. To be philosophically interested in language is to be interested in the range of possibilities of activity considered from one point of view.' Thus a linguistic philosophy which was more neutral than logical positivism towards metaphysics offered, in principle, new opportunities for dialogue with Continental thinkers. Similarly promising from the other side was, for instance, Merleau-Ponty's reinterpretation of phenomenological ideas about men's interaction with their surroundings. He suggested that this relationship be seen as a matter neither of passive contemplation nor of active construction, but rather as the process of endowing the world with meaning – a process involving linguistic usages that must be moulded within the very world which they reconstitute. Others such as Paul Ricoeur have been still more explicitly committed to spanning the gulf between analytical and metaphysical approaches. Nonetheless, even by the 1970s, there had been scant progress either via Husserl's bridge or via any similar structure. There might be now on the Continent more interest in the philosophy of language; but the mode of its pursuit tended still to differ greatly from the Anglo-Saxon one. That the two main camps in European philosophy found so little upon which to agree was not, in itself, fundamentally unhealthy. The deeper malaise related to the fact that, in a world of unparalleled complexity, they were so seldom capable even of mutual comprehension.

Problems of intelligibility also loomed large in the literary and artistic activity of non-communist Europe. During the first years of peace a whole spate of impressive creative work became public. Much of this was suffused by the Resistance spirit, and was embodied in items that could not be properly

presented, or completed, or even begun while Fascism
flourished. Only after this initial outburst did it become plain
just how heavy was the toll that the war had levied on the
creative spirit and just how rare would be works of lasting
worth. While Eastern European literary and artistic life
suffered from the excessive uniformity of state-inspired
realism, imaginative effort in non-communist countries was
complicated by a dearth of agreed guidelines. Among most
westerners there was certainly some similarity of mood. The
overthrow of Fascism prompted a shared sense of relief; and
soon there developed, more soberingly, an equally widespread
awareness of the depth to which Europe had been materially
and morally wounded and of the gravity of dilemmas and
threats ahead. Even so, there was far less consensus about
appropriate modes of response to these problems and perils.
Traditional lines of demarcation between genres were often
blurred, and styles were adopted and discarded with great
rapidity. Such variety and fluidity were sometimes stimulating, but more often they were merely confusing. Political
messages were still quite common, yet they became generally
harder to interpret. Much avant-garde culture, in particular,
seemed more than ever remote both from the concerns and
indeed from the comprehension of a mass public. Perhaps the
arts and literature now reflected only too well some wider
fragmentation in Western civilization.

By the end of the war no aspect of European culture seemed
to have suffered more disintegration than the German
literary tradition. Many regarded 1945 as *das Jahr null* – the
'zero-year' from which some fundamental reconstruction
must be dated. This would be all the slower and more painful
precisely because Nazism had succeeded so well in blunting
one essential tool, the language itself. Moreover it soon
became evident that little assistance could come from East
Germany, whose new rulers had their own engines of linguistic torture. Among the first widely-read contributions to a

cleansing of German prose were such factual accounts of recent persecution as Ernst Wiechert's *The Forest of the Dead* (1945) and Eugen Kogon's *Der SS-Staat* (1946; translated as *The Theory and Practice of Hell*). One remarkable, but rather neglected, sign of new vitality in the novel was Hermann Broch's *The Death of Vergil* (1945). This applied to German many of the prose-poetical techniques of Joyce, who had helped the author to flee from his native Austria. A more widely recognized sign of recovered dignity for the German novel was Mann's *Doctor Faustus*. Even so, the author chose to spend his last years in Switzerland rather than at home. He was not altogether wrong in fearing that something of Hitler's magic still survived. This was apparent from the reception given in 1951 to *The Questionnaire*, written by the scarcely repentant ex-Freikorps fighter Ernst von Salomon. Much of the German public was unduly enthusiastic about its success in deriding the Allies' clumsy efforts at 'denazification'.

The best of post-war German literature was unequivocal in its condemnation of Nazism. Yet increasingly writers felt obliged to warn also against newer superstitions, associated especially with the 'wonder' of economic recovery. Indeed, by the 1960s, nowhere was a literary intelligentsia more deeply alienated from the prevailing social ethos of material acquisitiveness than in West Germany. The moral emptiness often accompanying the country's miracle of prosperity had become a particular concern of 'Group 47', whose didactic radicalism found subtlest expression through Heinrich Böll and Günter Grass. The latter attained international renown with his novel *The Tin Drum* (1959), in which the simple vision of a childlike hero – the dwarf, Oskar – illuminated the hollowness of much conventional thought and behaviour. Grass was not alone in also capturing astutely the mendacities of Nazi-German language. Two particularly notable plays that manifested this same talent were Rolf Hochhuth's *The Representative* (1963) and Peter Weiss's *The Interrogation* (1965).

The Swiss-German dramatist Friedrich Dürrenmatt shared with Grass a taste for the absurd. Such plays as *The Visit* (1956) and *The Physicists* (1962) – where a madman is left dominating the world – suggested that only the grotesque could begin to do justice to the tragi-comic condition of contemporary man.

It was from France, however, that there came the most widely acclaimed contributions to the theatre of the absurd. Any who searched for a relevant national tradition could point to the Parisian associations of surrealism and Dada; and, even farther back, to Alfred Jarry's violent farce *Ubu Roi* (1896), which now won new fame. Neither of the leading post-war contributors was actually a native of France, but both chose to reside in that country and to write chiefly in its language. The Irishman Samuel Beckett first made great impact with a play that brilliantly transferred to the stage the stream-of-consciousness technique pioneered by Joyce, whom he had earlier followed to Paris and served as secretary. The two tramps from *Waiting for Godot* (1952) were simply the first in a whole line of Beckett characters – variously outcast, maimed, and humiliated – who have been condemned merely to fill in such time as remains before the final absurdity of death. They find speech valuable, less as an instrument of communication with others than as a means of reassuring themselves of their own continuing existence. Still more wildly absurd were the situations imagined by the Rumanian-born Eugène Ionesco, in such plays as *Amédée* (1954) and *Rhinóceros* (1960). Like Beckett, but with clearer reference to public and essentially anti-bourgeois themes, he suggested powerfully men's mutual isolation in the midst of anxieties about identity and mortality.

The popularity of the existentialist mood in early post-war France was an important factor towards making the supposed absurdity of life such a prominent literary topic. Especially vital here were the plays and novels both of Sartre and of Camus. Yet each became increasingly keen to venture beyond an initially rather negative concentration upon individual solitude and confusion. In this endeavour the Algerian-born Camus seemed the more successful. His sequence of novels – *The Outsider* (1942), *The Plague* (1947), and *The Fall* (1956) – revealed his developing determination to transcend mere nihilism. Characters such as Dr Rieux, who struggles in Oran against deadly epidemic, embodied Camus's growing insistence on the reality and moral value of humane fellow-feeling. It was the unequivocal translation of this into reformist and anti-Stalinist terms, particularly through his study of *The Rebel* (1951), that caused him to clash with Sartre. By the 1960s the most intellectually challenging novels had become far less concerned with such matters of social commitment. Indeed it was doubtful whether the 'new wave' of French writers working at their 'new novel' cared even about communication in any sense positively helpful to their audience. Readers were invited, rather, to become both collaborators and detectives – to impose their own frame of order upon a tantalizingly incomplete jumble of facts and perceptions. A sense of ambiguity and disorientation, of time and space untamed, pervaded such representative books as Alain Robbe-Grillet's *Jealousy* (1957), Claude Simon's *The Flanders Road* (1960), and Michel Butor's *Degrees* (1960). The cleverness and technical ingenuity of these authors was undeniable. Each was continuing in his own distinctive way that rebellion against naturalistic conventions about character, style, and narrative structure which had been launched by Proust and Joyce. Yet none of them even began to rival the achievement of those two great pillars of the modernist movement.

Masters of such stature were difficult to discern anywhere on the European literary scene after 1945. Still, judged by most other standards, the amount of interesting creative writing was respectable enough. A Nobel award to Halldór Laxness from Iceland or Ivo Andrić from Yugoslavia indicated that some of the smaller languages had developed a literature of valuable comment on contemporary anxieties. There were good artistic as well as political reasons for the West's welcome of work by Pasternak and Solzhenitsyn, and none could fairly scorn an epoch in which Camus, Grass, and Beckett also flourished. In Italy social realism recorded some notable achievements, particularly straight after the war. The tribulations of the backward South were displayed in Carlo Levi's novel *Christ Stopped at Eboli* (1945), inspired by banishment to Lucania under Mussolini. Urban misery prompted works like Moravia's *The Woman of Rome* (1947) and Vasco Pratolini's *A Tale of Poor Lovers* (1947). Among slightly younger authors, Pier Paolo Pasolini – soon film-maker too – was drawn by similar concerns into vividly exploiting the expressive qualities of colloquial language. The harshness or mere tedium of everyday life also constituted a major theme in British writing. Here the greatest stir was caused by the 'angry young men' who emerged during the 1950s. Their wrath often proved as impermanent as their youth. Nonetheless, they managed to ensure that gritty kitchen-sink realism would be a leading feature of national literary effort over the next twenty years. The stuffy 'Establishment' was an obvious enough target; more intriguing were the expressions of disillusionment even with the brave new world of the welfare state. John Osborne's play *Look Back in Anger* (1956) and John Braine's novel *Room at the Top* (1957) were classic products of the angry mood. This generation of writers tended not to fulfil its early promise. One exception was the dramatist Harold Pinter who, after success with *The Caretaker* (1959), won increasing international recognition for his 'comedies of menace'. No less than Chekhov, Pirandello, or Beckett he seemed bent on making failure of communication between characters into a *leitmotif* of modern drama.

Some believed that in recent decades the communicative power of literature itself had been dangerously eroded. Was not the printed word – and even much of language at large –

becoming secondary to a culture of electronic sound and vision rather less demanding of active intellectual response? And did not much of this culture seem increasingly defiant of verbal approximations? The young, whatever their reading habits, certainly provided a vast international market for 'pop' music. They derived almost narcotic relief from what the uninitiated heard mainly as over-amplified noise. Yet a certain cacophony seemed fashionable for much serious avant-garde music too. No sooner had Stravinsky shown sympathy for twelve-tone method than younger composers began to develop expressive techniques moving far beyond Schoenberg's own. Perhaps the most interesting of those who started experiments on randomness in writing and performance was the Frenchman Pierre Boulez. For him at least, such aleatory composition was not a total revolt against rules. Rather he hoped to inspire music that would be, within specified limits, 'a product not of pure chance but of non-determined choice'. The German Karlheinz Stockhausen was outstanding among those who used such flexibility while exploring the potential of electronic effects, with or without accompaniment from conventional instruments. He even met squarely the consequential challenge of devising new – more diagrammatic – schemes of notation and scoring. Eric Salzman describes thus the credo of the contemporary avant-garde:

More than ever, the problems, the materials, the premises and the forms, the expressive means and realizations, the psychological, artistic, aesthetic, and human meaning of the new music must be unique to each work of art – established anew with each act of creation and realization and yet universally valid in terms of the scope and universal potential of human experience and knowledge.

But, for better or worse, any such universality or validity was only rarely appreciated. By the 1970s many homes had the glories of the European musical tradition from Bach to Stravinsky instantly accessible on tape or disc. Yet, even here, there were very few who found post-war avant-garde compositions anything but remote, implausible, incommunicative.

Contemporary visual art was often equally confusing. Despite much frantic experimentation, its goals seemed uncertain
and its achievements very questionable. A notable fashion,
especially in the first decade after the war, was 'action painting' – otherwise known as abstract expressionism. This was
an art of splash and dribble which had the American Jackson
Pollock as a leading pioneer and the *tachisme* of the Frenchman
Georges Mathieu as its chief European manifestation. Indebted
to surrealist ideas on automatic creation, it reasserted the value
of the spontaneous promptings of the unconscious. This stress
on the authenticity of individual psychic expression had wide
international appeal, perhaps partly because recent events had
cast grave doubt upon more public values. There was also
some development in more carefully controlled and intellectualized forms of abstract art, concerned to balance clearly
defined areas of simple colour. An extension was Op (optical)
Art, whose complex patterns stimulated exploration of perceptual ambiguities. Though most avant-garde painting tended
towards the non-representational, another significant feature
of the post-war scene was 'the new realism', or Pop Art,
which began spreading from New York and London in the
later 1950s. This borrowed particularly from the art-work of
commercial advertising. The naturalistic painting of soup-tins
or detergent packets did perhaps have something, however
contemptuous, to say about certain standardized features of
contemporary life. From here it was only a small step towards
converting pre-existing objects into works of art – simply by
deeming a particular motor-cycle engine, or whatever, to be
such. There was in these echoes of Dada a certain falsity of
tone. Among the best-qualified to discern it was Duchamp,
that *enfant terrible* of the 1920s. As he commented in 1962: 'I
threw the bottle-rack and the urinal into their faces as a challenge, and now they admire them for their aesthetic beauty.'

In painting and sculpture, as in music, a great deal of the earlier twentieth century's creative promise appeared to have been betrayed. Much recent work was little more than pretentious and over-rated daubing or junk-collecting – a dismal parody of modernist inspiration. There was an abundance of narcissistic solipsism, of artists bent merely on 'doing their own thing'. This temptation was more resistible in the spheres of architecture and design, if only because of their more intrinsically social functions. Here, at least, the image of 'Europe rising from ruins' had literal application. In 1945 there was devastation – and opportunity. Some fifteen years later Basil Spence's Coventry Cathedral was being added to such earlier post-war architectural triumphs as Pier Luigi Nervi's exhibition hall at Turin and Le Corbusier's housing scheme at Marseilles. Among the cities that benefited from imaginative projects of extensive reconstruction were Rotterdam and Le Havre, while in Britain high priority was given to the development of a series of 'new towns'. As cars proliferated and suburbs sprawled, the problems of planning became more complex. Undoubtedly much building was, as ever, mediocre in design; and certainly there were some undertakings that proved quite disastrous in aesthetic and social terms alike. Yet the best architectural educators did reiterate the need to treat built forms as part of a total environment. Thus they testified to the continuing influence of ideas once cultivated by De Stijl and the Bauhaus. The impact of these movements was evident too in the further advances of an uncluttered, if frequently over-brutal, functionalism. By the late 1950s even the Soviet authorities were beginning to prefer this to the monumental wedding-cake idiom employed for numerous prestige products of the Stalinist era. The International Style, pioneered in the United States and Europe, deserved its name and had many merits. Nevertheless it was regrettable that in every continent so much major building should now lack distinctive vernacular character.

Another force towards more international culture was film, increasingly dependent on a far-flung network of financial, artistic, and distributive resources. The standard recipe for commercial success was not very different from the pre-war one, even though mass audiences now expected their escapism to be technically far more sophisticated. The one major new feature of popular cinema was the profitability of the crudely erotic, which reflected an altogether wider stampede into sexual explicitness. To the extent that film-making could still be treated in national terms, it was noticeable that Frenchmen had been particularly prominent in directing works which aimed to make distinctively intellectual impact. François Truffaut and Jean-Luc Godard ensured that the cinema, as well as the novel, should enjoy a 'new wave'. Robbe-Grillet himself provided the screenplay for Alain Resnais' attempt to realize visually 'a world where everything happens at one and the same time', and their collaboration made *Last Year at Marienbad* (1961) one of the most hauntingly memorable creations of the post-war era. This was also the epoch when Italians made their first full impact on serious cinema. The neo-realism of novels by Levi or Pratolini was paralleled on the screen by such works as Roberto Rossellini's *Open City* (1945) and Vittorio de Sica's *Bicycle Thieves* (1948). Scarcity of resources inspired these directors to forsake studio sets for real streets, to exchange regular crowd-actors for ordinary people. But the results were all the more powerful, and conveyed lessons (not least, about low budgeting) that many successors eventually heeded. Other Italians, like Federico Fellini and Michelangelo Antonioni, would later contribute to a genre of film that explored realms of subjective fantasy, spheres of reverie and seeming absurdity. Such a spirit of enigma, often casting out all conventional considerations of plot, pervaded much that was most stimulating in post-war European cinema. None made it more chillingly manifest than the Swedish director Ingmar Bergman, whose densely allegorical realizations included *The Seventh Seal* (1956) and *Wild Strawberries* (1957).

The commercial, as well as artistic success, of those just mentioned should not conceal the fact that the cinema at large now had a leaner time than before the war. Above all, it was evident after about 1960 that in many European countries the older film industry was losing some of its most talented workers and much of its audience to television. The latter seemed to exert an ever stronger influence on attitudes, choices, and behaviour. By the early 1970s receiving-sets numbered around 28 million in the USSR, 18 million in Britain, 17 million in West Germany, 12 million in France, and 10 million in Italy. Especially in the West, these magical machines had come to dominate a great deal of the average European's expanded leisure time. Was television developing, however, more as opiate than as stimulus? In most lands its paymasters, whether governmental or commercial, appeared concerned that it should lull, as often as provoke, thought. No age had lacked trivial entertainments but television made these more instantly, hugely, and passively consumable than ever before. Not least of the reasons why cinemas were now less popular was that the newer medium had proved still better suited to providing pap on tap.

Yet there were also less gloomy signs. Television well exemplified how an instrument of mass communication might contribute to healthier as well as weaker aspects of contemporary cultural life. At its most salutary, it could confront millions with much that was liveliest in post-war drama and film-making (especially of the documentary kind), or with the character and convictions of innovative artists in many fields. It was therefore capable of helping to keep substantial that minority which showed interest in nurturing cultural development. The post-war boom in the number of those proceeding to advanced education was prominent among other forces tending this same way: one notable case of alliance was the use of television by Britain's Open University from 1971 onwards. In most European countries attendance at operas, concerts, and art exhibitions had never been greater – though one had to concede that such presentations were often heavily dependent on subsidy and that there was relatively slack demand for recent work. Until the mid-1970s at least, figures for the sale of books were similarly buoyant. The preceding twenty-five years had witnessed huge growth particularly in paperback production. Many of these volumes were vehicles merely for ephemeral hack-writing. But, at their best, they constituted a major educative force: thus, in English, the term 'Penguin' now referred as often to book as to bird.

Scepticism about the vitality of the printed word, or indeed the vitality of European culture at large, could not be stifled by any such statistics of sale or attendance. Rather, it was quality that stood essentially in doubt – the quality both of what was currently being produced and of the responses now being elicited to the creative work of this or any other age. Did Europeans appreciate the classics of the past as a still-living presence or merely nod towards them in rituals of hollow piety? Was the worth of collective cultural enterprise being exaggerated at the expense of individual talent? There was good reason to question whether Europe now relied over-much upon an 'instant' culture marketed in standardized packages and homogenized for easy consumption. The persistent arguments for greater regional independence – by Welshmen or Scotsmen, Basques or Bretons – expressed something more than merely political protest. They sprang also from anxiety about the erosion of variety in styles of life and self-expression.

Too many critics identified 'Americanization' as the major source of such weaknesses. This scapegoat proved self-flatteringly convenient, above all for French commentators during the Gaullist years who were obsessed with *franglais* and with other issues of Anglo-Saxon cultural menace. More helpful is Stuart Hughes's suggestion that 'Europe was not so much being influenced by the United States as travelling of its own will the same path that America had pursued a generation before. Consumption levels were rising and life was becoming democratized. The rest follows almost automatically.' Under such conditions one of the greatest risks was that high intellectual or artistic achievement might be readily derided precisely because of its necessarily élitist nature, while at the same time mass culture might be indiscriminately praised merely for its necessarily demotic one. To whatever extent this occurred there was likely to be more rather than less difficulty over a particularly sensitive area in the communication of ideas. As Roland Stromberg comments: 'Cultural distance between popular and advanced thought has always existed and perhaps always will; but there have been cultures wherein a general consensus or forum was closer to a possibility than in the vast democratic nations of today.'

Mutual intelligibility in post-war Europe was hindered by numerous obstacles of this and other kinds. Such phenomena as the narcissistic hermeticism of much avant-garde work in the arts, the schism in politics between communist and non-communist regimes, and the divide in philosophy between analytical and metaphysical modes all made communication harder. The sheer pace of social change was now such that dialogue between generations also became still more strained. None of this was eased, moreover, by the problems of language itself. To some extent these were still apparent in their most traditional form, that of disparity between tongues. Nonetheless the contribution of broadly national barriers, linguistic or otherwise, to difficulties of communication was probably diminishing in relative significance. The senses in which the older complication of translation now played a reduced role were hinted most forcefully in the advance of English as a medium of international discourse, diffused on a scale unknown even in the days when Latin or French had linked a smaller lettered élite. Nearer the heart of the difficulty with language was the continuance of that verbal debauchment already noted, something manifest in the half-truths of political or commercial propaganda carefully fashioned for mass consumption. And at the very core was the fact that many endeavours had become specialized to the point where they outstripped the capacity of any language at all to communicate effectively beyond exclusive bands of initiates and experts. Late twentieth-century man might well inhabit what Marshall McLuhan called 'a global village', where knowledge could be given instant electronic transmission from continent to continent. Yet, paradoxically, the wizardry that made this possible belonged to scientific and technological domains which, from another standpoint, exemplified perfectly the sheer frailty of communication in some deeper sense.

The matter was often treated as a gulf between 'the two cultures', of the scientist and the non-scientist. The former justly complained about the survival of so many supposedly educated circles in which total ignorance of the laws of thermodynamics or the principles of genetic coding was condoned far more readily than merely patchy knowledge of art or literature. Many pivotal scientific findings might admittedly now be communicable to the uninitiated only through adulterating forms of analogy or metaphor. However, even this process was highly preferable to any perpetuation of the illusion that one could be 'cultured' while lacking tenacious curiosity about the leading ideas of natural science. No sphere of intellectual endeavour was marked by more vitality, and none impinged more insistently upon every facet of daily life. The issues raised by critical positivism remained absorbing. It was necessary still to consider how far the procedures of natural science were relevant to those of social understanding, and even how far scientific insights might beneficially stimulate the literary or artistic imagination. Discussion simply in terms of two cultures was nonetheless misleading. In particular, the real issue was often the altogether more detailed fragmentation caused by unprecedented specialization within many spheres of mind. This tested none more severely than the scientist himself. For he was likely to experience difficulty in communicating not merely with non-scientists but also with many fellow-scientists. Here he was bothered relatively little by foreignness in the ordinary sense. The language of mathematics, so often vital, still spurned all national boundaries; and, within fields largely unconnected with state-security, there had never been fuller international contact between researchers. The problem related, rather, to the sheer pace of advance. This was frequently such that any particular scientific discipline might be spawning new theories, concepts, and technical jargon at a rate to which few scientists from other specialisms could readily adapt.

This kind of collaborative adjustment was essential, however, in work along the very frontiers of knowledge where the relations between different branches of science needed to be faster than ever replotted. The scale, complexity, and costliness of research had grown notably during the inter-war period, but the rate of increase mounted still more strikingly after 1945. Governments, as well as commercial concerns, now realized with even more force than before that major economic advance had become inseparable from scientific and technological success. This recognition was a driving force behind the post-war enlargement in Europe of tertiary and advanced secondary education, centred on institutions whose curricula tended to reflect shifts of emphasis away from the humanities. In no previous age had higher mathematics been more relevant to explaining so much. Thus numeracy was becoming almost as indispensable as literacy. Computers, electronically storing huge quantities of statistics and other information, played a progressively wider role in everyday transactions. The benefits they brought were often less evident than the threat they offered. Certainly they appeared to many people as the harbingers of a civilization in which the mass of men might be made mere ciphers, the helots of a very highly numerate élite or even of some machine-intelligence itself.

In the physical sciences the overall challenge remained that of absorbing and exploiting earlier fundamental insights. As G. H. A. Cole writes:

The new discoveries and changes of attitude up to 1939 were breathtaking in both their depth and beauty, and they have not been equalled since. Perhaps this is not surprising. A period of such change and trauma must be followed by a period of stock-taking and relative quiet, and the period since 1945 can be looked at in these terms.

Often the task was to develop projects already much stimulated by the war itself. Britain and France were the first second-rank powers to join the USA and the USSR as holders of nuclear weaponry. A lesser degree of anxiety surrounded the application of atomic science to peaceful purposes. Here it was possible to have quite extensive international collaboration, as demonstrated by the success of the European Centre for Nuclear Research (CERN) established near Geneva in 1953. Air travel was to be made safer and faster through the general application of once-secret work on radar and the jet-engine. The rocketry of the earlier 1940s was a basis for the less obviously useful exploration of space. This won great public interest, from the launching of the first Russian sputnik in 1957 until the American landing of men on the moon in 1969.

There was a less nationalistic flavour to certain other forms of macrocosmic study, where the general European scientific community was able to make a rather bigger contribution. Here the discoveries were sometimes only superficially less sensational than the spectacle of men and machines in space. Above all, astrophysical investigations served essentially to underline the sheer vastness and mysteriousness of the universe itself. The 1950s saw substantial division of opinion about its evolution, though later the arguments for a 'steady-state' theory of continuous creation seemed much less plausible than those attributing the expansion of the universe to an initial 'big bang'. Continuing progress in optical astronomy was overshadowed by research into the emission from space of X-rays, radio waves, and other forms of radiation. This work brought, for example, the identification of extra-galactic 'quasars' (quasi-stellar sources), receding at such vast speed that many were beyond the range of visibility. The further discovery inside our own galaxy of stars whose radio signals pulsate with great rapidity ('pulsars') suggested cases where huge gravitational forces might have caused a large body of matter to collapse into an extremely compressed state dense with neutrons. It seemed theoretically conceivable that in some instances the collapse might have gone still further, to a stage at which the gravitational field became too powerful even for light itself to escape. Scientists could do little more than guess at the physical laws that might be applicable to any such 'black holes' of the universe.

The most outstanding of many post-war achievements in science emerged from a more socially relevant field. The latter covered a range of work on the chemistry and physics of living organisms, and only against this background can one appreciate the great triumph of James Watson and Francis Crick in revealing the molecular structure of the chemicals governing genetic replication. The principal broad feature of progress in biochemistry was still its contribution towards better medicine. By the late 1940s penicillin was in wide use, streptomycin was yielding remarkable results against tuberculosis, and – principally through American research and investment – a whole battery of other antibiotics was being developed. One difficulty proved to be the resistance of mutant bacteria. Another related to the fact that it was easier to record the results produced by antibiotics and other drugs than to describe the actual manner of such operation. While there persisted large ignorance about how even simple chemical agents worked on the body there was significant risk of 'iatrogenic' disorders – ones caused by treatment itself. This consideration affected, for instance, the early development of 'the pill' – after 1960 a progressively larger force in encouraging less restrictive attitudes towards sexuality and especially towards women's activities in society at large – which acted contraceptively only through changing the balance of hormones in the female. The greatest mysteries of all surrounded chemotherapy's dealings with 'mind'. Drugs were used increasingly not only to alleviate major symptoms of mental disorder but also to relieve or cure commoner conditions of tension and anxiety. An unprecedented proportion of Europeans had their thoughts and behaviour conditioned, to varying degree, by prescribed stimulants and tranquillizers. Were these drugs a valuable means to contentment, or merely some prelude to a dehumanizing dystopia? Far too little was known of the workings of the brain and of the central nervous system to support any reassuring answer. What did become clearer were the dangers incurred by scientists and philosophers alike in treating as axiomatic any broadly Cartesian dichotomy between matter and mind. It was wiser not to prejudge the location, or even the existence, of any boundaries between physical and psychological causation. There was need to demonstrate, not just presuppose, areas of immunity to chemical and physical action. Thus Freudian psychoanalysis seemed, in retrospect, to have involved too many detours – however bracingly imaginative – from the highroad of physiological and experimental psychology.

The dismantling of older conceptual and departmental barriers was particularly evident in the kind of confluence between physics and life-science well exemplified by molecular biology. Early in the 1950s geneticists already knew that the crucial carrier of the chemical messages of inheritance across generations was deoxyribonucleic acid (DNA). The race was now on to provide a convincing model of its molecular structure. None could have hoped to achieve this without assistance from crystallographic studies of X-ray diffraction patterns, a field of research inaugurated just before the First World War by Max von Laue in Germany and W. H. and W. L. Bragg (father and son) in Britain. Biochemical interpretation of such scattering by a London team under the New Zealander Maurice Wilkins made a notable contribution to final success. This work, as well as that of the great American structural chemist Linus Pauling, underlined the likelihood that the DNA molecule would be found to possess some kind of spiral structure. The conclusive breakthrough, announced in April 1953, resulted from only eighteen months of collaboration in Cambridge between the biophysicist Crick and the twenty-five-year-old American viral chemist Watson. They were obviously much indebted to many efforts of twentieth-century collective science; nonetheless their own brilliant solution also showed how vital had remained the interpretative flair, and even the aesthetic sense, of the gifted individualistic researcher. Their detailed structural description of the molecule involved two intertwining sugar-phosphate spirals, linked by complementary bases of adenine-thymine and guanine-cytosine which provided the key to particular genetic codings. There was immediate acclaim. Crick and Watson had not merely come up with a model – more especially, they had produced a model that instantly indicated the very method of exact genetic replication. It was realized now that, when a cell divides, the spirals unwind from each other; and that, then, each half-molecule guides the reconstitution of its lost complement. Biological science still faced huge agenda for the future, but in its history Crick and Watson had assured themselves of a place alongside Darwin. They had managed, in Jacob Bronowski's words, 'to express the cycles of life in a chemical form that links them with nature as a whole'.

The triumphs of twentieth-century science were patent. But so also was its accentuation of moral dilemmas. Knowledge of the destructive and contaminative effects of the atomic bomb – and of the even more powerful thermonuclear hydrogen weapons first tested in the early 1950s – made it easy to suppose that physicists should suffer the greatest anxieties. Some of them did indeed turn away from research on nuclear reactions because of political or ethical qualms. Yet, eventually, it became rather clearer that this constituted only one of the areas tending to provoke unease. The alliance of science and technology in the development of computers or supersonic airliners, for example, meant also the generation of grave menaces to reasonable privacy and tranquillity. Noteworthy too were the subtler and more insidious threats arising from various kinds of broadly biological work. What were the ethical principles to be followed during further research into the transplantation of human organs, or into genetic manipulation, or bacterial warfare, or drugs capable of inducing artificial behaviour, or into the whole biochemistry of thought and emotion? Were there even areas of science where, at last, it was better not to indulge that restless curiosity which for centuries had spurred the European intellectual achievement?

The suspicion that many scientists viewed mankind merely as the raw material for ever more ingenious experimentation certainly hardened, and perhaps did so particularly among young people. These were prominent in the movements that brought ecological issues to the fore from the late 1960s onwards. There was an explosion of urgent concern at such features of modern mass society as noise, overpopulation, the pollution of air and water, and the reckless exploitation of natural resources. This showed some belated recognition of the manner in which science had sought to win domination over nature rather than to stimulate men's awareness of their responsibilities towards nature. There developed pressure to consider 'the environment' as a general system of delicately interlocking relationships, and to restrict supposed advances which severely disturbed the balance of the whole. On many accounts the condition of science in later twentieth-century Europe simply reinforced the need to question the Enlightenment's broad assumptions about smooth symbiosis between intellectual progress and the improvement of civilization at large. Most paradoxically of all, the millions of Europeans who lived longer and in better physical health than ever before had also to cope with the knowledge that their collective annihilation might be only minutes away. There could be no more vivid illustration of the discontinuities possible between scientific conquest and social contentment.

Nor had science satisfied the expectations, so widespread a century earlier, about its capacity to inspire some framework of synthesis. Stunning achievements in particular areas were not enough to produce the kind of total picture that had seemed to be emerging before the epoch of Planck and Einstein. The areas of new or reconnected dialogue between physical and biological science hinted at the continuing possibility of some systematic unifying principle. Yet, even after the breakthrough on DNA and related questions, it could not be supposed that the promulgation of such a principle was any longer imminent. Above all, both the microcosmic and the macrocosmic brands of investigation continued to present, not only separately but also in relation to each other, many fundamentally mysterious problems. Moreover, the persistence of such obstacles to conceptual order within science itself could only strengthen doubts about any bolder aspirations it might have to provide a compass for intellect at large. There was, however, no reason why any of this should diminish the actual yearning for over-arching systems of explanation.

Sustained essays in synthesis, aimed at restoring some lost sense of intellectual wholeness, might now be encountered less commonly, and be undertaken usually with less confidence and naïvety, than in the mid-nineteenth century. Nonetheless, there existed in post-war Europe ample evidence that the quest itself was still far from lifeless.

Its most conspicuous manifestation was the vogue of 'structuralism', which spread through much of Western Europe during the 1960s. This style of thinking took its earliest and firmest hold in France, where eventually it surpassed even existentialism in popularity among the *literati*. Especially appealing was the offer of resistance against forces of intellectual fragmentation. Very broadly, structuralism strove to elucidate the elements of conceptual order and cohesiveness that were deemed hidden beneath the many superficially disparate modes of human experience. Thus it was committed, in essence, to communication between disciplines. Much of the original structuralist impetus came, however, from work on linguistics in particular. Even before the First World War the Swiss Ferdinand de Saussure was probing for certain models of structure valid in every language; and he had coined the term 'semiology' to cover his fundamentally general science of signs, or of the principles governing communication. During the 1920s the language of children was very perceptively investigated by his fellow-countryman Jean Piaget. Over the following decades the latter made this one of the foundations for a general psychology of human development that became highly influential among educational theorists.

A key figure in the history of structural linguistics between the wars was the Russian-born Roman Jakobson. He worked first in Moscow, then during the early 1930s migrated to found 'the Prague School' of structural linguistics, and finally fled to teach in the United States. It was indeed a native American, Noam Chomsky, who after 1960 most greatly stimulated the intensified European speculation on the universal in language. Central here was his explanation both of the facility with which a normal child first learns language and of our ability ever to translate between languages. He contended that these attainments must depend on the existence of some universal grammar; that this grammar must reflect certain 'innate mental structures' common to all mankind; and that, in turn, these must be determined biologically and conveyed genetically from generation to generation. Whether Chomsky was right or wrong, this whole field of investigation raised questions of immense significance not only for students of language and literature but also for philosophers, biologists, and psychologists. Structural linguistics inspired, for instance, efforts by the French psychoanalyst Jacques Lacan to update the Freudian account of mental processes and of the therapy these required.

If language was indeed to be treated as merely one aspect of men's complex behaviour then the social implications of work by figures such as Chomsky seemed virtually unlimited. A model of universal grammar might hold the key to the description of some unconscious infrastructure influencing every kind of action in society. This general line of thinking was most boldly pursued by the French anthropologist Claude Lévi-Strauss. During the 1930s he taught in Brazil and did some field work on its Indian populations. In 1941 he left defeated France and settled for six years in the United States, where he was influenced especially by Jakobson. Lévi-Strauss eventually expounded the view that cultures not merely resemble languages but, in a certain sense, actually are languages. They amount to systems of communication which, no less than grammar, must conform to some universal logic and so express the modes of mental operation common to all men. He pursued this argument with particular reference to primitive structures of kinship and belief. His quest for synthesis was supremely evident in the four volumes of *Mythologiques* (1964–71), a prodigious survey of the field of reference shared by some eight hundred Indian fables drawn widely from the whole American continent. Not since Frazer had such a remarkable web been woven; and *Mythologiques* excelled even *The Golden Bough* in the richness of its hints about the origins and evolution of all language, belief, and custom.

As post-war Europe's most audacious prophet of synthesis Lévi-Strauss had only two real rivals, neither of whom adopted any distinctively structuralist approach. One was the British historian Arnold Toynbee, who between 1934 and 1954 published *A Study of History* in ten volumes that professional colleagues distrusted for their Spenglerian sweep. Nonetheless this attempt to describe the laws determining the rise and fall of some twenty or so civilizations did attract wide international readership, especially after the issue of a skilful abridgment. As the grand project drew to a close, it became increasingly clear that for Toynbee any theory of progress must relate ultimately to the enrichment of religious experience: only through some renewed, probably syncretistic, awareness of God might Western man now escape from 'schism in the soul' and stave off the doom of his civilization. Appeals to the mystical were made even more readily by the second figure, the French Jesuit and palaeontologist Pierre Teilhard de Chardin. Being suspected of heterodoxy by his ecclesiastical superiors, he was unable to publish many of his most controversial ideas during his own lifetime. But after his death in 1955 – and particularly after the appearance in 1959 of *The Phenomenon of Man* – there was much excitement about Teilhard's unique approach towards reconciling religion and science. This was the most vital aspect of his attempt at restoring wholeness to what he called 'the noösphere', or realm of mind, which had been rent asunder by the advance of mere secularization. His humanist contemporary Julian Huxley referred, quite admiringly, to 'a threefold synthesis –

of the material and physical world with the world of mind and spirit; of the past with the future; of variety with unity, the many with the one'. Teilhard was focusing especially on the convergence between natural and spiritual evolution, in a cosmic progress through the stages from matter to life, from life to man, and from man to God. His vision was notable more for undaunted imaginative power than for solid scientific authority, but above all it suggested the profundity of one man's craving to recapture some total view.

In the past religious thinking had done much to satisfy this yearning for all-embracing synthesis. Now increasingly even theologians hesitated to deal in certainties. This did not signify, however, any total victory for secular scepticism; it suggested, rather, the greater tentativeness that might properly accompany greater subtlety. Indeed, there is much to be said for the proposition that the religious thinkers of post-war Europe have shown an intellectual vigour second to none. Since the turn of the century science too had learned how difficult it was to purvey convincing final solutions to riddles of the universe. In the process many of the battle-lines between natural and supernatural philosophy had been dissolved, often to the mutual benefit of scientist and theologian. Similarly stimulative was the growing interpenetration of humanist agnosticism and so-called Christian agnosticism. Undoubtedly there continued some overall growth of religious indifference, particularly as measured through neglect of formal worship. Yet this did not amount to any really precipitate erosion in the number of those who regarded the Churches as the surest anchorage amidst the storms of a troubled world, nor indeed in the number of those who sustained a more diffuse kind of religiosity near the boundaries with secular humanism. Even the governments of the Soviet bloc, all of whom in some degree persecuted believers, had to continue taking practical account of the fact that they ruled many whose attachment to God remained very far from dead.

There was in post-war Europe only one institution that could rival atheistical communism as an internationally organized force for the inculcation of values: the Roman Catholic Church. Sometimes, as in Poland, it acted as a brave bulwark against oppressive government; sometimes, as in Spain during the greater part of Franco's rule, it assisted the denial of reasonable liberties. During the 1960s Catholicism underwent a belated but extensive intellectual regeneration. The kind of ecclesiastical bigotry that imposed silence upon Teilhard became far less characteristic of the new epoch. This was inaugurated under the papacy of John XXIII (1958–63), who pointed the way towards a less restrictive and more creative concept of authority. Catholic thinkers were given a greater freedom of debate and speculation, a degree of release from dogmatic neo-Thomism; meanwhile the generality of bishops and clergy (and even the laity) was granted some more active role in the consultative procedures of the Church. Pope John's whole policy of *aggiornamento*, or updating, necessitated a trial of strength between reactionary and progressive forces. This became outstandingly evident at the Second Vatican Council (1962–5). Neither side swept the field, not least because the new Pope, Paul VI, seemed bent upon compromise.

By the mid-1970s the Vatican was still just managing to maintain bridges over some remarkable gulfs: for example, between the obscurantist tendencies of its Irish hierarchy and the startling institutional and theological radicalism being developed in the Netherlands. Tension in the Church was plainest on questions with a sexual bearing. These had become particularly pressing once it was obvious that 'permissive' attitudes were advancing throughout much of Europe – and in such a way that the many sensitive arguments developed during the twentieth century for less repressive physical relations, both between and within the sexes, were often endangered by considerations of mere hedonism. Catholic debate on priestly celibacy was largely drowned by the uproar following the encyclical of 1968 in which Pope Paul denounced 'artificial' contraceptive techniques. *Humanae Vitae* certainly had roots in a tradition of natural law thinking that had always emphasized human dignity. Yet so abstract was its treatment of 'true human values' and its 'total vision of man' that the document became widely condemned even by Catholics, particularly for its unrealistic approach towards urgent problems in the poorer continents. The crisis was all the more deeply felt precisely because it suggested that John XXIII's work had prompted others to harbour naïve expectations about the rapidity of future change in the Church. Even so, without his commitment to *aggiornamento* and without the freer atmosphere thereby engendered the prospects for Catholicism would surely have been altogether less healthy in the longer term.

One promising product of this changing ambience was a greater collaboration with the Protestant churches in thought, worship, and service to society. Barth's influence upon their most sophisticated spheres of thinking remained considerable, but after 1945 a still greater force was exerted by Bultmann. Indeed, especially from the 1960s, many Catholic circles too showed great interest in his plea for 'demythologization'. This involved something more radical than the Barthian neo-orthodoxy which he had earlier espoused. The difficulty with the New Testament, Bultmann now argued, was not merely that it incorporated a mythological world-view remote from modern sensibility but also, more deeply, that it presented existential truths as though they were objective facts. Perhaps the stories of the Incarnation or Resurrection ought to be considered in terms not of their historicity but of their capacity, as myths, to stimulate insight into the significance of the human condition. Thus Bultmann was not so much discarding myth as attempting to clarify how it suggested Christianity's grasp of specifically existential verities. Also influential in Europe were the broadly comparable arguments of Paul Tillich, who had made his home in the United States after the Nazi takeover of Germany. For him, as Anthony Quinton writes,

faith is simply the ultimate concern that all but the most vapid and trivial of men must experience. A personal God is just a symbol of the Ultimate that is the object of this concern, an apt one since personality, human existence is man's primary point of contact with reality, certainly much more adequate than idolatrous, secular conceptions of the ultimate, a state, a party or a class.

Nothing did more to alert a wide international public to this whole area of avant-garde theology than the Anglican John Robinson's *Honest to God* (1963), which illustrated forcefully the general drive towards revision of the very language through which men sought to express awareness of divinity. The reformulations in post-war religious thinking even went to the point where the phenomenon of 'Marxist' Christianity was not altogether uncommon. The general state of fermentation certainly promoted, and in turn benefited from, much freer contacts between Protestantism, Catholicism, and the Orthodox traditions. The ecumenical spirit spread even farther still, for Christians also showed a greater willingness to learn from the insights and expressive modes characteristic of Judaism, Islam, and the other great religions of the globe.

This was only one of the senses in which, during the latter half of the twentieth century, Europeans needed to reconsider their views of the wider world. There emerged also from the work of such figures as Teilhard, Toynbee, and Lévi-Strauss a vision that had been broadened by concern for the relativity of cultures and for the essential unity of mankind. At numerous points Europe was having to unlearn the self-congratulatory habits so dominant in earlier epochs. True, it had stood for many centuries – and remained even now – second to none in the scope and force of its intellectual achievements. The essential difference derived from the fact that any such proficiency could no longer be considered, implicitly or explicitly, as the simple product of some innate and perpetual excellence. It seemed, more than ever before, that the maintenance of real vitality in Europe's own civilization would depend upon a willingness to render less presumptuous her dialogues with other cultures. Such greater humility also accorded with the changing facts of global political might. The 'Great Powers' of the nineteenth century had all been European. Now from their number only Russia (in a sense, semi-Asian) survived in the first rank, there rivalled by the United States and, increasingly, by China. Most notably, the post-war years had witnessed a bout of European decolonization as dramatic as any phase in the earlier consolidation of Empire. Even Britain, so proud a force as the century began, now seemed dwarfed in power. Her membership from 1973 of the European Economic Community was some acknowledgement, however belated, of the wisdom already shown by France, Germany, Italy, and the Benelux countries in exploring the advantages of pooled resources. Yet for the foreseeable future 'the European idea', of which so much was heard in the West and of which the Community was the most remarkable practical result, appeared bound to concern itself chiefly with only half a continent. As the last quarter of the twentieth century opened, Europe at large was still quite profoundly divided. Above all the Iron Curtain, though corroded in places, remained an inescapable grim reality.

Such waning of Europe's global political authority did not involve, however, any fully commensurate weakening in the general impact of the continent's ideas. Much of the world still sought to imitate supposedly attractive features from those styles of living and thinking which Central and Western Europeans, and North Americans too, seemed broadly to share. It proved easier for the former colonies to attain political independence than to liberate themselves from reliance upon the economic, scientific, and technological expertise of their old masters. Even those movements that were keenest to reject the whole legacy of Europe often needed to employ concepts which that same continent had first fashioned. The Third World's bid for liberation was frequently accompanied by a rhetoric of equality, human rights, and national self-determination that had essentially European roots – and Marxist catchwords, in particular, cropped up in a host of exotic tongues. It was easier for anti-imperialists to discern the elements of duplicity within European slogans than to prevent themselves from exploiting very similar slogans with comparable bad faith. But this does not deny the reality of confrontation between Europe and the wider world, especially where differences of wealth and differences of colour roughly correlated. Nor does it suggest that the resentment of those who had been economically and racially deprived was quite lacking in therapeutic value for Europeans themselves. Most particularly, the latter had much to learn from the African or Asian who refused to continue viewing the past exclusively through the white man's self-flattering distortions.

Pleas for a new perspective, within which Europeans might better perceive the less fortunate features of their own tradition, became legion from the 1960s onward. Perhaps the most striking was made by Frantz Fanon, a coloured native of Martinique who trained as a psychiatrist in France and then joined the movement for Algerian independence. His principal work *The Wretched of the Earth* appeared in 1961 (the very year of his early death) with a pungent introduction from Sartre. This widely-read book stressed that violence could exist not merely as a matter of fist or gun but also as a subtler condition of attitude. At the heart of Fanon's indictment of the West was his image of imperialism as violence in this second sense, involving a brutality of attitude which could and did survive processes of formal decolonization. He declared,

When I search for Man in the technique and style of Europe I see only a succession of negations of man, and an avalanche of murders

... It is a question of the Third World starting a new history of Man, a history which will have regard to the sometimes prodigious theses which Europe has put forward, but which will also not forget Europe's crimes, of which the most horrible was committed in the heart of man, and consisted of the pathological tearing apart of his functions and the crumbling away of his unity.

According to this view, physical degradation and social separation fade in significance beside the still greater evil of a violence in attitude that amounts ultimately to mental apartheid. Fanon's writings undeniably lapsed all too often into exaggeration or mere hysteria. Yet, taken as a whole, they certainly had power to stimulate greater critical self-awareness among those Europeans whom he deemed to be already 'swaying between atomic and spiritual disintegration'.

The broad tradition of ideas developed in Europe over centuries was henceforth under heavy fire. In these circumstances it became all the more desirable for defenders to distinguish between what was worth preserving and what was not. Success in guarding the virtues might well depend upon franker admission of the vices that had managed to co-exist. Perhaps the tradition would prove resilient precisely because, at its best, it had already gone far towards encouraging an ethos of self-criticism. The history of civilizations recorded no greater display of constructive remorse than that which emanated from many Europeans in this post-colonial age. This was only one of the senses in which the tensions of the years since 1945 were potentially beneficial. Indeed, some such current of creative disorder had been a leading feature in the development of European ideas throughout the twentieth century. Many of the illusions now so painfully relinquished had gained strength from the Enlightenment. In particular, that movement had been better at recording the past history of human folly than at appreciating how much of the worst was still to come. On the other hand, the Enlightenment had also greatly fortified those habits of sober self-scrutinizing rationalism which might constitute the European tradition's best defence against its enemies. Men of the twentieth century clearly had more cause than those of the eighteenth to be alert to the limitations of reason. Yet the course of ideas and events, especially through the last hundred years, also served to underline that rational intelligence, despite all its frailties, remained essential to any form of progress.

Now less than ever could men afford to undervalue those qualities which over millennia their ancestors had developed to a degree unique in the animal realm. These included the capacity to ponder upon themselves and their world, to communicate the results of such contemplation, and thereby to reduce in some degree the seeming chaos of existence. No single civilization could make exclusive claim to this achievement. However, there was little doubt that during recent centuries Europe, all its errors notwithstanding, had made especially imposing contributions. As the last quarter of the twentieth century began, this whole process of rational adaptation was imperilled from within as well as without. Nothing could more endanger all that remained most valuable in Europe's heritage than the loss of nerve, the waning of belief in the worth of reason, which was now often discernible among some of its very own inhabitants. When discussing their tradition with the wider world, these really had no cause at all thus to replace the older attitude of mindless self-satisfaction with a newer one of equally mindless self-abasement. Somewhere between there must exist a more truly reasonable approach to the history of European thought and behaviour. This would begin by balancing the rich records of triumph and failure alike, and possibly conclude by declaring that no other continent had yet produced such wealth both of wisdom and of folly.

NOTES ON FURTHER READING

THIS guide is limited to books in English. Those under the Penguin imprint are published from Harmondsworth. Unless indicated otherwise, London is the place of publication for the rest.

The many works mentioned in the main text of this volume themselves constitute the most valuable kind of further reading. Those who wish to approach them via anthologies will be helped by J. Cruickshank, ed., *Aspects of the Modern European Mind* (Longmans, 1969); R. N. Stromberg, ed., *Realism, Naturalism, and Symbolism: Modes of Thought and Expression in Europe, 1848–1914* (Harper, New York, 1968); and W. W. Wagar, ed., *Science, Faith and Man: European Thought since 1914* (Harper, New York, 1968). Each contains extracts from a wide range of authors.

The rest of these notes deal solely with some of the most helpful secondary sources.

Among general histories of this period which allow due weight to the role of ideas are the following: D. Thomson, *Europe since Napoleon* (revised ed., Penguin, 1966); J. Joll, *Europe since 1870: an International History* (Penguin, 1976); G. Barraclough, *An Introduction to Contemporary History* (Penguin, 1967); H. S. Hughes, *Contemporary Europe: A History* (Prentice-Hall, Englewood Cliffs, N. J., 1961); G. Lichtheim, *Europe in the Twentieth Century* (Weidenfeld & Nicolson, 1972); and W. Laqueur, *Europe since Hitler* (Penguin, 1972). 'The Rise of Modern Europe' series, edited for Harper of New York by W. L. Langer, contains three volumes having this same merit: C. J. H. Hayes, *A Generation of Materialism, 1871–1900* (1941); O. J. Hale, *The Great Illusion, 1900–1914* (1971); and R. J. Sontag, *A Broken World, 1919–1939* (1971). Lively thematic essays are allied with lavish illustration in two outstanding works from Thames & Hudson: A. Briggs, ed., *The Nineteenth Century: the Contradictions of Progress* (1970); and A. Bullock, ed., *The Twentieth Century: a Promethean Age* (1971).

Adequate broad surveys concerned predominantly with the

development of ideas remain surprisingly rare. The most widely used textbook, R. N. Stromberg's *An Intellectual History of Modern Europe* (Appleton-Century-Crofts, New York, 1966), is quirky and uneven. However, it may be found helpful at least in suggesting certain longer-term patterns of cultural continuity and change. W. M. Simon, *European Positivism in the Nineteenth Century: an Essay in Intellectual History* (Cornell U.P., Ithaca, N.Y., 1963); O. Chadwick, *The Secularization of the European Mind in the Nineteenth Century* (Cambridge U.P., 1976); G. L. Mosse, *The Culture of Western Europe: the Nineteenth and Twentieth Centuries* (Murray, 1963); G. Masur, *Prophets of Yesterday: Studies in European Culture, 1890–1914* (Weidenfeld & Nicolson, 1963); H. S. Hughes, *Consciousness and Society: the Reorientation of European Social Thought, 1890–1914* (MacGibbon & Kee, 1959); J. Passmore, *The Perfectibility of Man* (Duckworth, 1970); and J. H. Plumb, ed., *Crisis in the Humanities* (Penguin, 1964), all offer especially rewarding reading. *The Fontana Dictionary of Modern Thought* (1977), edited by A. Bullock and O. Stallybrass, deserves to become established as an indispensable work of general reference. Most aspects of modern cultural development are subjected to lively Marxist critique in A. Hauser, *The Social History of Art* (vol. 4, Routledge, 1962). Every page of George Steiner's brief work *In Bluebeard's Castle: Some Notes Towards the Re-definition of Culture* (Faber & Faber, 1971) is also characteristically provocative. C. B. Cox and A. E. Dyson have edited three volumes called *The Twentieth-Century Mind: History, Ideas, and Literature in Britain* (Oxford U.P., 1972) whose geographical ambit is often broader than the sub-title suggests. The Methuen 'Companions to Modern Studies' also offer information on a wide range of intellectual and artistic activity: note particularly D. G. Charlton, ed., *France: a Companion to French Studies* (1972) and M. Pasley, ed., *Germany: a Companion to German Studies* (1972). Rewarding treatment of a further area is found in W. M. Johnston, *The Austrian Mind: an Intellectual and Social History, 1848–1938* (California U.P., Berkeley, 1972).

There are a large number of intellectual biographies devoted to figures who feature in this book. Any selection of modern classics from this genre must include M. Meyer, *Ibsen* (abridged ed., Penguin, 1974); G. Painter, *Marcel Proust: A Biography* (2 vols., Chatto & Windus, 1959–65); and E. Jones, *The Life and Work of Sigmund Freud* (abridged ed., Penguin, 1964). An admirable collection of shorter studies is being developed, under Frank Kermode's editorship, in the Fontana 'Modern Masters' series. Its worth is particularly evident from such items as these: E. Leach, *Lévi-Strauss* (1970); J. Gross, *Joyce* (1971); R. Williams, *Orwell* (1971); D. Pears, *Wittgenstein* (1971); A. J. Ayer, *Russell* (1972); J. Bernstein, *Einstein* (1973); B. Magee, *Popper* (1973); R. Shattuck, *Proust* (1974); and A. Danto, *Sartre* (1975).

Every major field of modern science is treated in the second and third of J. D. Bernal's four volumes on *Science and History* (Penguin, 1969). Even despite its attachment to the most naïve forms of Marxist explanation, this work retains real value. An example of excellent scientific popularization is J. Bronowski, *The Ascent of Man* (BBC, 1973). A strong historical sense is also shown by Isaac Asimov in the admirable *Asimov's Guide to Science* (2 vols, Penguin, 1975). Helpful introductions to particular areas of development are C. C. Gillispie, *The Edge of Objectivity: an Essay in the History of Scientific Ideas* (Princeton U.P., 1960); L. Barnett, *The Universe and Dr Einstein* (second revised ed., Bantam, New York, 1968); W. Heisenberg, *Physics and Philosophy: The Revolution in Modern Science* (Allen & Unwin, 1959); J. Watson, *The Double Helix: a Personal Account of the Discovery of the Structure of DNA* (Penguin, 1970); R. Thomson, *The Pelican History of Psychology* (Penguin, 1968); and J. A. C. Brown, *Freud and the Post-Freudians* (revised ed., Penguin, 1964). C. P. Snow, *The Two Cultures: And A Second Look* (Cambridge U.P., 1964) is one classic point of departure for discussion of the relationship between science and the wider world.

All the reliable general guides to recent philosophical trends make rather heavy demands on the reader. Three admirable, but very contrasting, treatments are J. Passmore, *A Hundred Years of Philosophy* (Penguin, 1968); I. M. Bochenski, *Contemporary European Philosophy* (California U.P., Berkeley, 1956); and F. Coplestone, *Contemporary Philosophy: Studies of Logical Positivism and Existentialism* (Burns & Oates, 1956). The integration of commentary with original texts is a useful feature of the 'Mentor Philosophers' series. The items in it relevant to this period are H. D. Aiken, *The Age of Ideology: The 19th-Century Philosophers* (New York, 1956); M. White, *The Age of Analysis: 20th-Century Philosophers* (1955); and H. Kohl, *The Age of*

Complexity (1965). For more advanced discussion the 'Library of Living Philosophers' collection, under the editorship of Paul Schlipp and published now by the Cambridge University Press, is indispensable. Especially noteworthy are the studies devoted to A. N. Whitehead (1941), Einstein (1949), Russell (third ed., 1951), G. E. Moore (second ed., 1952), Jaspers (1957), Carnap (1963), Buber (1967), and Popper (2 vols, 1974). Modern religious thought and institutions receive clear introductory treatment in A. Vidler, *The Church in an Age of Revolution: 1789 to the Present Day* (revised ed., Penguin, 1971). More detailed discussion of relevant intellectual issues can be found in J. Macquarrie, *Twentieth-Century Religious Thought: The Frontiers of Philosophy and Theology, 1900–1970* (revised ed., SCM, 1971), and in W. Nicholls, *Systematic and Philosophical Theology* (Penguin, 1969).

There is no shortage of secondary material on the history of social and political ideas. Among stimulating general studies are A. P. Thornton, *Doctrines of Imperialism* (Wiley, New York, 1965); H. Arendt, *The Origins of Totalitarianism* (second ed., Allen & Unwin, 1958); G. D. H. Cole, *A History of Socialist Thought* (5 vols in 7, Macmillan, 1953–60); G. Lichtheim, *Marxism: An Historical and Critical Study* (second ed., Routledge, 1964); and R. Crossman, ed., *The God that Failed: Six Studies in Communism* (H. Hamilton, 1950). Worth noting as well are two books by James Joll: *Intellectuals in Politics: Three Biographical Essays* (Weidenfeld & Nicolson, 1960), and *The Anarchists* (Methuen, 1969). The latter topic is also treated in G. Woodcock, *Anarchism: A History of Libertarian Ideas and Movements* (Penguin, 1962). D. Caute, *Communism and the French Intellectuals, 1914–1960* (André Deutsch, 1964) is best read in tandem with H. S. Hughes, *The Obstructed Path: French Social Thought in the Years of Desperation, 1930–1960* (Harper, New York, 1966). The exceptionally rich crop of distinguished work on Germany includes F. Stern, *The Politics of Cultural Despair: A Study in the Rise of the Germanic Ideology* (Anchor, New York, 1965); P. Gay, *Weimar Culture: The Outsider as Insider* (Penguin, 1974); W. Laqueur, *Weimar: a Cultural History, 1918–1933* (Weidenfeld & Nicolson, 1974); M. Jay, *The Dialectical Imagination: A History of the Frankfurt School …* (Heinemann, 1973); K. Bracher, *The German Dictatorship: The Origins, Structure, and Effects of National Socialism* (Penguin, 1973);

J. P. Stern, *Hitler: the Führer and the People* (Fontana, 1975); and International Council for Philosophy and Humanistic Studies, *The Third Reich* (Weidenfeld & Nicolson, 1955). George Mosse's relevant books include *The Crisis of German Ideology: Intellectual Origins of the Third Reich* (Weidenfeld & Nicolson, 1966) and the anthology *Nazi Culture: Intellectual, Cultural and Social Life in the Third Reich* (W. H. Allen, 1966). P. Hayes, *Fascism* (Allen & Unwin, 1973) is a sober introduction to a topic which can be explored later at a more demanding level through E. Nolte, *Three Faces of Fascism* (Weidenfeld & Nicolson, 1965). The evolution of academic social theory is discussed in R. Aron, *Main Currents in Sociological Thought* (vol. 2, Penguin, 1970); W. G. Runciman, *Social Science and Political Theory* (Cambridge U.P., 1963); I. M. Zeitlin, *Ideology and the Development of Sociological Theory* (Prentice-Hall, Englewood Cliffs, N.J., 1968); A. Giddens, *Capitalism and Modern Social Theory: An Analysis of the Writings of Marx, Durkheim and Max Weber* (Cambridge U.P., 1971); and T. Parsons, *The Structure of Social Action* (second ed., with new introduction, Collier-Macmillan, 1968).

Students of modern literature still find Edmund Wilson one of their most inspiring guides. *Axel's Castle: A Study in the Imaginative Literature of 1870–1930* (Fontana, 1961), which he published first in 1931, remains an excellent starting-point. Other especially lively contributions are R. Williams, *Culture and Society, 1780–1950* (Penguin, 1961); L. Trilling, *The Liberal Imagination: Essays on Literature and Society* (Penguin, 1970); E. Heller, *The Disinherited Mind* (Penguin, 1961); and G. Steiner, *Language and Silence: Essays, 1958–1966* (abridged ed., Penguin, 1969). Stimulating too are the pieces by Walter Benjamin collected as *Illuminations*, with an introductory essay by Hannah Arendt (Fontana, 1973). More works of the kind represented by R. Pascal, *From Naturalism to Expressionism: German Literature and Society, 1880–1918* (Weidenfeld & Nicolson, 1972) and B. Thomson, *The Premature Revolution: Russian Literature and Society, 1917–1946* (Weidenfeld & Nicolson, 1972) would be welcome. J. Cruickshank, ed., *French Literature and its Background* (Oxford U.P., vol. 5, 1969; vol. 6, 1970) is helpfully wide in scope. An indispensable aid to detailed reference is *The Penguin Companion to Literature*, especially vol. 1 'Britain and the Commonwealth' edited by D. Daiches (1971) and vol. 2 'European' edited by A. Thorlby (1969).

Note also two rewardingly wide-ranging works among the *Pelican Guides to European Literature*: F. W. J. Hemmings, ed., *The Age of Realism* (1974), and M. Bradbury and J. McFarlane, eds, *Modernism, 1890–1930* (1976).

Artistic movements receive authoritative survey in G. H. Hamilton, *Painting and Sculpture in Europe, 1880–1940* (Penguin, 1967). Briefer is A. Bowness, *Modern European Art* (Thames & Hudson, 1972). E. Lucie-Smith, *Movements in Art since 1945* (Thames & Hudson, 1969) helps unravel some of the complexities of the most recent period. R. Shattuck, *The Banquet Years: the Arts in France, 1885–1918* (Faber & Faber, 1959) and G. Masur, *Imperial Berlin* (Routledge & Kegan Paul, 1971) are model works of their kind. J. Willett, *Expressionism* (Weidenfeld & Nicolson, 1970) and D. Cooper, *The Cubist Epoch* (Phaidon, 1971) provide good studies of particular schools. N. Pevsner, *Pioneers of Modern Design: from William Morris to Walter Gropius* (Penguin, 1960) and H. R. Hitchcock, *Architecture: Nineteenth and Twentieth Centuries* (third ed., Penguin, 1968) are justifiably regarded as standard treatments. Two early and still valuable books on the cinema are P. Rotha, *The Film Till Now* (Cape, 1930; much enlarged ed., Spring Books, 1967) and R. Manvell, *Film* (Penguin, 1944). See also the latter's *New Cinema in Europe* (Studio Vista, 1966). Reliable surveys of the musical scene are G. Abraham, *A Hundred Years of Music* (third ed., Methuen, 1964) and, with more technical detail, E. Salzman, *Twentieth-Century Music: an Introduction* (Prentice-Hall, Englewood Cliffs, N.J., 1967).

The Times Literary Supplement (weekly) and *The New York Review of Books* (fortnightly) stand out among the many periodical publications which provide up-to-date comment across the whole spectrum of contemporary intellectual and cultural concerns in Europe and beyond.

INDEX OF NAMES

Dates are omitted for persons who died before 1870.

INDEX OF SUBJECTS